D0987166

TROLLOPE'S AUSTRALIA

* * * * *

A

TROLLOPE'S AUSTRALIA

A selection from the Australian passages in *Australia and New Zealand* by Anthony Trollope

* * * * *

edited by **HUME DOW**

THOMAS NELSON (AUSTRALIA) LTD

MELBOURNE and SYDNEY

THOMAS NELSON (AUSTRALIA) LIMITED
597 Little Collins Street Melbourne
321 Pitt Street Sydney

THOMAS NELSON AND SONS LTD
36 Park Street London W1

THOMAS NELSON AND SONS (AFRICA) (PTY) LTD
P.O. Box 9881 Johannesburg

THOMAS NELSON AND SONS (CANADA) LTD
81 Curlew Drive Don Mills Ontario

THOMAS NELSON AND SONS
Copewood and Davis Streets Camden 3 N.J.

Registered in Australia for transmission by post as a book
Printed by Halstead Press, Sydney

FOREWORD

The present volume has a clearly defined aim. It is a selection from a very much larger volume, Anthony Trollope's *Australia and New Zealand*. The guiding principle of selection is to give the flavour of Trollope's attitude to Australian life in the early 1870s and, in so far as he conveyed it, the flavour of that life itself. This book does not attempt to summarize all that Trollope's original volume contained; but it does contain most of those passages in the original volume which are of lively interest to the general reader today.

Australia and New Zealand was first published in two volumes by Chapman and Hall of London early in February 1873. Almost simultaneously, on 22 February 1873, the book began to appear serially in *The Australasian* in Melbourne, and shortly afterwards also in book form in separate parts, published by George Robertson of Melbourne; then, in June, Robertson brought out the whole work in one volume, the "Authorized Australian Edition". There were further editions in the 1870s (Chapman and Hall announced a second within a month of the first), but the book has not been republished in the last ninety years.

It is necessary to say what the present volume is—and what it is not. There are some 250,000 words in the Australian chapters of the original; the following pages give a selection from those chapters amounting to about one-third of the whole. Trollope wrote of the various colonies in turn, dealing with them in the order of his travels. As he states in his introduction:

> my book has been written as I went on. I do not know that I could have done my task otherwise. Queensland, and all that I had learned about that colony, her land-laws, her habits, and her prosperity, had been as it were dispatched and cleared out of my mind before I had reached Melbourne on my return journey. Tasmania and Western Australia were finished before I quitted Adelaide—and so on.

The present selection does *not* follow this sequence, but is rearranged in terms of subject-matter, the material under each heading being drawn from the separate accounts of all the various colonies. (The chapter headings and sub-headings are mine, not Trollope's.) I have also, in the Introduction, abstracted Trollope's comments on some subjects which do not appear in the selections that follow.

Trollope's colony-by-colony approach led to heavy and persistent repetition, the account of, say, the life of the squatters or the conduct of parliament in Victoria reiterating much that had been included in the Queensland and New South Wales sections. I have, of course, omitted such repetitions, though it has been necessary to retain a few repetitions of detail to avoid spoiling the flow of Trollope's wording. Apart from repetition, however, a great deal of the original is of interest today mainly to the scholarly historian. There is much, for him, in the detailed discussion of free-selection and land legislation, of the effect of border duties, of legislative and electoral procedures, of the cost of living in the various capitals, of the production figures for various industries, and so on; but the general reader is in a position neither to interpret such discussions nor fully to appreciate their interest.

This volume, then, is not a new edition of the original. The various versions which appeared in the 1870s in London and Melbourne differ in many details, and were cut about and modified for various publishing purposes. But no attempt has been made here to collate the various editions or the MSS. Everything in the body of the present volume is taken verbatim from Robertson's "Authorized Australian Edition" of 1873.

Two tasks remain to be done by others, tasks quite apart from the purposes of the present selection. One is to publish a properly collated, critical edition of the full text of Trollope's original book; this, I understand is being undertaken by scholars in Sydney and Brisbane, and will be invaluable for the social and political historian. The other, as suggested by G. F. James, of the University of Melbourne, the recognized authority on the history of Trollope's visits to the Australian colonies, is to make a critical assessment of his observations and opinions, which will entail, as James has said, a "thorough examination of the social and economic conditions of every colony in the early 1870's . . . an essential and formidable prerequisite".

It remains for me to state the formalities I have adopted in editing the present selections. Any comments I have interpolated are printed in italics; everything else which appears after the Introduction is in Trollope's own words, as they appear in the Robertson 1873 edition. The omission of any words within passages used is indicated by dots (except that I have not indicated the omission of such mechanical phrases as "I have said that" or "as I said before"). Punctuation and capitalization, irregular and inconsistent in the Robertson edition, have been simplified and (I trust) made consistent. At some points, additional paragraphing has been introduced. Trollope's spelling was apparently largely by ear: English editions give "Musclebrook" for "Muswellbrook", "gogobera" for "kookaburra", "Gullgong" for "Gulgong", but Robertson's edition corrects most of these; I have retained his spelling of place names, so we have "Gipps Land" and "Freemantle".

It is a pleasure to add my acknowledgment of the invaluable assistance of Miss P. Reynolds, Deputy Latrobe Librarian, and her assistants in the Latrobe Library, Melbourne, for their generous help and advice in the selection of the illustrations for this volume; to thank Mrs. Dorothy Fitzpatrick for lending me the copy of the Robertson edition from which I have worked—and to thank my wife not only for her help and advice but also for her patience with the nervous tension which the production of a book creates in a household.

HUME DOW

University of Melbourne,
May 1966.

[illegible] of [illegible]
Sorell and some [illegible]

It remains for me to [illegible]
during the present [illegible]
[illegible] in [illegible]
Introduction [illegible] Tollinger [illegible] have [illegible]
Robertson 1770 edition. The translation [illegible]
ages used is indicated by date except that I have [illegible]
the purposes of an [illegible] I have [illegible]
As I said before, the punctuation and capitalization [illegible]
[illegible] in the Robertson edition have been [illegible]
I trust [illegible]. At some [illegible]
[illegible] has been introduced. Tollinger's spelling [illegible]
largely [illegible] English editions give [illegible]
books' [illegible] for [illegible]
but Robertson's edition [illegible]
the spelling of place names, [illegible]
Freemantle.

It is a pleasure to add my acknowledgement [illegible]
assistance of Mrs. L. Reynolds [illegible] Library [illegible]
for assistance in the [illegible]. Mr. [illegible] for [illegible]
ous help and advice in [illegible] of the [illegible]
[illegible] to thank Mrs. [illegible] for [illegible]
copy of the Robertson edition [illegible] have [illegible]
to thank [illegible] not only for [illegible] and advice [illegible]
[illegible] with the [illegible]
a [illegible] that [illegible] hold.

[illegible]

University of Melbourne
May 1966

CONTENTS

LIST OF ILLUSTRATIONS

The illustrations used at chapter openings are also taken from contemporary prints.

INTRODUCTION

Anthony Trollope spent a full year in Australia, from 27 July 1871 until 29 July 1872. He was no casual traveller: a busy man, he did not waste time. He wrote the whole of a novel, *Lady Anna,* on the voyage out from England, finishing it the day before he landed in Melbourne, and he completed more than three-quarters of the Australian sections of *Australia and New Zealand* while he was still travelling around the colonies. He finished all but a few pages of the whole book before he arrived back in London on 20 December 1872.

What prompted this distinguished and successful novelist to undertake this task at the height of his career? As was usual with Trollope, it was an astute combination of profitable publishing and private pleasure. Trollope and his wife wanted to visit their son Frederick, who was established on a sheep station near the Lachlan River in New South Wales. At the same time, Trollope secured an agreement with Chapman and Hall, who would pay him £1,250 for a two-volume work on the Australasian colonies. What was remarkable was the extraordinary effort and sense of responsibility Trollope put into his task. Except for four or five weeks' respite on Frederick's property, Trollope hardly seems to have paused in his travels. This intrepid 56-year-old of 17 stone not only visited all colonies, but did so with conscientious thoroughness, tramping the cities, going through bush and over mountains by coach or horse, going down rickety mineshafts, killing a carpet-snake and learning to like the "gogobera", wading through underground caves, inspecting meat works and "lunatic asylums" meticulously, and always questioning, questioning everyone he met, ferreting out facts and figures, reactions and opinions. As he writes of his visits to asylums and gaols in Melbourne:

> Indeed I marvel when I look back at the diligence with which I walked through institutions of every kind in each of the

> colonies that I visited. I could tell how many inmates there were in each, and how much each inmate cost—no doubt with all that inaccuracy which a confidence in statistics customarily produces. But I doubt whether I should serve or interest any one by doing so.

And again:

> The fern-tree valleys on the road to the Huon are specially [lovely]—and in one of these I was shown the biggest tree I ever saw. I took down the dimensions, and of course lost the note.

Little wonder that, after a year of diligent observation, Trollope's patience was wearing thin, as is evident from his account of the last mine he visited:

> I went down a mine at Wallaroo, finding it always to be a duty to go down a shaft on visiting any mining locality—and I came up again. But I cannot say that I saw anything when I was down there. The descent was 450 feet, and I felt relieved when I was once more on the surface. I walked below among various levels, and had the whole thing explained to me—but for no useful purpose whatever. It was very hard work, and I think I should have begged for mercy had any additional level been proposed to me; as it was, I went through it like a man, without complaint—and was simply very much fatigued. As I rose to the air I swore I would never go down another mine, and hitherto I have kept my vow.

Yet, for all the thousands of details he packed into his book, it is hard to fault him. Touchy colonists who were angered by his comments found for the most part that they had to attack his opinions rather than his facts. His putting Balmain and Pyrmont on Sydney's North Shore is one of the few factual errors I can detect—he was apparently misled by the convolutions of Sydney Harbour.

Trollope was an extraordinarily sympathetic and, within his own limitations, humane observer, and a fascinating chronicler. But it is important to note that he was not merely writing a travel book for amusement. He was, quite deliberately, trying to provide the Englishman who was thinking of emigration with everything he should know. As he writes in his introduction:

> there are still many in England who have to learn whether Australia is becoming a fitting home for them and their children, and the well-being of Australia still depends in a great degree on the tidings which may reach them . . . . hoping that by diligence I might be able to do something towards creating a clearer knowledge of these colonies than at present perhaps exists, I have visited them all.

It is, of course, the very conscientiousness with which he carries out this purpose that leads to much of the tedium the modern reader finds in making his way through the complete work.

Comparisons between England and Australia are among his most interesting judgments. The low wages, bad housing, poor education, and appalling conditions of the mid-Victorian English factory and farm worker are implicit in much of Trollope's praise for Australian society.

> For members of parliament, and men with £5,000 a year, or with prosperous shops in Cheapside—for some even whose fortune is less brilliant than that—England is a very comfortable home. No land can beat it. But for Englishmen in general, that is for the bulk of the working population of the country, it is I think by no means the best place. A large proportion of our labouring classes cannot even get enough to eat. A still larger proportion are doomed so to work that they can think of nothing but a sufficiency of food. In all the Australian colonies, if a man will work, the food comes easily, and he can turn his mind elsewhere.

And it is this contrast which leads the usually mild Trollope to attack those who suggest that the glory of being at the centre of a great empire is compensation for poverty:

> You, my friend, want no shoes for your children. Though meat and coal may be dear, there is plenty of food and fuel at your hearth. Your daughter is not debarred from salutary social intercourse with those of the other sex. Your boys are not naked in the streets. Leisure and luxurious living allow you to indulge in glory. But for that poor man you know of, would not 5s. a day, with no song, be better than 2s. a day, and Rule Britannia? And for that young woman, would not £30 for a

year's services, and at the end of it a husband able to keep her, be better than £16 a year and no husband, even though no regimental band should go by the windows once a fortnight, playing "Steady, boys, steady" for the gratification of her patriotism?

It is with such feelings that Trollope, time and again, comes back to the observation that "the wages of a labouring man in Australia are about double the wages of his brother at home", and that he "eats meat three times a day in the colonies, and very generally goes without it altogether at home". And it is not only food and wages that he emphasizes; it is also the standard of what we have come to call social services:

> Could a pauper be suddenly removed out of an English union workhouse into the Melbourne Benevolent Asylum he might probably think that he had migrated to Buckingham Palace.

So Trollope discusses questions of emigration from England in great detail. It is strange to come across the sentence: "But I fear much success will not attend the giving of free or assisted passages." But, with the separate colonies competing, the analysis which emerges is sensible: Victoria and New South Wales, having the attraction of gold, do not need to tempt immigrants, while it is pointless for the other colonies, which need them, to offer passages because the men they bring out are soon off to Bendigo or Gulgong anyway. Trollope discusses the merits of each colony in turn—Queensland the best for the free-selector, Tasmania or the West for climate, and so on: if he were coming himself, incidentally, and could "choose the colony in which I was to live, I would pitch my staff in Tasmania".

He gives frequent warnings that only the hard-working should attempt to live in the colonies: "the land is cheap because the struggle required to make it useful is severe". His advice to the English is explicit:

> The old, the idle, the reckless, and the soft-handed will only come to worse grief in a colony than the grief which they will leave behind them. I am speaking now of intending emigrants who purpose to reach the colony without money in their pockets—and while so speaking I will say at once that the chances in any Australian colony are very bad both for men

and women who go thither with some vague idea of earning bread by their education or their wits. The would-be government clerk, the would-be governess, the would-be schoolmaster, lawyer, storekeeper, or the like, has no more probable opening to him in an Australian town than he has in London or in Liverpool. . . . But the young man with sinews and horny hands—the man who is young enough to adapt himself to new labour—will certainly find occupation. He is worth his rations, and high wages beyond his rations.

It is this quality of sound, balanced judgment which makes Trollope so intensely interesting to the historian. The book is not merely a collection of his detailed observations; there is a continuous sense that the author is soberly weighing up the significance of what he sees. One has the feeling that his conclusions must be respected; if they are to be rejected, as sometimes they must, it will only be after a well-substantiated argument is brought against them.

No subject was more thorny, more subject to emotion and prejudice, in the Australia of the 1870s than the conflict between squatter and free-selector; no subject better illustrates Trollope's balance and sound sense. It was not possible to include his comments on this issue in the body of the selections that follow—the comments are scattered here and there through hundreds of pages—but they seem to me to be such a good example of his tolerant and balanced judgment that I include them here in the Introduction.

Trollope makes his own position clear:

> it is almost impossible for the normal traveller not to sympathize with the squatter. The normal traveller comes out with introductions to the gentlemen of the colony, and the gentlemen of the colony are squatters. The squatters' houses are open to him. They introduce the traveller to their clubs. They lend their horses and buggies. Their wives and daughters are pretty and agreeable. They exercise all the duties of hospitality with a free hand. They get up kangaroo hunts and make picnics. It is always pleasant to sympathize with an aristocracy when an aristocracy will open its arms to you. We still remember republican Mrs. Beecher Stowe with her sunny memories of duchesses. But the traveller ought to sympathize with the

B

free-selector—always premising that the man keep his hands from picking and stealing his neighbour's cattle. He, we may say, is the man for whom colonial life and colonial prosperity is especially intended, and without whom no colony can rise to national importance.

The popular picture of all squatters as wealthy men is, Trollope realizes, an exaggerated one (his own son was not very prosperous):

> the growing of wool is, at the best, a precarious trade. Thousands have made their fortunes at it—but thousands also, with small capitals, have gone to the wall. . . . The year of favourable circumstances in regard to weather and climate may put him at his ease for life—and a year's drought may beggar him. This also tends to weed out the old men, and leave the young men in possession. At fifty the squatter can afford either to live in town or in England—or else he can no longer afford to live on his station.

As Trollope writes later:

> South Australian farmers simply live comfortably and die in obscurity by growing wheat; but South Australian squatters make splendid fortunes or are ruined magnificently by growing wool.

But, sympathetic as he is to the difficulties of the squatter, he does not readily accept the view that the risks the squatter must take justify the special privileges he constantly seeks.

> Very much has been said . . . of what is due to the squatters as the pioneers of Australian civilization. I do not think very much of the claim. When a man encounters danger manifestly for the sake of others—that knowledge may grow and science progress, and the world be opened to new comers, as did such men as Columbus and Cook, as many Australian explorers did, as Livingstone is now doing—he is entitled to public recognition and honour. But he can hardly with justice put forward the same claim because he seeks fortune for himself in stormy paths. He probably counts his chances, and, seeing personal security with ten per cent. at home, with forty per cent. and not improbable annihilation at the hands of a savage

> at the Antipodes, chooses forty per cent. and the Antipodes with his eyes open. I admire his courage, and applaud his decision. But I cannot admit his claim as a great public benefactor because he has thriven and others have followed him. . . . . I look upon the wool-growers of Australia as her aristocracy, her gentry, her strong men, her backbone. But in managing the affairs of this world, I do not like the theory of giving to those who have got much, and taking away from those who have got nothing.

And so we find Trollope telling the young English emigrant "that his best opening in colonial life is to buy a bit of land", to become a free-selector, despite the hatred the author's squatter friends have of such a view. Indeed, he goes so far as to state that "the encouragement of the free-selector—of the genuine free-selector who intends to cultivate and reside upon the land—is and should be the first aim of colonial government". It is of secondary importance that any laws which may interfere with the squatters' "pastoral and almost patriarchal views of life seem to him to emanate from democracy and the devil", that the squatter hates the free-selector "almost as thoroughly as the English country gentleman hates the poacher". Trollope is explicit:

> Personally, I love a squatter. I like to hear his grievances and to sympathize with them. I can make myself at home with him; and can talk to him of his sheep more comfortably than I can to a miner of his gold, or a merchant of his dealings. But on principle I take the part of the free-selector.

To the squatter, only wool matters, only wool can measure Australia's success; if land on his sheep-run is selected, it can only be to interfere with him and to steal his sheep. Trollope is not naïve about either side of the argument:

> That cattle-stealing and sheep-stealing are common practices is undoubtedly true; and the squatter is generally the victim, while the free-selector is as generally the thief. . . . But I look on the assertion that free-selectors are as a rule cattle-stealers as monstrous.

To Trollope the encouragement of the free-selector is in the interests not only of the colonies but of the squatters themselves:

"The more general he becomes, the less necessary will it be for squatters to depend for their work on the nomad tribe of wandering men which infest the pastoral districts . . ." As the free-selector "is a necessity, it must surely be wise to make the best of him"—and to use him in the shearing season instead of being at the mercy of "vagabond strangers". Indeed, the itinerant labourer carrying his swag seems to be the only typical Australian figure who failed to arouse Trollope's sympathetic understanding. But if, in this respect, Trollope was too ready to generalize, it should not obscure for us the extraordinary balance and objectivity of his account of the issue between squatter and free-selector.

There are many issues to which Trollope brings the same balanced judgment. In some cases, of course, his view is severely limited by the perspectives of his day. His conclusions on the question of the aborigines may horrify us (see Chapter VI, "The First Australians"), but there can be no doubt that his attitude was arrived at by what he saw as humane considerations. There is perhaps a less obvious but nevertheless unquestioned assumption of white superiority in his account of the use of Polynesian labour in Queensland ("From the South Seas"), but again we have an illuminating analysis of the issue, doubly illuminating because of what it tells us of the life and attitudes of the time; the origins of the White Australia Policy are here in embryo. And, if the imaginative sympathy of this most English of the English cannot quite extend to the itinerant labourer, it is all the more surprising that he is able to recognize that he has "never met more courteous men than the gold-miners of Australia".

There is a mature consideration in his (sometimes prolonged) disquisitions on social and economic affairs. He is not afraid to generalize, and it is surprising how often his generalization is apt—and, at the same time, it often reminds us how different our world was a hundred years ago. He sees that "the pastures of Australia are unlimited": if only the skill of man can "devise some plan by which meat can be carried as securely, and at the same time as cheaply, as other commodities", if "artificial freezing" is successful, the "flocks and herds would be multiplied for the supply of markets across the water". Again, the further development of wheat-growing is seen to be limited by the prevalence of rust; and we realize that Farrer's work was still far in the future. Sugar, on the other hand, is "produced largely, and will probably become the great rival of the wool trade".

He emphasizes the urgent need to discover and develop iron resources, and scorns the colonial gold fever in favour of developing coal mining. The few lucky diggers do not blind him to thousands who have lost their capital in the search for elusive nuggets:

> All that I have seen in Australia teaches me to believe that every ounce of gold raised has cost more in its raising than the price for which it has been sold.

The growing proportion of urban to rural population worried him. "Adelaide alone . . . contains very nearly a third of the life of the whole community of South Australia. This proportion . . . is very much in excess of that which generally prevails in other parts of the world." City populations in other colonies, too, are "excessive", and "cannot be taken as showing a healthy state of things". What would he think today—when more than half the people in four states are in their capitals?

The differences in Trollope's response to the various colonies tells us much of how Australia has changed. It is obvious that he has conflicting reactions—he admires the brash, youthful, American vigour of Victoria, but his more natural sympathies are with the slower, quieter, more English tone of Sydney or Hobart. Melbourne is "the great metropolis of our Australian empire". Victoria is the "younger and more energetic brother" of New South Wales: "In 1851 she was allowed to go alone, and is now, at any rate in her own opinion, the first in importance of all the colonial children of Great Britain."

With the Victorian railway approaching Albury and the line across the border reaching only from Sydney to Goulburn, Trollope pictures Sydney as fearful of joining the lines: Melbourne would take all the trade. Again:

> I feel myself bound to say that I doubt whether any country in the world has made quicker strides towards material comforts and well-being than have been effected by Victoria.

It is not only Melbourne; he is struck by the "uncouth prosperity" of Victoria's many country towns:

> You see them expanding and growing, as you do the young colonial girl of ten years old, who buds forth so quickly that the increase of her physical power becomes almost visible to you.

As will be evident from the selections in Chapter IX, Trollope held strong opinions about colonial government. The legislatures are too disorderly, there is too much log-rolling, payment of members (then true only of Victoria) is "injuriously powerful", and patronage "is indeed one of the greatest curses of the colonies". But his criticisms do not mean that he is against self-government; in Western Australia (still a crown colony, with almost 2,000 convicts)

> one hears of doings in days not far remote which lead one to think that any amount of ignorance in a legislator, that any amount of what I may, perhaps, call rowdyism in a chamber, is better than practically irresponsible power in the hands of a would-be mighty colonial officer, removed from home by half the world's circumference.

Perhaps Trollope's most carefully considered judgments—and the ones on which he was most strongly attacked in Australia—were on the question of separation from England. On the one hand he found that the colonists "do not in ordinary conversation speak with enthusiasm of Downing Street"; on the other, that "all the best minds among the colonists" were firmly against separation. Indeed, English statesmen were often attacked because it was thought that they were weakening the bonds between London and Australia.

Trollope is firm that the question of separation should "be considered solely in regard to the interests of the colonists":

> As long as the national prosperity of the colonies can be advanced by their dependence on England, that dependence England is bound, both morally and politically, to maintain. When the time shall come in which the colonies can serve themselves better by separation than by prolonged adherence, England, I think, should let them go.

He is somewhat too optimistic about the speed of Australia's growth:

> Does anybody believe that a population of twenty millions in Australia would remain subject to a population of forty millions in the British Isles? And the former number may be reached as quickly as the latter.

But his reasoning was sound. Border customs duties between the colonies, his *bête noire*, caused "confusion and grievous trouble". So he looked "first to a customs union, then to federation, and then after some interval . . . to Separation and Self-control":

> Australia must be one whole before she can settle herself and take a place among the nations. . . . The states must bind themselves together with the united object of making themselves a nation, and the men who now pride themselves on being Victorians, or South Australians, or Queenslanders, must learn to pride themselves on being Australians. At present they are very far from entertaining any such pride. The inhabitant of Melbourne thinks himself to be very much higher than the inhabitant of Sydney, and looks down from a great eminence upon the Tasmanian. In New South Wales there is a desire to maintain the distance between itself and Victoria—as though a gulf between the two, which could not be passed, would be for its good. Queensland, the youngest daughter of New South Wales, has but little respect for her parent. South Australia thinks herself better than her neighbours because she has never received a convict.

It would, indeed, be hard to find another commentator on the state of the Australian colonies in the nineteenth century who brought so much common sense and so much sound judgment to his task. But it is not only his judgment: we build up an impression from his side comments of a man whose edgy independence of mind and genuine understanding is mixed with tolerance, with humanity, and with humour. He is meticulous in recording facts, but his real interest is in people. As he said himself, "I wish to write of men and their manners and welfare, rather than of rivers and boundaries . . ." He is genuinely concerned with "the well-being of a people", and the result is a full-length portrait which not only tells us a great deal of what Australians were like in the 1870s, but may even tell us a little of what Australians are like today.

Trollope was at the height of his powers when he made his trip—it was on his return from Australia that he wrote *The Way We Live Now*—but no one would contend that *Australia and New Zealand* is a great book. What can be said is that among the repetitions, the long economic and political analyses, the details of cost of living and other advice to intending migrants, there is much good writing and some very good writing indeed.

1 RANDOM GLIMPSES OF COLONIAL SOCIETY

Some of the brief selections in this chapter are serious, others much less so; some are only random paragraphs. But, by way of introduction, they may together give the flavour of Trollope's attitudes—and of the society he was observing.

True Colonies

I have attempted in this volume to describe the Australian Colonies as they at present exist, and to tell, in very brief fashion, the manner in which they were first created. In doing so, it has been impossible to avoid speculations as to their future prospects —in which is involved the happiness of millions to come of English-speaking men and women. As a group, they are probably the most important of our colonial possessions, as they are certainly the most interesting. Their population is, indeed, still less than half that of the Canadian dominion; but they are very much younger than the Canadas; their increase has been much quicker—and we made them for ourselves. Canada and Nova Scotia—of which New Brunswick was then a part—we took, ready colonized, from the French. The Cape we got ready colonized from the Dutch, as also British Guiana. Jamaica and Trinidad we took from the Spanish. The early possession of Newfoundland was a moot point between ourselves and the French, till at last we obtained it by treaty from Louis XIV. Ceylon, which, in truth, is not a colony, though reckoned in our list of colonies, was possessed first by the Portuguese, and then by the Dutch, before it fell into our hands. The Mauritius we got from the French. Among the colonies, which we ourselves first colonized, Barbadoes and Bermuda are the most important that still remain to us—excepting those of which I am now about to speak.

When we make mention of "colonies" we should be understood to signify countries outside our own, which by our energies we have made fit for the occupation of our multiplying race. India is the possession of which we are most proud—but India is in no respect a colony. It should be our greatest boast respecting India, that we hold that populous country to the advantage of the millions by whom it is inhabited; but we do not hold it for the direct welfare of our own race, though greatly to the benefit of our own country. The Europeans who are spread over India, exclusive of the military, are less numerous than the inhabitants of Tasmania.

The United States are, in the most proper sense, a British colony; and it is the colony in which, of all others, Great Britain should feel the greatest glory, because therein has been achieved the highest prosperity by those who leave the shores of our islands from year to year. That India and the United States—so absolutely unlike each other in all the conditions of humanity, and yet each so prosperous after its own fashion—should, the one be governed from England, and the other speak the English language, is a combination which makes an Englishman conscious that, let the faults have been what they may, the race has been more successful than other races.

The Australias and New Zealand have been and still are colonies in every sense; and they are colonies which have been founded by ourselves exclusively—for the prosperity and the deficiencies of which we and the colonies are solely responsible. No French element, no Dutch element, no Spanish element can be pleaded by us as having interfered with our operations in Australia. And the real colonization of these Eastern lands, which did not in truth commence till the system of using them as penal settlements had been condemned, has been so recent that the colonists and the Government at home have had the advantage of experience, and have taken lessons both from the successes and the failures of earlier enterprises. . . .

The loyalty of the colonies is very strong. In England, to speak the truth, we do not know much about loyalty. We believe in our form of government; we believe in the Crown and in Parliament; and we believe in the practical sense of the people at large. We are satisfied that we are doing well, and we think that should we make any material change—such as would be the substitution of a democratic republic for the monarchy we possess—we should improve ourselves not at all, and might injure ourselves very much. We value trial by jury, primogeniture, and an hereditary House of Parliament, because they have helped to make us what we are; and we are generally contented with our position. This may be better than loyalty, but it is not loyalty. Now and again some spring may be touched, as when the Queen's household was attacked, or when the Prince was lying ill; but the feeling thus induced is not the normal condition of the British mind. England's greatness is too near to us at home to create sentiment—but in the far Antipodes loyalty is the condition of the colonist's mind. He is proud of England, though very generally angry with England because England will not do exactly what he wants. He reconciles this to his mind by telling himself that it is the England of the past of which he is proud, and the England of the present with which he is angry. But his hopes are as bright as his memories—or, at any rate, less dim than his insight into the evils of the day—and he still clings to the prospects of England in the future. He does not like to be told that he is to be divided from her. He is in truth loyal. He always speaks of England as home. He remembers the Queen's birthday, and knows the names of the Queen's grandchildren. He is jealous of the fame of Nelson and Wellington; and tells you in praise of this or that favourite colonial orator, that—he would be listened to in the House of Commons. All this is true loyalty—which I take to be an adherence to certain persons or things from sentiment rather than from reason.

* * *

It is impossible in Australia to forget the name of any past governor, or any Secretary of State for the colonies—almost impossible to forget that of any Under Secretary of State—so prone have been the colonists to name their districts, rivers, counties, towns, and streets from the men who have governed them. We have Phillip Street, Hunter Street, King Street, Bligh Street, and Macquarie Street in Sydney, not to mention the Macquarie River, and Hunter River, and Port Phillip. We have the city of Brisbane, and the Darling River, with various Darlings, and various Bourkes, and Gipps Land in Victoria, and the Fitzroy River in Queensland, and Port Denison quite in the north, and the town of Young; and the river Murray—and Belmore hotels are innumerable. I do not know that there is as yet any Kimberley County, but there are Caernarvons, Russells, Labouchere, Newcastles, Granvilles, Stanleys, Glenelgs, and Lyttons without stint, as also are there Merivales, Rogers, Elliots, Pelhams, and memorials of others who from time to time have been either politically or permanently great in Downing Street. Sir Hercules Robinson now reigns at Sydney, and when I left the city I heard enough to make me assured that before long there will be a Robinson district, a county Robinson, a town of Robinson, and a river Robinson.

* * *

I can imagine that it must be difficult for those who have never visited a British colony to realize life as it there exists—to realize in the first place the difference between colonial life and life at home, and then the likeness. The likeness is very close. The same language is spoken, and the same laws prevail for the protection of life, property, and character. This is the case also in the United States, but the people of the United States can hardly be said to be like Englishmen. In the Australian colonies the British mode of thinking prevails as to education, politics, and social position; whereas, in the United States the ideas of the people at large are not our ideas. In the States all the institutions of the country tend to the creation of a level, to that which men call equality—which cannot be attained because men's natural gifts are dissimilar, but to which a much nearer approach is made in America than has ever been effected in Europe. In Australia, no doubt, and especially in Victoria, there is a leaning in the same direction: but it is still so slightly in advance of that which prevails among ourselves as to justify an observer in saying that the colonies are rather a repetition of England than an imitation of America. When there is any divergence from the old John Bull proclivities, it is towards the American side; but the divergence is not great, and to many leading colonists the idea of any divergence is altogether distasteful.

Blowing—and Loafing

I may, perhaps, take this opportunity of saying one word as to colonial character which must be in the nature of censure—though of censure of the mildest form. . . . Colonists are usually fond of their adopted homes—but are at the same time pervaded by a certain sense of inferiority which is for the most part very unnecessary. But it exists. Men and women will apologize because they cannot do this or that as it is done in England. But this very feeling produces a reaction which shows itself in boasting of what they can do. And soon the boast becomes much louder than the apology—and very much more general. It arises, however, as does all boasting, from a certain dread of inferiority. In the Australian colonies it has become so common, that the salutary fear of being supposed to boast does not produce that reticence as to self which is considered to be good manners at home. You are told constantly that colonial meat, and colonial wine, colonial fruit, and colonial flour, colonial horses, and colonial sport, are better than any meat, wine, fruit, flour, horses, or sport to be found elsewhere. And this habit spreads from things national to things personal; and men boast of their sheep, their cattle, and their stations—of their riding, their driving, and their prowess. When one man asserts that he has shot 150 wild horses in a day, it is natural that another man should have shot 200. And so the thing grows, and means perhaps not a great deal. The colonists themselves have a term for it, and call it —"blowing". I met a gentleman who had once shot a bushranger. He had not been in my company five minutes before he had told me—nor an hour without his mentioning it half-a-dozen times. He always "blows" about that, said a friend who was with me; and those who heard him thought no more of it than if he bit his nails, or had a trick of stroking his beard. That gentleman always "blew". Now if I was sending a young man to the Australian colonies the last word of advice I should give him would be against this practice. "Don't blow", I should say to him.

* * *

Nothing strikes a visitor to the colony more forcibly than the desire to hold government place. I myself would certainly not have expected that this would be so among a young population, eager for independence, to whose energy unlimited acres are open, and among whom it cannot be said that the professions and pursuits of commerce are overcrowded. The government pay is not excessively liberal, and the positions when gained do not seem to be very enviable. Four or five hundred a year is a paradise of government promotion, to which but very few can hope to attain. But the thing when seen from a distance allures by its certainty—and I fear also by a conviction that the "government stroke" may be a light stroke of work. In colonial parlance the government stroke is that light and easy mode of labour—perhaps that semblance of labour—which no other master will endure, though government is forced to put up with it. With us the government stroke has happily taken quite another phase. It is to be hoped that it may gradually be made to do so in the colonies. That the longing for government employment, with the cringing and threats and back-door interest necessary to obtain it, should be made to cease also, is more perhaps than can be at once expected.

Is Plenty a Blessing?

The wages of a labouring man in Australia are about double the wages of his brother at home. Consequently the labouring man, let his labour be what it may, eats meat three times a day in the colonies, and very generally goes without it altogether at home. That is a plain, and, I think, a true statement of the case. . . .

I take it that plenty to eat is, all the world over, the first desire of man and woman. When a man has plenty to eat as a matter of course—when his food comes to him as does the air which he breathes—he is apt to think that his own first desires are of a sublimer nature; but any accident in the supplies for twenty-four hours will teach the truth on this subject to the most high-minded. I can imagine that a leg of mutton looms as large to an Essex delver, and is as glorious a future, as a seat in Parliament to a young barrister. There are legs of mutton, if only it might be possible to get at one! Let the delver get to Queensland and he will at any rate have legs of mutton. Meat three times a day is the normal condition of the Queensland labourer. In the colony mutton may be worth three halfpence per pound, or perhaps two-pence; but of the price the labourer takes no heed. He is provided as a matter of course with rations—fourteen pounds of meat a week is the ordinary allowance for a labourer in Queensland—and, as regards food for himself, he is called upon to take no thought of the morrow, any more than if he were a babe. Fourteen pounds of meat, eight pounds of flour, two pounds of sugar, and a quarter of a pound of tea, are allotted to him weekly. This in England would cost, at the lowest price, something over 12s. a week—more than the labourer can earn altogether—and this the labourer in Queensland enjoys as a matter of course before he comes to the question of wages.

I may, however, as well declare at once that the all but divine happiness of such a state of existence—as it will appear to the delver at home—seems very soon to lose its brilliance in the eyes of the man who is in Queensland. He has hardly eaten a few hundred pounds of colonial mutton, has not been on rations six months, before he has forgotten entirely that he was ever short of supply in the matter of animal food. The Irishman, who has come from the unchanging perpetuity of potatoes to a plethora of meat, teaches himself to believe within twelve months that he never sat down to dinner at home without a beefsteak or a roast fowl. I came to a little dispute once with a working man at Rockhampton. "If you knew what it was," he said, "to have eaten mutton three times a day, day after day, week after week, month after month, you would not come here and tell us that we ought to be contented with our condition." Looking at the matter in his light, I see that he has some justice on his side. I told him, jeering at him ill-naturedly, that if he would give up one meal a day, he would lessen his sorrow by at least a third—but I saw that I was not regarded as having the best of the argument. I would wish therefore that the would-be emigrating English labourer should understand that when he gets his meat in plenty it will not be to him a blessing so unalloyed as he now thinks it. Alas, is it not the same with all blessings? What is there for which we toil and sigh, which when gained does not become to us like mutton served thrice daily? The seat in parliament, the beautiful young wife, even accumulated wealth, all pall upon us; and we exclaim, as did my labouring friend at Rockhampton, "If you too had to eat this mutton three times a day you would not think your condition so blessed."

But there is the blessing—such as it is. The man who works in Queensland is at any rate sufficiently fed. The man who works at home is too often very insufficiently fed. I am of opinion that the English labourer looking at the question from this point of view, will make light of that Rockhampton objection which, nevertheless, I have felt it to be my duty to lay before him.

Three Kinds of Skill

I visited the largest of the Sydney public or common schools, and, as is usual on such occasions, I listened while the children were put through their facings. I never know how far to believe the wonders which I hear and see at such exhibitions. I endeavour to believe as little as possible, in order that I may be saved from a consciousness of disgrace at my own comparative ignorance. When a little boy gets up on his legs, and without any aid of pen or pencil, does a sum in half a minute which I know that I could not do myself if I were locked up for half a day with all necessaries, I hate that little boy, and feel disposed almost to hope that there must have been some fraud between him and his teacher. The following is the sort of question asked:—"If a man invest £197 7s. 6d. at $4\frac{1}{4}$ per cent., and get a rise in the rate of interest of $\frac{1}{8}$ per cent. at the end of 23 days, what will his income amount to at the end of 42 days?" Let me ask any ordinary English gentleman whether he would do that sum for the sake of getting the forty-two days' income? But the little boy does it out of head, looking innocently up to the ceiling for his answer, and getting not even praise when he gives it with presumed correctness. I suppose the answer was correct, and that the figures were not exhibited to the little boy in some manner that I could not detect.

And certainly a little girl whom I questioned myself must have understood what she was saying. A passage in Shakespeare had been read, in which the word "strategy" is used in its secondary, and not its technical sense. I asked the meaning of the word, and the little girl said that strategy was the art of military manœuvring. She was a very nice little girl, and I hope she may live to be the wife of the first commander-in-chief of the forces of New South Wales. The girls in some of these public schools are more wonderful even than the boys. They read better, and seem to have a clearer perception of things in general. I remember, at such an exhibition in New York, hearing a roomful of girls questioned by the mistress. She asked why the Romans ran away with the Sabine matrons. One girl suggested that it must have been because the Sabine matrons were pretty; but she was soon taken down by a clearer-headed maiden, who told us that it was done for the sake of population. The young girls at Sydney were perhaps not quite so far advanced as this; but nevertheless their condition amazed me. Putting aside all joking, I profess that the excellence of the teaching in the Fort Street School, at Sydney, was very high, though I doubt much whether all that be taught under its system is retained. Of course it will be understood that the school of which I am speaking is the school open to the people at large.

* * *

Undoubtedly, the crime of cattle-stealing—of cattle-stealing and sheep-stealing and horse-stealing—is one of the greatest curses of the Australian colonies. The pastures are so extensive, and therefore so little capable of being easily watched, that the thefts can always be made without difficulty. Every animal is branded, and the brands are all registered. One never sees even an unbranded horse in Australia, unless it be a wild animal in the woods. But the brands are altered, or else the carcasses are carried away while the skins are left. And there is undoubtedly a feeling in the pastoral districts of Australia, among the class of men who labour on the land, that the squatter is fair game for such depredations. We all know the difficulty which is felt in Ireland as to getting evidence against the perpetrators of agrarian violence. There is the same difficulty in these colonies with reference to the cattle-stealer. He has with him much of the sympathy of all men of his own class—and there are many who do not dare to give evidence against him. The law is severe, but is too often inoperative.

Very much that the squatter alleges against the free-selector is true. In arguing the question, as I have done with many a squatter, I always took the part of the free-selector, expressing a strong opinion that he was the very man whom the colony should be most anxious to encourage, and urging that if here and there a free-selector should become a thief, the law should be made to deal with him—but not the less did I feel that the gentleman with whom I might be conversing knew very well where his own shoe pinched him. A peculiar crime has grown up in Australia—and is attended by one of the worst circumstances which can accompany crime. It has assumed a quasi-respectability among the class of men who are tempted to commit it. It is like smuggling, or illicit distillation, or sedition, or the seduction of women. There is little or no shame attached to it among those with whom the cattle-stealers live. It is regarded as fair war by the small agriculturist against the ascendant squatter. A man may be a cattle-stealer, and yet in his way a decent fellow. I was once standing by, over a kangaroo which we had hunted, and which a free-selector who had made one in the hunt was skinning. There were two or three others also by. The man was a good sportsman, but I had been told that he liked other people's meat ."You have heard of the cattle-stealers, sir," he said, looking up at me. "This is the way they do it by moonlight, I'm told." He skinned the kangaroo with great skill and quickness, and I was sure that he was no novice at the business. He knew well enough by what he did and what he said he was owning himself to have been a cattle-stealer, but he was not a bit ashamed of it.

* * *

The impossibility of fixing a price for land, and yet the apparent necessity for doing so, has been the greatest difficulty felt in arranging the various schemes of Australian colonization. At first sight it may seem easy enough. Let the land be put up to auction, and let the purchaser fix the price. But when the work was commenced it was necessary to get new settlers on to the land, who knew nothing of its relative value, who could not tell whether they could afford to give 5s. or £5 an acre for it and then live upon it. These newcomers required to be instructed in all things, and in nothing more than as to the proper outlay of their small capitals. And the system of auction, when it did come to prevail in the sale of crown lands, was found to produce the grossest abuses—I think I may say the vilest fraud. Men constituted themselves as land agents with the express purpose of exacting blackmail from those who were really desirous of purchasing. "I will be your agent," such a one would say to the would-be purchaser. "I will buy the land for you, at a commission of a shilling an acre. You can buy it for yourself, you say. Then I shall bid against you." This system has prevailed to such an extent that the agency business has become an Australian profession, and men who did not want an acre of land have made fortunes by exacting tribute from those who were in earnest.

Church and Clergyman

Very much praiseworthy energy has been used throughout the colonies to bring religious teaching within the reach of the people under very disadvantageous circumstances. No doubt the fact of an endowed Church at home, and the theory of endowments which was brought from home to the colonies, has given rise there as well as here to an idea that religion and religious teaching and rites should be administered to a people without any demand upon them for direct payment. People in Australia will commonly make it a matter of complaint that no clergyman has ever been near them, that no religious aid has ever been sent to them, although they themselves have taken no measures and paid no money towards bringing a clergyman into their districts. For the doctor and the lawyer they know they must pay—as the Roman Catholic knows also that he must for his priest. But the normal English Protestant—even when dissenting from the Church of England—thinks that his spiritual pastor should be sent to him by some unknown authority which is supposed to have such matters in keeping. If the spiritual pastor be not sent, the Protestant goes on without clerical assistance, perhaps complaining—more probably troubling himself very little on the matter. He would go to church if there were a church near him; but if there be none within reach the fault does not rest with him, and thus his conscience is at ease. And again, the sparseness of the population and the great distances which lie between the small towns, add greatly to the difficulty. Clergymen of all denominations are, when employed in the pastoral districts, obliged to take charge of wide areas of country rather than of parishes—of areas so wide that services can be held by each perhaps only once a fortnight, and perhaps only once a month. The travelling also is expensive, laborious, and very disagreeable. It necessarily follows that in many places there is no religious worship set on foot with clerical aid; and that squatters, with their families and their attendant shepherds, stockriders, shearers, and the like, recognize Sunday only as a day of rest. . . .

I feel myself bound to record my opinion that religious teaching, and the exercise of religious worship, are held as being essential to civilization and general well-being by the people of Australia. Taking the inhabitants of the colonies all through, I think the feeling is stronger there than it is at home, first and chiefly because the mass of the population is better educated; secondly—and in a much less degree—because they who are foremost in education, rank, and society, are less highly educated. That the first should be the case will surprise no one, and will be generally admitted as a consequence, if it be allowed, that the colonial education is superior to that which we have as yet achieved at home. The tendencies and influences which send children to school, send them and their parents to church also—even though the schools be in all respects secular. Teaching produces prosperity; prosperity achieves decent garments—and decent garments are highly conducive to church-going. Among us in England that portion of our rural population which never goes to church; and which is utterly ignorant of all religious observances, consists of the unfortunates upon whom the kindly dew of instruction has never fallen, and who have been left in almost brute-like ignorance. Among all communities in the colonies the children are taught. Wherever there is any community, however small it may be, there is a school; and where there is a school the children attend it. And almost as universally, wherever there is a community there arises a church, or more commonly churches. Though there be only two or three hundred persons within a twelve-mile circle, affording perhaps an average church attendance of less than a hundred, there will be a Presbyterian and a Roman Catholic Church alongside of each other, or a Church of England and a Wesleyan church. Sometimes in a small township, containing ostensibly little in the way of buildings beyond the four public-houses, the blacksmith's shop and the bank, there will be three places of worship. The people are fond of building churches, and are proud of having them in their villages—though they are unfortunately less addicted to pay annually for their clergyman than to defray the cost of their churches. You can, too, go in debt for a church—but hardly for a clergyman. There is, I think, undoubtedly a general desire that the comfort and decency of religious teaching should be recognized in the colony, and this I attribute mainly to the healthy state of education.

It would be more difficult to show that a lower condition of education among the better educated classes in the colony than that which has been reached at home should have a similar tendency, but I think that such is the case. There can be but little doubt that education among the most favoured classes at home does range higher than in the colonies. It would indeed be most disgraceful to England with her wealth, and her endowed colleges and schools, if it were not so. And it has come about as one result of such advanced teaching—not in England only but in every country in which erudition has been valued—that the erudite have learned to disregard and in part to dispense with the services of a priesthood. I do not say that infidelity has been thus produced—but rather a tendency in the man's mind to think that he can best suffice to himself as his own priest. This feeling, operating from men to their wives, from fathers to sons, and from mothers to daughters—but ever more strongly among men than women—has in all highly intellectual communities had a certain tendency to weaken confidence in the administrations of church services. In the colonies this condition of society has hardly yet been reached. That it will come—whether it be for good of evil—is certain. In the meantime the absence of the condition has the tendency which I have alleged, of making the feeling in favour of religious teaching stronger among the higher classes in the colonies than it is among our higher classes at home.

The Women of Victoria

In describing Victorians of the upper classes, and of the two sexes, I would say that both in their defects and their excellences they approach nearer to the American than to the British type. And in this respect the Victorian is distinct from the colonist of New South Wales, who retains more of the John Bull attributes of the mother country than his younger and more energetic brother in the South. This is visible, I think, quite as much in the women as in the men. I am speaking now especially of those women whom on account of their education and position we should class as ladies; but the remark is equally true to all ranks of society. The maid-servant in Victoria has the pertness, the independence, the mode of asserting by her manner that though she brings you up your hot water, she is just as good as you—and a good deal better if she be younger—which is common to the American "helps". But in Victoria, as in the States, the offensiveness of this—for to us who are old-fashioned it is in a certain degree offensive—is compensated by a certain intelligence and instinctive good sense which convinces the observer that however much he may suffer, however heavily the young woman may tread upon his toes, she herself has a good time in the world. She is not degraded in her own estimation by her own employment, and has no idea of being humble because she brings you hot water. And when we consider that the young woman serves us for her own purposes, and not for ours, we cannot rationally condemn her.

The spirit which has made this bearing so common in the United States—where indeed it is hardly so universal now as it used to be—has grown in Victoria, and has permeated all classes. One has to look very closely before one can track it out and trace it to be the same in the elegantly equipped daughter of the millionaire who leads the fashion in Melbourne, and in the little housemaid—but it is the same. The self-dependence, the early intelligence, the absence of reverence, the contempt for all weakness—even feminine weakness—the indifference to the claims of age, the bold self-assertion, have sprung both in the one case and in the other from the rapidity with which success in life has been gained. The class of which I am now specially speaking is an aristocrat class; but it is an aristocracy of yesterday; and the creation of such an aristocracy does away with reverence and puts audacity in its place. The young housemaid does not shake in her shoes before you because you have £10,000 a year, and the young lady has no special respect for you because you are her father's old friend. Her father and her father's friends have had their time. It is her time now. It is for her to stand in the middle and for them to range themselves on one side. She will do her duty by her father and mother—but she does it as a superior person attending on those who are inferior. To her grandfather and her grandmother she alludes as poor things of the past, to whom much tenderness is due. But the attention is paid after a fashion which seems to imply that old folk, in the arrangements of life, should not interfere with their betters who are young. Luckily for fathers and grandfathers in Victoria the power of the purse remains with them—otherwise they would I fear be ciphers in the houses that were once their own. The Australian girls and young married women are not cruel, false, or avaricious, and I will not call them Gonerils and Regans; but I have seen old men who have put me in mind of Lear.

There is a manifest difference between women who have come out from England and those who are "colonial-born", which is not at all points in favour of the former. If we are to take personal appearance as the good thing most in request by the female sex, I think that the girls born in the colony have the pre-eminence. As a rule they are very pretty, having delicate sweet complexions and fine forms. They grow quickly, and are women two years earlier in life than are our girls—and consequently are old women some five years sooner. They are bright and quick, hardly as yet thoroughly educated, as the means of thorough education for women do not grow up in a new country very readily; but they have all achieved a certain amount of information which they have at their fingers' ends. They never appear to be stupid or ignorant—because they are never bashful or diffident. We do not criticize very accurately the law as laid down to us by a pretty woman—being thankful for any law from bright eyes and ruby lips. Sometimes at home we can get no law, no opinion, no rapid out-flow of sweet-sounding words, because some modest sense of the weakness of feminine youth restrains the speech. It must be admitted, however, that even at home this failing is less general than it used to be.

Women, all the world over, are entitled to everything that chivalry can give them. They should sit while men stand. They should be served while men wait. Men should be silent while they speak. They should be praised—even without desert. They should be courted—even when having neither wit nor beauty. They should be worshipped—even without love. They should be kept harmless while men suffer. They should be kept warm while men are cold. They should be kept safe while men are in danger. They should be enabled to live while men die in their defence. All this chivalry should do for women, and should do as a matter of course. But there is a reason for this deference. One human being does not render all these services to another—who cannot be more than his equal before God—without a cause. A man will serve a woman, will suffer for her—if it comes to that will die for her—because she is weaker than he and needs protection. Let her show herself to be as strong, let her prove by her prowess and hardihood that the old idea of her comparative weakness has been an error from the beginning, and the very idea of chivalry, though it may live for awhile by the strength of custom, must perish and die out of men's hearts. I have often felt this in listening to the bold assertion of American women—not without a doubt whether chivalry was needed for the protection of beings so excellent in their own gifts, so superabundant in their own strength. And the same thought has crept over me when I have been among the ladies of Victoria. No doubt they demand all that chivalry can give them. No ladies with whom I am acquainted are more determined to enforce their rights in that direction. But they make their claim with arms in their hands —at the very point of the bodkin. Stand aside that I may pass on. Be silent that I may speak. Lay your coat down upon the mud and perish in the cold, lest my silken slippers be soiled in the mire. Be wounded that I may be whole. Die, that I may live. And for the nonce they are obeyed. That strength of custom still prevails, and women in Victoria enjoy for a while all that weakness gives, and all that strength gives also. But this, I think, can only be for a day. They must choose between the two, not only in Victoria but elsewhere. As long as they will put up with that which is theirs on the score of feminine weakness, they are safe. There is no tendency on the part of men to lessen their privileges. Whether they can make good their position in the other direction may be doubtful. I feel sure that they cannot have both, and I think it unfair that they should make such demand. For the sake of those who are to come after me—both men and women—I hope that there may be no change in the old-established fashion.

I write these words in fear and trembling, lest the ladies of Victoria should condemn my book, and set me down as one who had accepted and betrayed hospitality. Let them remember all that I have conceded to them. They are lovely, bright, quick-witted, and successful. If, having said so much on their behalf, I venture to add a few words of counsel, they should remember that unqualified praise is always egregious flattery.

"Knocking Down His Cheque"

If we may take 17s. 6d. as the average money wages of a labouring man, he will receive in the year something over £45, besides his food. It must be understood also that in most of the occupations shelter is afforded—a place, that is, in which to cook, to sleep, and to eat. The man brings his own blankets, but he has a bunk on which he can lie, and the use of a hut. If, therefore, a man be unmarried and really careful, he can very quickly save enough money to enable himself to start as a buyer of land. I now presume myself to be addressing some young English labourer; and the young English labourer is doubtless certain that, when the circumstances described become his own, he will be prudent. I hope he may. There is no reason whatever why he should not. Those among whom he works will respect and even like him the better for it—and those for whom he works will of course do so. He will have every facility for saving his money, which will be paid to him in comparatively large sums, by cheques. Perhaps he will do so. I am bound to tell him that I have my doubts about it. I shall very much respect him if he does; but, judging from the habits of others of his class, and from the experience of those who know the colony, I think that he will take his cheque to a public-house, give it to the publican, get drunk, and remain so till the publican tells him that the cheque has been consumed. The publican will probably let him eat and drink for a fortnight, and will then turn him out penniless, to begin again. He will begin again, and repeat the same folly time after time, till he will teach himself to think that it is the normal condition of his life.

A Queensland gentleman told me the story of a certain shearer who had shorn for him year after year, and had always gone through the same process of "knocking down his cheque", as the work is technically called. He liked the man, and on one occassion remonstrated with him as he handed him the paper, explaining to him the madness of the proceeding. Would he not on that occasion be content to get drunk only on a portion of his money, and put the remainder into a savings-bank? No—the man said that when he had earned his money he liked to feel that he could do what he pleased with it. So he took his cheque, and started for the nearest town. On the following day he returned—to the astonishment of his employer, who knew that the knocking down of so substantial a cheque should have occupied perhaps three weeks—and told his story. Having a little silver in his pocket, and having thought much of what had been said to him, he had "planted" his cheque when he found himself near the town. In the language of the colonies, to plant a thing is to hide it. He had planted his cheque, and gone on to the publican with his silver. To set to work to get drunk was a matter of course. He did get drunk—but the publican seemed to have had some doubt as to the propriety of supplying him freely. Why had not the man brought out his cheque in the usual manly way at once, instead of paying with loose silver for a few "nobblers" for himself and the company? The publican put him to bed drunk, stretching him out on some bunk or board in the customary hospitable manner; but he had his suspicions. Could it be that his old friend should have no cheque after shearing? It behoved him, at any rate, to know. The knocking down of an imaginary cheque would be dreadful to the publican. So the publican stripped him and examined all his clothing, looked into his boots, and felt well through the possible secrets of every garment. The man, though drunk and drugged, was not so drunk or drugged but what he knew and understood the proceeding. He had not paid enough for a sufficient amount of drugs and liquor to make him absolutely senseless. The cheque had been securely planted, and nothing was found. On the next morning he was turned out ignominiously by the justly-indignant owner of the house; but in the tree by the roadside he found his cheque, and returned with it to the station a wiser and a better man.

Heat and the Mosquitoes

On the 29th of September [1871] I left Brisbane for Sydney, going south from Queensland to New South Wales, so as to accommodate myself to the heat. I may however say here once for all that I found Australian heat to be a bugbear of which no Englishman fresh from England need be afraid. I remained in New South Wales on this occasion till the middle of December, and encountered no weather in which I could not take exercise. I had been especially warned as to the hot winds of Sydney, having been told both in Victoria and Queensland that of all effects of weather in the colonies the hot winds of New South Wales were the worst. They ought to blow in December, coming from the north-west over the central deserts of Australia, bringing with them all the heats of those vast plains. But they did not come when I was there; and people in Sydney, though they fear the heat, seemed to lament that the hot winds of the present were not like the old hot winds. Folk were not scorched now as they used to be scorched, nor suffocated, nor forced to shut themselves up in dark rooms with every window closed lest the enemy should enter—as they were wont to do in the good old times twenty years ago. Such was the tone of the wailing which prevailed. Early in January I certainly did find it very hot in Victoria, but the heat was intermittent, lasting only for a few days; and though I am told that the mercury rose occasionally to 90° in the shade, I was not seriously oppressed by it. And I may add to this that Australian mosquitoes, of which I had heard much and which I feared greatly, were never quite so venomous to me as mosquitoes have been in other countries, nor are they in force for so large a proportion of the year. The mosquito of Australia is a poor, impotent and contemptible creature as compared, for instance, with the mosquito of the United States. If a man wants to find his master—a master whom he cannot evade or subdue, a tyrant under whose lash he will have to quail with a sense of unceasing inferiority and trembling subjection—let him remain in Washington through the month of July. Then the horn of the animal will be to him as the trumpets of ten thousand coming foes, against whom no struggles, no defence can avail aught. Night and day he will be as Job was, till all his manhood will depart from him. And afterwards, if he survive, he will think of himself as of one who has gone through worse than an Egyptian plague. He will be justified in no such feeling in reference to the Australian mosquito, whom I declare to be comparatively a poor creature entitled to but little attention. So much—as a traveller recording his experience—I feel bound to say, because the animal has succeeded in acquiring some reputation. To write a book about Australia and make no allusion to the mosquito would be improper.

The Wine of the Country

Australia makes a great deal of wine—so much and so cheaply that the traveller is surprised at finding how very little of it is used by the labouring classes. Among them some do not drink at all, some few drink daily—and many never drink when at work, but indulge in horrible orgies during the few weeks, or perhaps days, of idleness which they allow themselves. But the liquor which they swallow is almost always spirits—and always spirits of the most abominable kind. They pay sixpence a glass for their poison, which is served to them in a cheating false-bottomed tumbler so contrived as to look half-full when it contains but little. The dram is swallowed without water, and the dose is repeated till the man be drunk. The falseness of the glass seems to excuse itself, as the less the man has the better for him; but the fraud serves no one but the publican, for though the "nobbler" be small—a dram in Australia is always a nobbler—there is no limit to the number of nobblers. The concoction which is prepared for these poor fellows is, I think, even worse than that produced by the London publican. At home, however, beer is the wine of the country, and beer is the popular beverage at any rate with the workmen of this country. In all the Australian colonies, except Tasmania, wine is made plentifully, and, if it were the popular drink of the country, would be made so plentifully that it could suffice for the purpose. All fruits thrive there, but none with such fecundity as the grape. One Victorian wine-grower, who had gone into the business on a great scale, told me that, if he could get 2s. a gallon for all that he made, the business would pay him well. The wine of which he spoke was certainly superior both in flavour and body to the ordinary wine drank by Parisians. It is wholesome and nutritious, and is the pure juice of the grape.

Accustomed to French and Spanish wines—or perhaps to wines passed off upon me as such—I did not like the Australian "fine" wines. The best that I drank was in South Australia, but I did not much relish them. I thought them to be heady, having a taste of earth, and an after flavour which was disagreeable. This may have been prejudice on my part. It may be that the requisite skill for wine-making has not yet been attained in the colonies. Undoubtedly age is still wanting to the wines, which are consumed too quickly after the vinting. It may possibly be the case that though Australia can grow an unlimited quantity of wine, she cannot produce wines capable of rivalling those of Europe. On these points I do not pretend to have an opinion. But I regard a wholesome drink for the country as being of more importance than fine wines, even though they should equal the produce of the vineyards of the South of Spain or the South of France. France and Italy are temperate because they produce a wine suitable to their climate. Australia, with a similar climate, produces wine with equal ease, and certainly—I speak in reference to the common wine—as good a quality. There is now on sale in Melbourne, at the price of, I think, threepence a glass—the glass containing about half a pint—the best vin-ordinaire that I ever drank. It is a white wine made at Yering, a vineyard on the Upper Yarra, and is both wholesome and nutritive. Nevertheless, the workmen of Melbourne, when they drink, prefer to swallow the most horrible poison which the skill of man ever concocted.

* * *

I have drank fairly good wine made in Australia, but none made in Queensland. If on this head any wine-growing Queensland squatter should accuse me of falsehood—remembering the assenting smile which seemed to acknowledge that his vintage was excellent—let him reflect how impossible it is for the guest to repudiate the praises with which the host speaks of his own cellar. All the world over it is allowed to the giver to praise his own wine—a privilege of which Australians avail themselves—but it is not allowed to the receiver to deny the justness of such encomium, except under circumstances of peculiar intimacy. Here, in these pages, truth must prevail; and I am bound to say that Queensland wine was not to my taste. I am delighted to acknowledge that their pine-apples were perfect.

2 THE COLONIES AND THEIR TOWNS

Queensland

After a few days spent in Melbourne, the great metropolis of our Australian empire, I went direct to Queensland, in order that I might see and hear what was to be seen and heard in that semi-tropical colony before the great heat commenced. I arrived there on the 11th August, 1871. The hot weather is supposed to begin in October and to last till the end of April. The subject of heat is one of extreme delicacy in Queensland, as indeed it is also in the other colonies. One does not allude to heat in a host's house any more than to a bad bottle of wine or an ill-cooked joint of meat. You may remark that it is very cool in your friend's verandah, your friend of the moment being present, and may hint that the whole of your absent friend's establishment is as hot as a furnace; but though you be constrained to keep your handkerchief to your brow, and hardly dare to walk to the garden gate, you must never complain of the heat then and there. You may call an inn hot, or a court-house, but not a gentleman's paddock or a lady's drawing-room. And you should never own to a mosquito. I once unfortunately stated to a Queensland gentleman that my coat had been bitten by cockroaches at his brother's house, which I had just left. "You must have brought them with you then," was the fraternal defence immediately set up. I was compelled at once to antedate the cockroaches to my previous resting-place, owned by a friend, not by a brother. "It is possible," said the squatter, "but I think you must have had them with you longer than that." I acquiesced in silence, and said no more about my coat till I could get it mended elsewhere. It was winter, so called, when I reached Queensland, but I found Brisbane very warm—warmer than when I left it two months later. . . .

On my first arrival at Brisbane I spent but a few days there, and then hurried up north to Rockhampton, again endeavouring to anticipate the heat. Brisbane is a commodious town, very prettily situated on the Brisbane River, with 12,000 inhabitants, with courts of justice, houses of parliament, a governor's residence, public gardens, and all the requirements of a capital for a fine and independent colony. I had an opportunity of seeing a new governor sworn in. The ceremony was not very august, and I was chiefly amused with the vain endeavours of an unfortunate photographer to bring his instrument to bear upon the performance. It may be interesting to know that the governor took his oath manfully in a tight-fitting, tight-buttoned blue uniform, which was no doubt prescribed to him by official rule, but which seems to be as ill adapted to the climate as any dress that could possibly be desired. But I envied him his house, which was airy, spacious, well-built, and pretty. His house will be there for him always till his term of government be over, and no doubt he can put off his blue uniform on occasions. . . .

Of Gladstone I will say a few words now. It is a seaport in the so called Port Curtis district, and a prettier spot or more melancholy town than Gladstone one could hardly find in any country, new or old. It received its name, of course, from our own statesman, and is said to have been peculiarly favoured by him. It has been spoken of as the future capital of Queensland, and there are many in Queensland—including the present Premier of the colony—who think that it should be selected, as was Ottawa in Canada, because it has the double advantage of a somewhat central position—on the coast—and of possessing nothing to offend the jealousies either of Brisbane to the south or Rockhampton to the north. Other apparent fitnesses for a capital it has none—except that of a fine harbour. Though it has been essentially fostered by the affections of certain politicians, that first primary necessity of a city, population, has refused to cleave to it. The busy part of the town, consisting of a little wharf, two or three stores, and a custom-house, stands about a quarter of a mile up a small creek just broad enough to allow the steamboats to be turned in it. The creek opens into a magnificent harbour—magnificent in scenery certainly, and equally so, I should imagine, for the use of ships lying at anchor; but for vessels to lie against the shore, the little muddy creek at present affords the only useful spot. But a fine harbour and beautiful scenery will not make a city—or even help to make one, unless people can find on its shores the means of earning their bread. Gladstone is landlocked by mountains, and has no back country to support it. There is nothing there to produce trade, or to induce people to choose the place as a domicile favourable to their hopes in life. Consequently the streets, which are many, spacious, and long, are simply beautiful glades running through the wild woods, with here a cottage and there a house, so sparsely scattered as to give to each habitation the appearance of having been rudely built for some Paul and his Virginia. They inflict on the forest no look of invading humanity.

In passing through the western districts of the United States, in Canada, and also in these Australian colonies, visitors are accustomed to find large straggling collections of straight, fenced roads, from which the last relics of the primeval forests have not as yet disappeared, and to hear them graced with the names of streets though the houses be as yet unfrequent. These are baby towns; but they are babies strong with signs of increasing life. The grass has given way to the pressure of men's feet. The happiest sites, the corners and double frontages, are generally occupied. The pioneers have got the better of the forest, and population is manifestly alive and afoot. But, again, there are selected spots in which it is too clearly evident that man's endeavour in regard to that enterprise is destined to failure. The wildness of the woods is too strong for the amount of energy which the limited advantages of the place can produce. Sometimes these failures in the founding of cities are most wretched to the eye. Perhaps the most miserable which I ever beheld was Cairo, in Illinois—the Eden of Charles Dickens. There was nothing on that spot but mud, idleness, whisky, and despair. Cairo, no doubt, had more of life in it than Gladstone; but Gladstone is

D

beautiful to the eye, and is thus redeemed to the traveller. From green glades within a quarter of a mile of the wharf, one looks down upon a sea lake surrounded by wooded mountains, and feels all the pride of distant desolation and forest silence.

* * *

Rockhampton is a town lying exactly on the line of the tropic of Capricorn, some miles up the Fitzroy River, with about seven thousand inhabitants, which considers itself to be the second town of the colony, and thinks a good deal of itself. It has been seized with the ambition to become a capital, and therefore hates Brisbane. It is so hot that people going from it to an evil place are said to send back to earth for their blankets, finding that evil place to be too chilly for them after the home they have left. But the Rockhamptonites are energetic as become the aspirants to metropolitan honours. They do, in truth, do those things which are necessary for the well being of a community. They have a hospital—and an excellent hospital it is; also a jail, not so excellent; a good hotel—or, as I was assured, one or two good hotels; wide streets, a grand post-office—they ought to keep it open for the accommodation of the public after six o'clock in the evening, and no doubt would do so if they knew that here in England post-offices are not closed at the earliest before nine. They have excellent shops, a good quay, and they have a railway. Perhaps the railway is the crowning glory of Rockhampton.

I must say a word of the Rockhampton railway, and it certainly will not be a word in praise. I have my regrets, for I was carried over it free of charge, and was accompanied by the gentleman who manages it, and who made himself very pleasant on the occasion. Nevertheless I can say nothing good of the Rockhampton railway. It was made as a job, and now that it is made it is not only useless but infinitely worse than useless. It would be a great saving to the colony if it could be shut up and abandoned. I asked in my innocence whether, independent of the cost of making, it supported itself—whether it paid for its own working. I was told that it about paid for the grease used upon it. Now, the cause and meaning of the Rockhampton railway may be described as follows:—Queensland, a colony vast in extent, was at first populated in her southern districts, those which were contiguous to New South Wales, from which she had succeeded in separating herself. But even at the time of her separation, a small and scattered few had driven their cattle up to the hotter northern lands. Then there were gold rushes, and boiling down establishments, and so the town of Rockhampton was formed, while the population and prosperity of Queensland was as yet in her southern borders—round Brisbane, and the towns of Ipswich, Warwick, and Toowoomba, and on the Darling Downs. It was then deemed expedient that there should be a railway in the South—not running out of Brisbane, which has easy water communication with Ipswich; but from Ipswich to the other towns above named, and so across the Darling Downs, where are the grand sheep-walks of that country. It must be understood that railways in Australia, with one or two exceptions, have been made by Government—as hitherto have all roads, river clearances, and the like. The Government makes the railway and works it, taking and expending the money, and doing all by the hands of official servants. That it should be so is to me distressing. Whether or no the practice is necessary shall not be discussed now, but at any rate such is the fact. But the Government can only make its railway when the Legislature has sanctioned the making of it, and the borrowing of the money for the purpose.

When the making of the Darling Downs railway was mooted—by which undoubtedly the produce of a very fine district would be brought down to the sea, and the people of various towns would be brought within easy reach of the metropolis—no very strong objection seems to have been raised to the scheme. It was not much debated whether or no the young colony could or could not bear the weight of the borrowed millions. But this was debated, and made very clear in debate—that if the southern division of the colony had its railway, then also must the northern. The southern population were ten times greater than the northern no doubt. Well—then let the southern railway be ten times greater than the northern. But if the Darling Downs people were to have their railway, then should Rockhampton have its railway. On no other terms would any northern member dare to vote the appropriation of the money. Unless this were done, Rockhampton, which is not a meek place nor forbearing in its nature, would make such a row that the colony should split to pieces with it. It had to be done, and hence there are thirty miles of a railway that barely pays for its own grease. It goes out thirty miles to three public-houses in the forest which call themselves Westwood; but it does not get the traffic incident to these thirty miles, because for so short a distance it is not worth the while of waggoners, who take down wool and bring back stores, to unload their burden. The squatters can communicate with Rockhampton cheaper by the old way than by using thirty miles of railroad. . . .

That question of levying taxes and spending public money for other purposes than those of direct government, including the defence and protection of the nation, is very seducing and very dangerous. . . . When a government can make ever so much a year by monopolizing telegraphs, it may seem to be very well—but when a government has to lose ever so much a year by distributing railways it is surely very bad. The Rockhampton and Westwood railway is the very bathos of such attempts.

And this brings me to the great subject of Separation, which I found to be in every man's mouth at Rockhampton. Separation now-a-days in Queensland means the division of that colony into two colonies, as in old days it meant the division of New South Wales into two or more colonies. Though Queensland is hardly in her teens she is already held by the people of her northern districts to be ready for further division. Let there be Queensland and—Albertland some wish to call the would-be future colony. Why should taxes levied in the north go to make roads round Brisbane? Why should northern legislators travel four, five, six, and seven hundred miles to a southern town built on the very borders of New South Wales? Why should we northerners with our unlimited area, our high ambition, with a great future looming upon us in gold and sugar, be sacrificed to Brisbane and the Darling Downs? Brisbane is hated at Rockhampton, but I think that the Darling Downs are more odious. It must be remembered always that the Darling Downs squatters are the aristocrats of Queensland, and are about as much in favour at Rockhampton as a marquis is at Manchester. We have, say these northern men, ten, fifteen, or twenty thousand inhabitants—according as the line may be drawn. Let us have a governor of our own—and, above all, the privileges of legislation. We are old enough to go alone, and go alone we will. The sweat of our brow shall no longer go to Brisbane.

But where shall the line be drawn? Just south of Rockhampton say the Rockhamptonites, so that the new colony, the finest that will bear the flag of England, may have this well built, elegantly organized, and populous town for its capital—a town with real streets, and hotels, with a grand post-office and a railroad. What more can a colony desire? But in that case Rockhampton also would be at the extremity, and the people north of that—ay, five hundred miles to the north of it, as any man may see by looking at the map—would have to send the sweat of his brows to that city. The coming golden era of sugar and northern gold is destined to bless a region nearer to the sun even than Rockhampton. Let Cape Palmerston be the point, and Bowen or Townsville the new capital. And so the matter is debated. . . .

There must be politicians among young colonists, and there must be houses of legislation, but the less there is of ambition in that direction, the quicker will fortunes be made and families established. The future sugar grower of Port Mackay will not be so much injured by sending taxes to Brisbane as by having to devote his time to some nearer little parliament whether in Rockhampton or Townsville. Parliaments, with their debates and all that volubility of words which Mr. Carlyle hates with such genuine vigour, are dear to my heart. Parliaments are to me the very salt of the earth. But I doubt the expediency of a fresh parliament for ten thousand people—the population of a one-membered borough at home—when that ten thousand has so little of which to complain as have at present the inhabitants of Northern Queensland.

After visiting Gympie (see pp. 114-118), Trollope returned to Brisbane and set out for the Darling Downs.

Thence I went to the little town of Warwick, which in that part of the world is held to be the perfection of a town. "You will think Warwick very pretty," everybody said to me. I did not think Warwick at all pretty. It is unfinished, parallelogrammatic, and monotonous; and the mountains are just too far from it to give it any attraction—as is also the sluggish Condamine River. It is not so rugged as are many of the towns. And though here, as in other colonial towns, the houses are intermittent and every other lot apparently vacant, there has been an eye to decency. But when I am told that such a place is pretty, I do not know what the speaker means. That it should be clean is creditable; that it should be progressive is satisfactory—but that it should be ugly is a necessity of its condition. I found Warwick to be clean, and I believe it to be prosperous; and, which was very much to my purpose, I found in it an excellent inn, kept by one Bugden. And I found there Chang, the great Chinese giant, about to show himself at 2s. a head on the evening of my arrival. But I had not come from London to Warwick to see Chang, and I neglected an opportunity which, perhaps, may never occur to me again.

Sydney

I despair of being able to convey to any reader my own idea of the beauty of Sydney Harbour. I have seen nothing equal to it in the way of land-locked sea scenery—nothing second to it. Dublin Bay, the Bay of Spezia, New York, and the Cove of Cork are all picturesquely fine. Bantry Bay, with the nooks of sea running up to Glengariff, is very lovely. But they are not equal to Sydney either in shape, in colour, or in variety. I have never seen Naples, or Rio Janiero, or Lisbon; but from description and pictures I am led to think that none of them can possess such a world of loveliness of water as lies within Sydney Heads. The proper thing to assert is that the fleets of all nations might rest securely within the protection of the harbour. How much acreage of sea the fleets of all nations might require I cannot even surmise—but if they could be anchored together anywhere, they could surely be so anchored at Sydney.

As I thought of this, steaming up the harbour to Sydney Cove—having just heard the boast from a stout Sydney citizen—I felt assured that whenever the experiment should be tried, the English fleet would enter first with proud pre-eminence; and range themselves with haughty courtesy close under the Governor's house and all round the town. Then would come the Danish, the Swedish, the Spanish, the Portuguese, the Turkish, the Russian, and the Austrian ironclads. And we should glow with national pride as we told ourselves that, added together, all these foreign ships of war amounted to about half our collected force. The French and the Prussian fleets would place themselves in the broad expanse between Manly Beach and Watson's Bay, watching each other with ill-concealed hatred. In the very mouth of the harbour would be four or five American Alabamas—who would thus be enabled to hurry off to Europe, to burn Liverpool, and carry off all the ropes of pearls which lie hidden between Bond Street and the Tower of London. By the time that they had disposed of the spoil in New York, we should be extricating ourselves from our position. The Americans after a while would apologize. The captains would probably have misunderstood their instructions, and would have gold swords given to them. But they would not pay for a single rope of pearls, and Liverpool would rebuild itself.

In none of the books which I have seen respecting the early settlement of the colony, or of its subsequent difficulties in progress, is much stress laid on the scenery of Sydney Harbour, or of the Hawkesbury River which is near it. Nor is much said of the glorious defiles of the Blue Mountains. Such books have been generally circumstantial and statistical—either despondent or hopeful, according to the opinions of the writers. They have always insisted much—and have done so with well-deserved zeal—on the great efforts made by Australian discoverers. They have told us of the drawbacks of the land—which are very great, as the soil is often poor, is encumbered with forests, deficient in water, and subject to a climate which is not propitious to cereals. On the other hand, we have heard from them much of Australian wool, and for the last twenty years of Australian gold. We gather from these books many facts as to the past events of Australia, and many opinions as to its future. But we hear very little of Australian scenery. Consequently we, at home in England, are inclined to believe that Australia, as a country, is displeasing to the eye. The eternal gum-tree has become to us an Australian crest, giving evidence of Australian ugliness. The gum-tree is ubiquitous, and is not the loveliest, though neither is it by any means the ugliest of trees. But there are scenes of nature in Australia as lovely as are to be found in any part of the world; not so closely congregated as in Western Europe, but quite as much so as in North America. They are often difficult of access—and must remain so, till the population is large enough to stretch itself about the country, and to make railways, and to run river steamers.

The people of Sydney are by no means indifferent to the beauty of their harbour, and claim for it the admiration of strangers with something of the language, but not with the audacity of Americans, when they demand the opinions of their visitors as to their remarkable institutions. There is something of shamefacedness, a confession of provincial weakness, almost an acknowledgment that they ought not to be proud of a thing so insignificant, in the tone in which you are asked whether, upon the whole, you do not think Sydney Harbour rather pretty. Every Sydney man and every Sydney woman does ask you the question—as does every American ask that other question; but it is asked in Sydney with bated breath, and with something of an apology, "Of course you have been bothered out of your life about our harbour; but it is pretty—don't you think so?" It is so inexpressibly lovely that it makes a man ask himself whether it would not be worth his while to move his household gods to the eastern coast of Australia, in order that he might look at it as long as he can look at anything. . . .

I doubt whether I ever read any description of scenery which gave me an idea of the place described, and I am not sure that such effect can be obtained by words. Scott in prose, and Byron in verse, are both eloquent in declaring that this or that place is romantic, picturesque, or charming; and their words have been powerful enough to send thousands to see the spots which they have praised. But the charm conveyed has been in the words of the writer, not in the beauty of the place. I know that the task would be hopeless were I to attempt to make others understand the nature of the beauty of Sydney Harbour. I can say that it is lovely, but I cannot paint its loveliness. The sea runs up in various bays or coves, indenting the land all around the city, so as to give a thousand different aspects of the water—and not of water, broad, unbroken, and unrelieved—but of water always with jutting corners of land beyond it, and then again of water and then again of land. And you, the resident—even though you be a lady not over strong, though you be a lady, if possible, not over young —will find, unless you choose your residence most unfortunately, that you have walks within your reach as deliciously beautiful as though you had packed up all your things and travelled days and spent pounds to find them.

One Mrs. Macquarie, the wife, I believe, of Governor Macquarie, made a road, or planned a road, or at any rate gave her name to a road, which abuts on the public domain, and is all but in the town. A mile and a half from the top of Hunter Street carries the pedestrian all round it. Two shillings does as much for him or her who prefers a hansom cab—and the Sydney hansoms are the very best cabs in the world. At the end of it is Mrs. Macquarie's chair—with a most ill-written inscription—but with a view that affords compensation even for that. The public gardens, not half a mile from the top of Hunter Street, beat all the public gardens I ever saw—because they possess one little nook of sea of their own. I do not love public gardens generally, because I am called on to listen to the names of shrubs conveyed in three Latin words, and am supposed to interest myself in the locality from which they have been brought. I envy those who have the knowledge which I want; but I put my back up against attempts made to convey it to me, knowing that it is too late. But it was impossible not to love the public gardens at Sydney—because one could sit under the trees and look out upon the sea. There is a walk from the bottom of Macquarie Street—not Mrs. Macquarie's Road, but the old Governor's own street—leading round by the fort, under the Governor's house, to the public gardens. The whole distance round may be a mile and a half from the top of Hunter Street, which opens on to Macquarie Street. It runs close along the sea, with grassy slopes on which you may lie and see the moon glimmer on the water as it only glimmers on land-locked coves of the ocean. You may lie there prostrate on the grass, with the ripple close at your feet within a quarter-of-an-hour of your club. Your after-dinner cigar will last you there and back if you will walk fairly and smoke slowly. Nobody ever is there at that hour, the young men of Sydney preferring to smoke their cigars in their arm-chairs. Then there is the little trip by steam ferry over to the north shore, where lives that prince of professors and greatest of Grecians, Doctor Badham, of the university. I should like to be the ferry-man over that ferry to Lavender Bay on condition that the Doctor met me with some refreshment on each journey. Sydney is one of those places which, when a man leaves it knowing that he will never return, he cannot leave without a pang and a tear. Such is its loveliness.

The town itself, as a town, independently of its sea and its suburbs was, to me, pleasant and interesting. In the first place, though it is the capital of an Australian colony, and therefore not yet a hundred years old, it has none of those worst signs of novelty which make the cities of the New World unpicturesque and distasteful. It is not parallelogrammic and rectangular. One may walk about it and lose the direction in which one is going. Streets running side by side occasionally converge—and they bend and go in and out, and wind themselves about, and are intricate. Philadelphia, which has not a want in the world, and is supplied with every luxury which institutions can confer upon human nature, is of all towns the most unattractive, because it is so managed that every house in it has its proper place, which can be found out at once, so long as the mind of the seeker be given to ordinary arithmetic. No arithmetic will set the wanderer right in Sydney—and this, I think, is a great advantage. I lived at 213½ in a certain street, and the interesting number chosen seemed to have no reference to any smaller numbers. There was no 1, or 5, or 20 in that street. If you live at 213 in Philadelphia, you know that you are three doors from Two Hundred and Ten Street on one side, and seven from Two Hundred and Twenty Street on the other. Information conveyed in that manner is always to me useless. I forget the numbers which I should remember, and have no aid to memory in the peculiarity either of the position or of the name.

The public gardens at Sydney deserve more than the passing mention just made of them. The people of Australia personally are laudably addicted to public gardens—as they are to other public institutions with which they are enabled to inaugurate the foundation of their towns, by the experience taught to them by our deficiencies. Parks for the people were not among the requirements of humanity when our cities were first built; and the grounds necessary for such purposes had become so valuable when the necessity was recognized, that it has been only with great difficulty, and occasionally by the munificence of individuals, that we have been able to create these artificial lungs for our artisans. In many of our large towns we have not created them at all. The Australian cities have had the advantage of our deficiencies. The land has been public property, and space for recreation has been taken without payment of any cost price. In this way a taste for gardens, and, indeed, to some extent, a knowledge of flowers and shrubs has been generated, and a humanizing influence in that direction has been produced. There are, in all the large towns—either in the very centre of them or adjacent to them—gardens rather than parks, which are used and apparently never abused. Those at Melbourne in Victoria are the most pretentious, and, in a scientific point of view, no doubt the most valuable. I am told that in the rarity and multiplicity of the plants collected there, they are hardly surpassed by any in Europe. But for loveliness, and that beauty which can be appreciated by the ignorant as well as by the learned, the Sydney gardens are unrivalled by any that I have seen. The nature of the land, with its green slopes down to its own bright little sea bay, has done much for them, and art and taste combined has made them perfect. It may be said that of all drawbacks to public parks distance is the greatest. We know that in London Hyde Park is but of little service to those who live at Mile End. The great Park at New York, though it is connected by omnibusses with the whole city, requires an expedition to reach it. The gardens of the Crystal Palace at Sydenham are so far off from the multitude that the distance rather than the cost of entrance deters the crowd which might take delight in them. Even the Bois de Boulogne are too remote for daily purposes. But the gardens of Sydney are within easy reach of every street of the combined towns of Sydney and Woolloomooloo. A little beyond the gardens, almost equally near to the town, are the sea baths—not small, dark, sequestered spots in which, for want of a better place, men and women may wash themselves, but open sea-spaces, guarded by palisades from the sharks which make bathing in the harbour impracticable, large enough for swimming, and fitted up with all requisites. It is a great thing for a city to be so provided; and it is a luxury which, as far as I am aware, no other city possesses to the same degree. There is no place for bathing in England like it, or at all equal to it. That at Kingstown in Ireland is perhaps as good; but Kingstown is six or seven miles from Dublin, and has to be reached by railroad. A man or a woman may walk to the bathing place at Sydney in a quarter of an hour.

I was much surprised at the fortifications of Sydney Harbour. Fortifications, unless specially inspected, escape even a vigilant seer of sights, but I, luckily for myself, was enabled specially to inspect them. I had previously no idea that the people of New South Wales were either so suspicious of enemies, or so pugnacious in their nature. I found five separate fortresses, armed, or to be armed, to the teeth with numerous guns—four, five, or six at each point—Armstrong guns, rifled guns, guns of eighteen tons weight, with loopholed walls, and pits for riflemen, as though Sydney were to become another Sebastopol. I was shown how the whole harbour and city were commanded by these guns. There were open batteries and casemented batteries, shell rooms and gunpowder magazines, barracks rising here and trenches dug there. There was a boom to be placed across the harbour, and a whole world of torpedoes ready to be sunk beneath the water, all of which were prepared and ready for use in an hour or two. It was explained to me that "they" could not possibly get across the trenches, or break the boom, or escape the torpedoes, or live for an hour beneath the blaze of the guns. "They" would not have a chance to get at Sydney. There was much martial ardour, and a very general opinion that "they" would have the worst of it. For a time I could not gather who "they" were to be. But "indirect damages" were on men's tongues, and so I knew who were the "they" at that moment uppermost in the thoughts of my companions. It would be the same in regard to any other enemies of England, either in *esse* or in *posse*. I hope that New South Wales may never have to fight for England, and certainly that she may not have to fight America. But the feeling of loyalty in the colony is so strong, that were there a fight on hand, she would be unhappy not to be allowed to take some share in it. But in viewing these fortifications, I was most specially struck by the loveliness of the sites chosen. One would almost wish to be a gunner for the sake of being at one of those forts.

Three different localities are combined to make Sydney. There is the old city—old as the age of cities is as yet counted in Australia—in which are George Street and Pitt Street, so called from George III and his minister, running parallel to each other, from the centre. . . . To the south of these rises the important town of Woolloomooloo—as to the remarkable spelling of which name the reader may take my assurance that I am right. Woolloomooloo has become almost as big as Sydney and much more fashionable; and beyond Woolloomooloo, on and over various little coves of the sea, Elizabeth Bay, and Rose Bay, and Double

Bay, and Rushcutter's Bay, cluster the various villa residences of the wealthy families. It is here that the rising generation of Sydney desires to dwell, and there is much to justify its choice.

Then there is the "North Shore", less fashionable, but almost as beautiful as the hills round the southern coves. The North Shore has to be reached by steam ferry from Sydney Cove, which now is better known as the Circular Quay, where is congregated the shipping of the port. When the wool ships from England are here, lying in a circle all round the margin, no port has a pleasanter appearance. This is during the summer months; from October perhaps up to March. I was at Sydney both in summer and winter; but during the winter the port seemed to be deserted. Crossing the main harbour from the Circular Quay, the inhabitants of the North Shore reach their side of the town in ten minutes. Here are St. Leonard's, which is fairly fashionable; Balmain, which is less so; and up higher, the township of Pyrmont which will perhaps hardly excuse me if I say that it is not fashionable at all. But then, on the other hand, Pyrmont is reached by a bridge, while the inhabitants of St. Leonard's are driven to use the ferry. I can hardly complete this attempted description of the city, without explaining that the Government House stands between the Circular Quay and the public gardens, with grounds sloping down to the sea. The position is one of great beauty, and the house has an air of magnificence about it, such as should belong to the residence of a viceroy. I have been told, however, that as a house it is not as good as it should be. Looking at it with the eyes of a humble private individual I thought that it was all that a house need be.

The antiquity of Sydney—perhaps I should say the comparative antiquity—strikes an Englishman as being almost absurd, as he remembers that in his father's lifetime the place was covered by gum trees and peopled by savages. There are houses so old that they are in almost ruinous condition—seeming to be as low, as comfortless, and almost as picturesque, as do some dilapidated tenements in the old streets of our old towns. These are chiefly of wood; but the eyes become so used to wooden houses that this speciality is not observed. Two or three were pointed out to me, each as being the oldest in the town, and which certainly were built when the hearts of the young colonists were heavy with many troubles. Little was thought then of beauty of position, of gardens down to the water's edge, and of views over the land-locked sea. How were the inhabitants to make themselves safe against black savages, against convicts who were still more savage, and against fire. It seems that the first comers into any land have rarely thought much about scenery. Trouble as to food and security is too heavy on the minds of pioneers to allow them to indulge in the luxury of landscapes, and the taste for scenery is one of latter-day growth. In the last century Englishmen travelled to see cities, and to see men, and to study the world—but in those days mountains were troublesome, and dark valleys were savage, and glaciers were horrible. Much is said by those who first landed at Botany Bay and Port Jackson on the trees and plants and herbs of the new country—what I believe is now called "the Flora"—but I do not remember a word in praise of its loveliness.

Among other old buildings at Sydney there is an old church, and a very old hospital. The hospital, I was assured, is quite antiquated. It seemed to be airy, easy, and as pleasant as is compatible with the nature of such an institution. St. James's church is pewed round with high dark panels, and is as much like an English comfortless church of the last century, as though it stood in a second-rate town in an Eastern county. I went there once, and found it impossible to hear a word, either from the gentleman who read the lessons, or from him who preached. But it is a fashionable church, and is supposed to be that at which the Governor and his family should say their prayers. The cathedral, on the other hand, is new, and very well arranged. I heard an excellent sermon there, in which I was told that it was the practice of St. Paul to teach his own religion rather than to abuse that of others—a lesson which is much needed at home, and by no means unnecessary in the Australian colonies. . . .

The glory of Sydney in the way of education is its university and certainly a great deal of spirit has been shown by the colony in the creation of the institution and in the erection of the building. As regards the building, I think no one will dispute the assertion when I say that the college-hall—or public room, for it is put to none of the comfortable festive uses for which college-halls have been built at our universities—is the finest chamber in the colonies. If I were to say that no college either at Oxford or Cambridge possesses so fine a one, I might probably be contradicted. I certainly remember none of which the proportions are so good. In regard to the Sydney University itself, it must be remembered that it has been instituted simply for education, and not as a place of residence either for fellows, scholars, or commoners. It consists, therefore, of the hall, library, lecture-rooms, museum, and a residence for one of the professors. It knows nothing of gaudy days, of high tables, of sweet Latin graces, or of audit ale. It lacks the social charms to which the frequenters of Oxford and Cambridge have been accustomed; but perhaps the education on that account is not the worse, and certainly it is very much less expensive. . . . There is no institution in the colonies which excites and deserves the sympathies of an English traveller more completely than does the Sydney University.

New South Wales Towns

The country towns of Australia, generally, are not attractive, and it is hardly to be expected that they should as yet be so. There are, of course, exceptional instances—Ballarat, Geelong, and Beechworth in Victoria, are exceptions, as are also Launceston in Tasmania, and Strathalbyn and Mount Gambier in South Australia, which, from peculiarity of situation, or the energy of individuals have become well-built cities or pleasant little towns. No doubt there are others which I was not able to visit. But, generally, there is a raw newness about these congregations of houses, an initiation of streets which as yet are no more than initiated, a deficiency in pavement and macadamization which leads either to dust or mud, an apparent mixture of pretension and failure which is indeed indispensable to towns founded with hopes of future greatness, but which creates a feeling of melancholy sadness in the mind of a stranger. It could hardly have been otherwise, and yet it grieves us to see that they who have diligently made their plans, intending to produce comfort, social neatness, and sometimes even urban magnificence, should as yet have succeeded in producing only discomfort, untidiness, and insignificance.

In old countries, such as our own, towns have grown up almost without an intention on the part of any founder. Cities have formed themselves out of villages, because it has suited first this man and then that to earn his bread in this or that locality. Consequently our streets have been narrow and crooked, our spaces confined and often ill-arranged, and our supplies of water and air insufficient for an increasing population. We are daily compelled to pull down that we may rebuild—and are almost angry with ourselves or with those who went before us, in that there has been so little foresight among us as to the wants of mankind. But it has resulted from all this that we are not, as a rule, incomplete, pretentious, or unpicturesque. The new countries, however, have taken a lesson from the deficiencies of the old countries, and have commenced their towns on a certain plan, with wide streets, and large spaces, and straight long lines, so that coming generations of thronging men may be able to build their houses in spots properly prepared, and to move about without knotting themselves into inconvenient crowds as men have to do in the old cities. When the generations shall have come, this will be very well, and the wisdom of the founders will be acknowledged —but in the meantime the new towns are ugly, and generally dirty.

They who have travelled in the United States beyond the big cities—who have seen something besides New York, Boston, and Chicago—must have felt this ugliness very strongly. It was the appreciation of this deformity, excited to its greatest intensity by the unfortunate youthfulness of the place then under inspection, and by the imagination of the artist, which produced that portion of a town in the wilderness which Dickens painted and called Eden. The founders of his Eden had sought the confluence of two great navigable rivers, and had planned long quays and broad streets—but up to Dickens's day, had produced nothing but mud and ague. I have seen no Australian town so bad as Eden, which certainly when I visited it still deserved all the evil things which have been said of it. Such a picture of any Australian town, even if I could draw it, would be untrue. But I cannot say that as yet these communities possess many beauties to recommend them to the eye, or have much to please a stranger. I visited not a few of these in New South Wales, and found, almost invariably, the same characteristics—broad streets, and many of them but streets very imperfectly filled with houses, a look of scattered, straggling incompleteness, and an air of disappointment, as though men were beginning to fear that their Eden was not becoming that city of Elysium which they had fondly anticipated.

And yet in these towns there is ample evidence of energy. The population of such places may be said to vary from 7,000 to 500, the great majority having less than 2,000 inhabitants. Exclusive of Sydney there are but six towns in the whole colony of New South Wales which have a population over 2,000, and, of these, four, Newcastle, Maitland, Parramatta, and Bathurst, have a population varying from 5,000 to 7,500. In all these towns—even in places with less than 500 souls—there is a bank. In most of them there are two or three banks. In all these there is a church—in most of them there are churches. The hotels are more numerous even than the banks and churches, and—though I heard them abused as inns are always abused in all countries—I found them fairly comfortable and very much better than I had expected from the sparseness of the population over so wide a district. Almost all inns in Australia, however small, have a bath room, though it may be of rude construction. I wish I could convey this information to hotel-keepers in England. I found, too, that the shops were better than they looked, and that the means of comfortable life were to be found in towns which were not attractive in their appearance.

In England it is sometimes very difficult to discover the *raison d'être* of a community called a town. One cannot understand why that especial lot of human beings have formed themselves together and determined to live in that particular place. It seems that the tailor lives on the butcher, the butcher on the baker, the baker on the publican, and so on. In many of our towns, probably in all the greater cities, there is some particular industry, but in others, especially in the South and East, there is no such cause. I never could understand why Wincanton or Ilminster should continue to exist, or Chelmsford, or Bury St. Edmunds. There were causes when the towns were new, and in new countries the causes are still to be recognized. In New South Wales many of the towns have been absolutely created by the goldfields, and are still being created. Some of the goldfield towns are already in a state of decay, and are almost passing away. Still something of life remains, but of all the sad places I ever saw they are the most melancholy. They are "bush" towns. Readers who desire to understand anything of Australian life should become acquainted with the technical meaning of the word "bush". The bush is the gum-tree forest, with which so great a part of Australia is covered, that folk who follow a country life are invariably said to live in the bush. Squatters who look after their own runs always live in the bush, even though their sheep are pastured on plains. Instead of a town mouse and a country mouse in Australia there would be a town mouse and a bush mouse—but mice living in the small country towns would still be bush mice. A young lady, when she becomes engaged to a gentleman whose avocations call upon him to live far inland always declares that she prefers "bush life".

The mining towns are comprised of the sudden erections which sprung from the finding of gold in the neighbourhood, and are generally surrounded by thick forest. But in their immediate vicinity the trees have been cut down either for firewood or for use under ground—but have not been altogether cleared away, so that the hideous stumps remain above the surface. Around on all sides the ground has been stirred in the search for gold, and ugly bare heaps of clay are left. The road to and from such a place will meander causelessly between yawning holes, in each of which some desponding miner has probably buried his high hopes—and which he has then abandoned. One wonders that every child in the neighbourhood does not perish by falling into them. At different points around the centre which have once been supposed to be auriferous, there are the skeleton remains of wooden habitations, with here and there the tawdry sign-boards of deserted shops from which high profits were once expected. In some few of these skeleton habitations there are still inhabitants—men and women who having a house have been unwilling to leave it, even when the dreadful fact that gold is not to be found in paying quantities has been acknowledged. In the centre there is still the town, though day by day its right to the name is passing from it. There are still the publicans, and still the churches, though the services become rare and still more rare, and there is the bank holding its position as long as an ounce of gold is to be extracted from the unwilling soil. Here congregate Chinese in gangs, who are content to re-wash the ground which has already been perhaps twice washed by European or Australian Christians, and who, with the patient industry which is peculiar to them, will earn perhaps each 1s. 6d. a day by the process. I will name no such town, because by doing so I might offend the susceptibilities of some still hopeful denizens of the place specified, but they are easy to find by those who travel in New South Wales. There are, however, other mining towns in the colony full of life. Men are still crowding to them; and, at these, habitations cannot be put up fast enough to cover the eager seekers after wealth, nor shops opened quick enough to supply their wants. Of them I will say a few words in another chapter.

Melbourne

Melbourne has made its place for itself, and is the undoubted capital, not only of Victoria but of all Australia. It contains together with her suburbs, 206,000 souls, and of these so called suburbs the most populous are as much a part of Melbourne as Southwark is of London—or were I to say as Marylebone is of London, my description would be true, as there is no line of demarcation traceable by any eyes but those of town-councillors and the collectors of borough rates. There are very many cities in the world with larger populations—so many that the number does not strike one with surprise. But I believe that no city has ever attained so great a size with such rapidity. Forty years ago from the present date (1873), the foot of no white man had trodden the ground on which Melbourne now stands, unless it was the foot of Buckley the escaped convict, who lived for thirty years with a tribe of native savages.

Melbourne is not a city beautiful to the eye from the charms of the landscape surrounding it, as are Edinburgh and Bath with us, and as are Sydney and Hobart Town in Australia, and Dunedin in New Zealand. Though it stands on a river which has in itself many qualities of prettiness in streams—a tortuous, rapid little river with varied banks, the Yarra Yarra by name—it seems to have but little to do with the city. It furnishes the means of rowing to young men, and waters the Botanical Gardens. But it is not "a joy for ever" to the Melbournites, as the Seine is to the people of Paris, or the Inn to the people of Innspruck. You might live in Melbourne all your life and hardly know that the Yarra Yarra was running by your door. Nor is Melbourne made graceful with neighbouring hills. It stands indeed itself on two hills, and on the valley which separates them; and these afford rising ground sufficient to cause considerable delay to the obese and middle-aged pedestrian when the hot winds are blowing—as hot winds do blow at summertime in Melbourne. But there are no hills to produce scenery, or scenic effect. Though you go up and down the streets, the country around is flat, and for the most part uninteresting. I know no great town in the neighbourhood of which there is less to see in the way of landscape beauty.

Nevertheless the internal appearance of the city is certainly magnificent. The city proper—that Melbourne itself which is subject to the municipal control of the mayor, and which in regard to all its municipal regulations is distinct from its suburbs—is built on the Philadelphian, rectangular, parallelogrammic plan. Every street runs straight, and every other street runs either parallel to it or at right angles with it. . . .

It is the width of the streets chiefly which gives to the city its appearance of magnificence—that, and the devotion of very large spaces within the city to public gardens. These gardens are not in themselves well kept. They are not lovely, as are those of Sydney in a super-excellent degree. Some of them are profusely ornamented with bad statues. None of them, whatever may be their botanical value, are good gardens. But they are large and numerous, and give an air of wholesomeness and space to the whole city. They afford green walks to the citizens, and bring much of the health and some of the pleasures of the country home to them all.

One cannot walk about Melbourne without being struck by all that has been done for the welfare of the people generally. There is no squalor to be seen—though there are quarters of the town in which the people no doubt are squalid. In every great congregation of men there will be a residuum of poverty and filth, let humanity do what she will to prevent it. In Melbourne there is an Irish quarter, and there is a Chinese quarter, as to both of which I was told that the visitor who visited them aright might see much of the worse side of life. But he who would see such misery in Melbourne must search for it especially. It will not meet his eye by chance as it does in London, in Paris, and now also in New York. The time will come no doubt when it will do so also in Melbourne, but at present the city, in all the pride of youthful power, looks as though she were boasting to herself hourly that she is not as are other cities.

And she certainly does utter many such boasts. Her population is not given to hide its light under a bushel. I do not think that I said a pleasant word about the town to any inhabitant of it during my sojourn there, driven into silence on the subject by the calls which were made upon me for praise. "We like to be cracked up, sir," says the American. I never heard an American say so, but such are the words which we put into his mouth, and they are true as to his character. They are equally true as to the Australian generally, as to the Victorian specially, and as to the citizen of Melbourne in a more especial degree. He likes to be "cracked up", and he does not hesitate to ask you to "crack him up". He does not proceed to gouging or bowie knives if you decline, and therefore I never did crack him up.

I suppose that a young people falls naturally into the fault of self-adulation. I must say somewhere, and may as well say here as elsewhere, that the wonders performed in the way of riding, driving, fighting, walking, working, drinking, love-making, and speech-making, which men and women in Australia told me of themselves, would have been worth recording in a separate volume had they been related by any but the heroes and heroines themselves. But reaching one as they do always in the first person, these stories are soon received as works of a fine art much cultivated in the colonies, for which the colonial phrase of "blowing" has been created. When a gentleman sounds his own trumpet he "blows". The art is perfectly understood and appreciated among the people who practise it. Such a gentleman or such a lady was only "blowing"! You hear it and hear of it every day. They blow a good deal in Queensland—a good deal in South Australia. They blow even in poor Tasmania. They blow loudly in New South Wales, and very loudly in New Zealand. But the blast of the trumpet as heard in Victoria is louder than all the blasts—and the Melbourne blast beats all the other blowing of that proud colony. My first, my constant, my parting advice to my Australian cousins is contained in two words—"Don't blow".

But if a man must blow it is well that he should have something to blow about beyond his own prowess, and I do not know that a man can have a more rational source of pride than the well-being of the city in which he lives. It is impossible for a man to walk the length of Collins Street up by the churches and the club to the Treasury Chambers, and then round by the Houses of Parliament away into Victoria Parade, without being struck by the grandeur of the dimensions of the town. It is the work of half a morning for an old man to walk the length of some of the streets, and to a man who cannot walk well the distances of Melbourne soon become very great indeed. There seems to be this drawback upon noble streets, and large spaces, and houses with comfortable dimensions, that as the city grows the distances become immense. They are now far longer in Melbourne with its 200,000 inhabitants clustered together than in Glasgow with 500,000; and as the population increases and houses are added to houses, it will become impossible for pedestrians to communicate unless they devote the entire day to travelling. There will, no doubt, be railways about the town, as there are about London, but it seems strange that half a million of people should not be able to live together within reach of each other. It must be remembered also that when the hot winds are blowing in Melbourne from the north in December, January, and February, a very little walking is equal to a great deal of exercise. . . .

Melbourne is the centre of a series of railways, but the city has the advantage of a local line—belonging to a private company and not worked by the government as are the colonial lines generally—which passes from St. Kilda and Emerald Hill on one side, through Melbourne to Richmond, Prahran, Brighton, and other suburbs on the other side, which is so generally used that Melbourne itself is nearly as hollow as London. I may almost say that no one lives in Melbourne. Of this, one consequence is disagreeable. When you dine out you are generally under the necessity of returning by railway—which is an abomination. But in other respects the railway is a great blessing. People even of moderate means live in the country air and have gardens and pleasant houses. On two sides, south and east, Melbourne is surrounded for miles by villa residences.

There is now being built, very close to the town, a new Government House, which is intended to be very magnificent. The governors who occupy it will probably find it by far too much so. The present house, which is four miles out of town, is very much abused as being inadequate to its purpose. It certainly is much less grand than those at Sydney, at Hobart Town—which is first among government houses—or even at Perth in poor Western Australia. Nevertheless, I was present there at a public ball, at which all Melbourne was entertained with true vice-royal munificence. Were I appointed governor of a colony I should deprecate very much a too palatial residence. I think it may be admitted as a rule that governors find it hard to live upon the salaries allotted to them, and generally do not do so. Men used to accept bishoprics and governorships with a view to making fortunes. It is beginning to be admitted now that men with private means are wanted for both.

There are excellent clubs at Melbourne, having all the comforts of London clubs, with the additional accommodation of a large number of bedrooms for their members. At all the Australian clubs great hospitality is shown to strangers—a hospitality which, unfortunately, the London clubs cannot reciprocate with equal profusion. Were they to do so the strangers admitted would outnumber the members, and destroy the clubs, so great is the continued influx of visitors into London. Nevertheless, it is impossible for a London man not to feel half ashamed of himself when he accepts with freedom a generous hospitality which he knows that he cannot return with the same full hand. I have bitterly experienced the same regret in reference to Americans in London, who in their own country are very liberal in conferring on Englishmen the use of their clubs, and who find a difficulty in obtaining similar entertainment among us. We are the greatest travellers on the earth, and I am disposed to think that something might be done by a not injudicious relaxation of our own rules.

When in Melbourne—which, as I travelled backwards and forwards, I visited half-a-dozen times—I generally stayed at Menzies' hotel, of which I am bound to say that I never put myself up at a better inn in any part of the world. Scott's hotel is the rival house, and the Scottites declare that to be as good—a thorough Scottite will perhaps say better. As I was never in Scott's hotel I am unable to form a comparison, but from prejudice, I am prepared to fight for Menzies. But at Melbourne, as elsewhere, good hotel accommodation is accompanied by a good price.

Were I to finish my account of Melbourne as a city without speaking of the Yan Yean water, I should be thought to have omitted the greatest glory of the glorious town. Melbourne is supplied from a distance of about twenty miles with millions of gallons of water—with so many millions that every one says that the supply cannot be exhausted. It is laid on to every house in the town and suburbs, and is supposed to be the most perfect water supply ever produced for the use of man. Ancient Rome and modern New York have been less blessed in this respect than is Melbourne with its Yan Yean. I do believe that the supply is almost as inexhaustible as it is described to be. But the method of bringing it into the city is not as yet by any means perfect. During the very heart of the summer of 1871, when the hot winds were blowing as they blow only in Melbourne, I moved from a house in the town to a friend's residence in the country; and neither at the one nor the other could a bath be filled. The Yan Yean was not "running". In those days the Water Commissioners must, I think, have had a bad time. I will also add that the Yan Yean water is not pleasant to drink—a matter of comparatively small consideration in a town in which brandy is so plentiful.

There is perhaps no town in the world in which an ordinary working man can do better for himself and for his family with his work than he can at Melbourne. There may be places at which wages are higher, but then at those places the necessaries of life are dearer, and the comforts of life less easily attainable. There are others undoubtedly at which living is cheaper—but there also are wages lower, and the means of living less salutary and commodious. . . . A working man in Melbourne no doubt pays more for his house or for his lodgings than he would in London; but then in Melbourne the labourer or artisan enjoys a home of a better sort than would be within the reach of his brother in London doing work of the same nature, and in regard to house-rent gets more for his money than he would do at home.

Ballarat

Ballarat is certainly a most remarkable town. It struck me with more surprise than any other city in Australia. It is not only its youth, for Melbourne also is very young; nor is it the population of Ballarat which amazes, for it does not exceed a quarter of that of Melbourne; but that a town so well built, so well ordered, endowed with present advantages so great in the way of schools, hospitals, libraries, hotels, public gardens, and the like, should have sprung up so quickly with no internal advantages of its own other than that of gold. The town is very pleasant to the sight, which is, perhaps, more than can be said for any other "provincial" town in the Australian colonies. When the year 1851 commenced, Ballarat was an unknown name except perhaps here and there to a few shepherds. These words are written in the house of Messrs. Learmonth—younger men than I, and therefore not old men to me—who were the first pioneers in the country, and who ran the sheep which they brought with them from Van Diemen's Land over the hills adjacent to Ballarat. They have given way to the gold-seekers, and establishing themselves far enough from mines for rural serenity and pastoral comfort, are regarded as the territorial aristocrats of the district. Breathing their air and listening to their ideas, one feels as one does in the almost feudal establishment of some great English squire, who watches with a regret he cannot quite repress the daily encroachments made upon his life by the approaching hordes of some large neighbouring town.

The phase of life which is present to us at home in England, and which there has come from centuries of slow progress, the changes not only in action but in thought which are going on around us, and which we regard, according to our various political creeds, as tending to national ruin or to a millennium of national happiness, are already in action here in Victoria. The vitality of city life with its somewhat vulgar form of expressions, its occasionally dishonest ambition, its quick-witted but sometimes short-sighted policy, its majorities, popular instincts, and general rowdiness, is already in full force at Ballarat, and is already odious to those who eschew cities. And, in the country districts around, the feudal conservative instinct is already equally prevalent. And yet Ballarat as a city dates only from 1852, and has had nothing but gold to produce it. Nature has done for it little or nothing.

It has no navigable river. It is seventy or eighty miles from any possibility of sea-carriage. The land immediately around it is not fertile. It is high above the river, and runs in gentle hills which twenty years since were thinly covered with gum-trees; and here wandered the flocks of a few patriarch pioneers. Then came first one or two rough seekers after gold, then half a dozen, then a score, then a rush—and Ballarat was established as one among the few great golden cities of the young world. I do not think that there is any city equal to it that has sprung from gold alone.

I myself believe in cities—even though there should be dishonest ambition, short-sighted policy, and rowdiness. The dishonesty, the folly, and the rowdiness are but the overboiling of the pot without which cannot be had the hot water which is so necessary to our well-being. I heard much abuse of Ballarat from Ballaratters. There are three towns conjoined, Ballarat, Ballarat East, and Sebastopol, with three town-halls, three municipalities, and the like. The smaller towns will not consent to merge themselves. There are in them men of obstruction, and things cannot be done as they should be done. Money is wasted; municipal funds are expended foolishly—perhaps fraudulently on an occasion. If this class would only see with the eyes of that class, what a paradise it might be. But they see with quite other eyes —and what a pandemonium it is becoming. So say the men of Ballarat. . . . No words which can here be used are strong enough to describe the iniquity which some MacEvoy attributes to some O'Brien, or some Murphy to some Jones or Smith. Population is falling off, so that shortly Ballarat will be as a city of the dead. Such are the accounts a stranger hears either from this side or from that. One gentleman, who certainly was very much in the dark as to the statistics of his town, assured me that 20,000 people had gone out of Ballarat in two years. Another was angry with me because I hesitated to believe that the place was ruined. I was assured that I might hire 1,500 vacant houses at an hour's notice if I wanted them. As for gold at Ballarat, everybody knew that that game had been played out!

Such were the records of some men. As far as the eye went, I saw nothing but prosperity. Here I found that most of the mines were worked by companies at wages paid to the men—and that a miner's wages averaged from 40s. to 48s. a week—the man working eight hours a day, and thus reaching that acme of the workman's bliss—

Eight hours for work, and eight for play,
Eight for sleep, and eight shillings a day.

And the necessaries of life, and the comforts, are at any rate as cheap at Ballarat as they are in England, in spite of protective duties.

Gipps Land

The land between Melbourne and Gipps Land, through the county of Mornington, is very poor; as it is also for some distance in Gipps Land itself. Then the timber becomes less thick and the grasses rich. When first taken up the country was used for sheep; but it was not found to be good for wool, and the sheep have now given place to cattle. A large proportion of the beef with which Melbourne is fed is fattened on the Gipps Land runs. Here, as throughout Victoria, all the best of the soil has been already purchased, and is for the most part in the hand of large owners—of men whose successors will be lords of vast territorial properties, and not of small free-selectors or farmers. Throughout the colony it is impossible not to see how futile have been the efforts of legislation to prevent the accumulation of large domains in the hands of successful men. It has been thought by one ministry after another to be wise—or, at any rate, to be expedient—to break up the holdings of the great squatters, so that there should be no territorial magnates. The law has done all that it could be made to do, compatibly with justice—sometimes perhaps more than it could do with that condition—to make the colony a paradise for small landowners, and a purgatory for wealthy men who should attempt to accumulate acres. Politicians ambitious of being statesmen, who can reach power only by the aid of universal suffrage, are prone to look for popularity, and popularity in Victoria has much depended on adherence to the interests of the free-selector. As I have said elsewhere, the interests of the small buyer of land are entitled to warmer sympathy than those of the would-be territorial magnates. One still dreams of a happy land in which every man with his wife and children shall live happily and honestly on his own acres, owing neither rent nor submission to any lord. It may be that this feeling has been stronger with Victorian politicians than the love of political power. It is at any rate the feeling by which they claim to have been actuated, and they have worked hard to carry out their theory. But the wages of commerce and the enterprise of the intelligent have been stronger than any bonds which statesmen or legislators could forge. Wealth has been accumulated by a few, and wealth has procured the land in spite of the laws. Though cabinet ministers and land commissioners have had the land in their hands to sell under such laws as they have pleased to pass, though they have had a power entrusted to them as managers and agents greater than any confided by us to our ministers at home, though it has been declared by politicians that there should be no land magnates in Victoria, the rich have bought the land; and now vast territories are possessed by individuals which more than rival in area—and in course of time will rival in value—the possessions of great families at home. This is hardly so in the United States—is not so certainly to the same extent. There men seek to build up wealth in the cities rather than in the country, and prefer shares and scrip and commercial speculation to land. Why there should be this difference in the same race, when settled away from home in different regions, some one some day no doubt will tell us.

To fatten cattle is the present business of the Gipps Land squire. Cattle, no doubt, are bred there, but it seemed to be more usual to buy them young from some other district, and have them driven up over long distances to the Gipps Land pastures. I do not pride myself on having a good eye for a bullock, but those I saw seemed to be very big and very fat, very tame and very stupid. Why a bullock who has a paddock of seven or eight thousand acres in which to roam should make so little of himself as these beasts do in Australia I cannot understand. At home I think they are more troublesome and have higher hearts. I went out one morning at four a.m. to see a lot drafted out of a herd for sale. "Cutting out" is the proper name for this operation. Two or three men on horseback, of whom I considered myself to be by far the most active, drove some hundreds of them into a selected corner of the paddock called a "camp". There was no enclosure, no hurdles, no gates, no flogging, very little hallooing, and very little work. This camp happened to be in a corner; but camps for cattle generally are in the centre of the field, a bare spot—made bare by its repeated use for this purpose—to which the bullocks go when they are told, and on which they stand quietly till the operation of cutting out is over. On the occasion on which I was assisting, the owner himself was the "cutter out". He rode in among the herd, and selecting with his eye some animal sufficiently obese for market purposes, signified to the doomed one that he should leave the herd. There was a stock-rider to assist him, and the stock-rider also signified his intention. It seemed to be done altogether by the eye. The beast went out and stood apart, till he was joined by a second selected one and then by a third. On this occasion some thirty or forty were selected, either as many as were fit or as the owner desired to sell.

These were at once driven off on the way to Melbourne, and the others were allowed to go back to their grazing. I had looked for racing, and cracking of stock-whips, and horses falling, and some wild work among the forest trees. I would not knowingly have left my bed at four o'clock to see so tame a performance. At least for half its distance the road up to Melbourne is not fenced off from the timber, and consists of devious forest tracts; but these tame brutes never make their way out into the woods on the journey, as they might do.

Tasmania

It seems hard to say of a new colony, not yet seventy years old, that it has seen the best of its days, and that it is falling into decay, that its short period of importance in the world is already gone, and that for the future it must exist—as many an old town and old country do exist—not exactly on the memory of the past, but on the relics which the past has left behind it. England has towns of her own at home and colonies of her own abroad—it would be invidious to name them—of which this may truly be said. On visiting them the stranger feels assured that the salt of life has gone out of them. Trade dwells in them no longer, and prosperous men do not move about their streets. Their inhabitants are contented to be obscure, and generally have neither fears nor hopes. Society is mild and dull, and the remnant of the people who are left are for the most part satisfied to sit and wait. But a young colony should have young, sparkling, eager life. She should be hopeful, impetuous, and loud, and with a belief in her destiny; and if she be given somewhat to boasting, she will not, indeed, thereby show herself to be possessed of an actual virtue, but will give evidence even by that vice of the strength of youth which makes a community at first buoyant, and then prosperous. Such essentially are Queensland and Victoria, which force even upon unwilling ears a conviction of their strength by the loudness of their self-assertion and the vigour of their confidence. I by no means say that the dreamy, dusty quiescence of decay, the imbecility of old age which does not become actual death because so little of the energy of life is expended on the work of living from day to day, have become the lot of young Tasmania; but I do say that Tasmanians are almost united in declaring so of themselves, and that they have said so till the other colonies are quite united in repeating the story.

Tasmania as Tasmania is very young—so young that many old-fashioned folk at home hardly recognize her under that name, and still know her as Van Diemen's Land. That name is now odious to the ears of Tasmanians, as being still tainted with the sound of the gaol and harsh with the crack of the gaoler's whip; but it was under that name that the island was prosperous. England sent her convicts thither, and with her ruffians sent £350,000 a year for their custody and maintenance. The whole revenue of the island, including Customs, Inland Revenue, and Land Fund, does not now exceed £280,000. And the money sent from England was by no means all the wealth which the convicts brought with them. They had their thews and sinews, and the free squatters of Tasmania knew well how to turn such God-sends into money. And public works were done magnificently by them—on the doing of which sufficiently, quickly, and without too close a regard to any immediate return of money, the welfare of a growing colony almost depends. Roads were made, and buildings erected, and river banks were cleared, and forests were cut down with a thoroughness which proved that convicts were at any rate useful. But though useful they were disgraceful. The Van Diemonians—as colonists from other colonies are wont to call them in jeering mirth—had a spirit of their own which could not be at ease within a prison, even though they themselves were the masters and wardens, and kept the keys of the prison. It began to be unendurable to them that their beautiful island, the sweetest in climate, the loveliest in scenery, the richest in rivers and harbours, the most accessible of all Great Britain's eastern colonies, should be known to the world only as Great Britain's gaol. So she spoke her mind, and of course had her way—as has been the case with all Great Britain's children since the tea was thrown overboard at Boston. The convicts were made to cease, and Van Diemen's Land became Tasmania—Tasmania with free institutions of its own, with representative government, with Lords and Commons, with a public debt, with its own taxes, and a right to govern itself by its own laws—so long as it should exact no laws contrary to the spirit of the laws of England. It became, in fact, as were and are the other colonies, all but independent, and it threw off from itself its convict stain. But then, as a matter of course, it threw off from itself also the £350,000 a year which in one shape or another the convicts used to bring with them from England, and it could make no more roads and put up no more public buildings, except in the normal way of the world, by paying the market price for the works accomplished. . . .

The "Van Diemonians" were all but united in the declaration of their determination that no more convicts should be sent to them. They are now almost equally united in their declaration that the cessation of the coming of the convicts has been their ruin. They think that England has been hard to them in the measure of justice which she has meted. There might have been a regiment or at any rate a company of soldiers left in the island—a few red jackets, if only to enliven the streets and gladden the eyes of the women. Was it to be expected that all the money would be withdrawn at once—or if not quite at once with so great rapidity?

* * *

It is acknowledged even by all the rival colonies that of all the colonies Tasmania is the prettiest. This is no doubt true of her as a whole, though the scenery of the Hawkesbury in New South Wales is, I think, finer than anything in Tasmania. But it may be said of the small island that, go where you will, the landscape that meets the eye is pleasing, whereas the reverse of this is certainly the rule on the Australian continent. And the climate of Tasmania is by far pleasanter than that of any part of the mainland. There are, one may almost say, no mosquitoes. Other pernicious animals certainly do abound—but then they abound also in England. Everything in Tasmania is more English than is England herself. She is full of English fruits, which grow certainly more plentifully and, as regards some, with greater excellence than they do in England. Tasmanian cherries beat those of Kent—or, as I believe, of all the world—and have become so common that it is often not worth the owner's while to pull them. Strawberries, raspberries, gooseberries, plums, and apples are in almost equal abundance. I used in early days to think a greengage the best fruit in the world; but latterly, at home, greengages have lost their flavour for me. I attributed this to age and an altered palate; but in Tasmania I found the greengages as sweet as they used to be thirty years ago. And then the mulberries!

There was a lady in Hobart Town who sent us mulberries every day such as I had never eaten before, and as—I feel sure—I shall never eat again. Tasmania ought to make jam for all the world—and would do so for all the Australian world were she not prevented by certain tariffs. Now the Australian world is essentially a jam-consuming world, and but for the tariffs Tasmania could afford to pick, and would make a profit out of, the cherries and raspberries. And this is not the only evil. The Victorians eat a great deal of jam. No one eats more jam than a Victorian miner—unless it be a Victorian stock-rider. But they eat pumpkin jam flavoured with strawberries—and call that strawberry jam. The effect of protection all the world over is to force pumpkin jam, under the name of strawberry jam, down the throats of the people.

* * *

Hobart Town, the capital of the colony, has about 20,000 inhabitants, and is as pleasant a town of the size as any that I know. Nature has done for it very much indeed, and money has done much also. It is beautifully situated—as regards the water, just at the point where the river becomes sea. It has quays and wharves, at which vessels of small tonnage can lie, in the very heart of the town. Vessels of any tonnage can lie a mile out from its streets. It is surrounded by hills and mountains, from which views can be had which would make the fortune of any district in Europe. Mount Wellington, nearly 5,000 feet high, is just enough of a mountain to give excitement to ladies and gentlemen in middle life. Mount Nelson is less lofty, but perhaps gives the finer prospect of the two. And the air of Hobart Town is perfect air. I was there in February—the height of summer—having chosen to go to Tasmania at that time to avoid the great heat of the continent. I found the summer weather of Hobart Town to be delicious. . . .

So much in regard to the gifts bestowed by nature upon the capital of Tasmania. Art—art in the hands of convicts—has made it a pretty, clean, well-constructed town, with good streets and handsome buildings. The Government House, is, I believe, acknowledged to be the best belonging to any British colony. It stands about a mile from the town, on ground sloping down to the Derwent, which is here an arm of the sea, and lacks nothing necessary for a perfect English residence. The public offices, town hall, and law courts are all excellent. The supreme court, as one of the judges took care to tell me, is larger than our Court of Queen's Bench at Westminster. The Houses of Parliament are appropriate and comfortable, with every necessary appliance. They are not pretentious, nor can I say that the building devoted to them is handsome. There is a Protestant bishop, of course, and a cathedral—which a stranger, not informed on the subject would mistake for an old-fashioned English church in a third or fourth-rate town. I was told that it is tumbling down; but a very pretty edifice is being erected close by its side. The work is still unfinished and funds are needed. Perhaps a generous reader might send a trifle. . . .

I went up the Derwent to New Norfolk, and Fenton Forest, and across from Hobart Town to the Huon River and a township called Franklin, finding the scenery everywhere to be lovely. The fern-tree valleys on the road to the Huon are specially so—and in one of these I was shown the biggest tree I ever saw. I took down the dimensions, and of course lost the note. It was quite hollow, and six or seven people could have sat round a table and dined within it. It was a gum-tree, bigger I imagine in girth, though not so tall, as that which I described as having been found in Victoria, near the road from Woods Point to Melbourne. The River Huon is a dark, black, broad stream, running under hanging bushes—very silent and clear, putting me in mind of the river in *Evangeline*.

* * *

That Tasmania is going gradually to the mischief seems to be the fixed opinion of Tasmanian politicians generally. That such a belief as to one's country should not be accompanied by any personal act evincing despair has been the case in all national panics. English country gentlemen have very often been sure of England's ruin; but I have never heard of the country gentleman who, in consequence of his belief, sold his estate and went to live elsewhere. Speculative creeds either in politics or religion seldom prove their sincerity by altered conduct. Modern prophets have more than once or twice named some quick coming date on which the world would end; but the prophets have made their investments and taken their leases seemingly in anticipation of a long course of future years. So it is in Tasmania. Even they who are most unhappy as to the state of things live on comfortably amidst the approaching ruin. What the stranger sees of life on the island is very comfortable.

Western Australia

An ingenious but sarcastic Yankee, when asked what he thought of Western Australia, declared that it was the best country he had ever seen to run through an hour-glass. He meant to insinuate that the parts of the colony which he had visited were somewhat sandy. It is sandy. The country round Perth is very sandy. From Freemantle, the seaport, the road up to Perth, the capital, lies through sand. From Albany, the seaport at which the mail steamers stop, the distance to Perth is about 260 miles, and the traveller encounters a good deal of sand on the way. The clever Yankee who thought of the hour-glass probably did not go beyond Perth. There is much soil in Western Australia which is not sandy—which is as good, perhaps, as any land in the Australian colonies—but it lies in patches, sometimes far distant from each other; and there is very much desert or useless country between. In this is, probably, to be found the chief reason why Western Australia has not progressed as have the other colonies. The distances from settlement to settlement have been so great as to make it almost impossible for settlers to dispose of their produce. This has been the first great difficulty with which Western Australia has had to contend; and to this have been superadded others: the absence of gold—an evil not so much in itself as in the difference created by the presence of gold in the other colonies, whereby the early settlers in Western Australia were induced to rush away to Adelaide and Melbourne; its remoteness from the populous parts of the Australian continent; the fact that it is not the way from any place to any other place; the denseness and endlessness of its forests; its poisonous shrub, which in many places makes the pasturing of sheep impossible; and the ferocity of the aboriginal tribes when they first encountered their white invaders. These causes have made the progress of Western Australia slow, and have caused the colony to be placed in a category very different from that in which the other colonies are reckoned, and to be looked at from an exceptional point of view. . . .

She was colonized because she was there—not because she was wanted for any special purpose, either by the community at large or by any small section of it. We had claimed, and made good our claim, to call all New Holland, hardly by this time known by the name of Australia, as our own. We had done something on the east coast, something in the southern island; some small attempts had been made to utilize the south generally. There were still the west and the north open to us. . . .

Western Australia is an enormous country, and its scanty population is spread about it by hundreds. The so-called settled districts are twelve in number, and the average area of each is more than half as big as England. The average population of each district is only just above 2,000. Let the English reader conceive the ten northern counties of England with 2,000 inhabitants between them! And in saying this I am speaking of the settled districts—not of the distant regions which are claimed by the colony as belonging to it, and which will remain probably for centuries, perhaps for ever, uninhabited. An influx of population is necessary to Western Australia, not only that there may be enough of men and women to form a community and administer to each other's wants, but that the very nature may be changed of those upon whose industry the colony now depends.

* * *

The craving for gold has continued—and is still strong as ever. It is the opinion of many that nothing but gold can turn the scale, can bring joy out of despondency, can fill the land with towns, and crowd the streets with men. And there is much truth in the belief. It is not the gold that does it—the absolute value of the metal which is extracted—but the vitality to trade, the consumption of things, the life and the stir occasioned by those who, with the reckless energy of gamblers, hurry hither and thither after the very sound of gold. The men come, and must live—and must work for their livelihood, if not in getting gold then on some other work-field. The one thing wanted is population. Gold, if really found in paying quantities, would be a panacea for all evils in the colony; but, if that be impossible, even tidings of gold, tidings loud enough to gain credit, might turn the scale.

It may easily be conceived that such hopes as these—hopes which might be gratified any day by an accident, but which could not assure themselves of success by steady industry—would lead to a state of feeling which I may perhaps best describe as the Micawber condition. If only gold would turn up! Gold might turn up any day! But as gold did not turn up—then would not Providence be so good as to allow something else to turn up! This feeling, than which none can be more pernicious, is likely to befall every population which seeks after hidden and uncertain gains. The gain may come any day—may come in any quantity—may turn squalid poverty into wealth in an hour. The splendid transformation has been made over and over again, and may be repeated. Why should it not be repeated here, with me, on my behalf? And, if so, how vain, feeble, and contemptible would be a paltry struggle after daily wages? No doubt there was much of the Micawber spirit in the colony, and many waited, thinking that gold would turn up—or if not gold, pearls, or coal, or copper, or gas made out of blackboys. For there have been promises made by the cruel earth of all these brilliant things.

* * *

I reached the colony from Melbourne at Albany, and I left the colony starting from the same town for Adelaide in South Australia. Albany is a very pretty little town on King George's Sound—which is, I believe, by far the best harbour on the southern coast of the continent. It is, moreover, very picturesque, though not equally so with Port Jackson and the coves around Sydney. In Albany there are a few stores, as shops are always called, a brewery, a depôt for coals belonging to the Peninsular and Oriental Company, a church, a clergyman, two or three inns, and two or three government officers. Among the latter I found an old schoolfellow of my own, who filled the office of resident magistrate, and in that capacity acted as judge in all matters not affecting life for a district about as big as Great Britain. His training for these legal duties he had gained by many years' service in the Prussian army, and, I was told, did his work uncommonly well.

Albany itself is very pretty, with a free outlook on to a fine harbour, with bluff headlands and picturesque islands. The climate is delightful. The place is healthy. I was assured that the beer brewed there was good. The grapes were certainly good. For a few moments I thought that I also would like to be a resident judge at Albany, with unlimited magisterial power over perhaps a thousand people. It is pleasant, wherever one's lot is cast, to be, if not the biggest, at least among the biggest. But I was told that even at Albany there were squabbles and factions, and that the rose colour of the place did not prevail always. And then, though grapes grew there, and other fruits, and some flowers, I could not find anything else growing. The useless scrub covered the stony hill-tops close up to the town. The capital was distant 260 miles, and between it and the capital there was nothing. The mails came and went once a month. At each of my visits to Albany the mail excitement was existing. The Tichborne case was at its highest, and people had much to say. When I was departing, there were two bishops there. I fancy that I saw the best of Albany, and that it would be rather dull between the mails.

* * *

Perth I found to be a very pretty town, built on a lake of brackish water formed by the Swan River. It contains 6,000 inhabitants and of course is the residence of the chief people of the colony, as the governor is there, and the legislative chamber, and the supreme judge, and the bishop. The governor's house is handsome, as is also the town-hall. The churches—cathedrals I should call them—both of the Protestants and Roman Catholics are large and convenient. On my first arrival I stayed at an inn, which I did not indeed like very much at first, as the people seemed to be too well off to care for strangers; but which in its accommodation was better than can be found in many towns of the same size in England. I must acknowledge, however, that I was much troubled by mosquitoes, and did not think the excuse a good one when I was told that a mosquito curtain could not be put up because it was Sunday.

I found that crime of a heavy nature was not common in Perth or the districts around it, though so large a portion of the population consisted of men who were or had been convicts. Men were daily committed for bad language, drunkenness, absconding, late hours, and offences of like nature. For men holding tickets-of-leave are subjected to laws which make it criminal for a man to leave his master's employ, or to be absent from his master's house after certain hours, or to allude in an improper manner to his master's eyes. And for these offences, sentences of punishment are given which seem to be heavy, because it is difficult to bear in mind the difference between free men and prisoners who are allowed partial freedom under certain conditions.

I have heard it said, more than once or twice, in reference not specially to Perth, but to the whole colony, that the ticket-of-leave men are deterred from violence simply by fear, that they are all thieves when they dare to steal, and that the absence of crime is no proof of reformation. The physiognomy, and gait, and general idleness of the men, their habits of drinking when they can get drink, and general low tendencies, are alleged as proof of this. It cannot be supposed that convicts should come out from their prisons industrious, orderly men, fit for self-management. The restraint and discipline to which they have been subject as convicts, independently of their old habits, would prevent this. The Bill Sikes look is produced rather by the gaol than by crime. The men are not beautiful to look at. They do spend their money in drink, filling the bars of the public-houses, till the hour comes at which they must retire. But it is much in such a community that they should not return to crimes of violence.

For myself, I must say that I spent my time in Perth very pleasantly. I remember being reminded once of the injustice done to a certain poor community by a traveller who had wandered thither and had received hospitable treatment. "They cannot be so poor," the traveller had said, "because they gave me champagne every day." Doing honour to the stranger, they had broached their last bottles of the generous wine, and though poor, had put their best foot foremost in exercise of genuine hospitality. I was told how cruel this was. "We were poor," said my informant, "but we gave what we had freely, and were then twitted with making false complaints." I cannot but think of this as I tell my experiences of Perth. I heard very much of the poverty of Western Australia, but I found that people there lived as they do elsewhere. There were carriages and horses, and good dinners, and, if not liveried servants—a class which is not common in the colonies—men waiting with white cotton gloves, who in London would be presumed to be greengrocers, but who in Perth were probably "lags". They seemed to hand the dishes very well.

* * *

I fear that it will seem that in what I have said I have given a verdict against Western Australia. I have intended rather to show how great may be the difficulties attending the establishment of a young colony, which in its early years finds no special or unexpected aid from remarkable circumstances. The same struggles with equal hardship and similar doubts have no doubt been made before, and nothing has been said of them. The strugglers have lived through and fought their way to prosperity, and but little has been heard of the details of the fight. When the Puritans were landed on the shores of Massachusetts men did not rush about the world and write books. It may probably be that they too, at their first starting, had but few glimpses of the glory of the coming Yankee world. It was perhaps only by hard fighting with adverse circumstances, that they could get corn and labour, and money. But they went on, and the glories of Yankee-dom are now patent to the whole earth.

It is to the gold that has been found in Eastern Australia that the eastern colonies have owed their rapid rise and great name—and in a great measure the want of reputation under which Western Australia labours is due to the golden achievements of her sisters. She would not have been thought to have done so badly had not those sisters done so well. . . .

And then, in another way, the gold-diggings of the eastern colonies have been detrimental not only to the reputation, but to the very existence, of Western Australia. Men have constantly gone after the gold. It became almost useless to land emigrants on the western shore. Tidings came of this rush and of that rush, and the new-comers disappeared, soon turning up, as new chums again, in the golden land. . . .

In speaking of the future of Western Australia I shall not receive the thanks or sympathies of many of its inhabitants, if I express an opinion that that future is to be independent of gold. The idea is deep-rooted that there should be gold and must be gold—that Providence cannot have been so unjust as not to have put gold there. Why not in the west as well as in the east? . . . Doubtless gold may turn up in Western Australia, but I trust that the colony will be too wise to wait for it. Should it come, let the favour be accepted from the gods—but I do not think that men should live expecting it.

In the meantime what other measures may serve to turn the tide, and produce some life and action? The land is good, and if properly tilled will produce all that is necessary for man's life. And the land that will do so, though widely scattered, is abundant. I need hardly say that at home in England there are still among us millions of half-starved people—half-starved certainly according to the dietary of the poorest even in this poor colony —to whom the realization of rural life in Western Australia would seem to be an earthly paradise if it could be understood—to whom it would be a paradise if it could be reached. . . .

But how shall the rural labourer out of Sussex, Suffolk, Essex, or Cambridgeshire get to Western Australia? If there were no pecuniary difficulty in the journey—if every labourer were empowered by Act of Parliament to go to some parish officer and demand to be sent across the ocean—it is probable that a very large fleet of transport ships would soon be required, and that English farmers would find it difficult to get in their seed. This can never be the case, but something towards it is done. The colonies assist intending immigrants, and the mother country too assists, or, in some cases, pays the entire expense of emigrants. We sent out those ill-born and ill-bred women who were wanted as convicts' wives—and who, when received, were found to be mere Irish. But it is ill bringing a man out who will not stay when he is brought. If you, my philanthropical reader, send out some favoured tenant or parishioner, your object is fairly achieved whether the man make himself happy in Western Australia or Victoria. But it is by no means so with the colony, when the colony pays. When a colony has paid for three or four hundred immigrants, and finds after a few months that they have all disappeared, and gone to more fortunate lands, the colony not unnaturally becomes disgusted. Then it is that the colony feels that nothing will do but gold.

* * *

I cannot finish this chapter without giving a copy of a certificate which was handed to me by a policeman at Albany, just as I was about to leave the colony:—

> I hereby certify that the bearer, A. Trollope, about to proceed to Adelaide per A.S.N. Co.'s steamer, is not and never has been a prisoner of the Crown in Western Australia. (Signed)..
>
> Resident Magistrate.

It is perhaps something of a disgrace to Western Australia that the other colonies will not receive a stranger from her shores without a certificate that the visitor has not been a "lag". Such a resolution on their part must remind the poor Western Australians grievously of their disgrace. So many have been convicts, that the certificate is demanded from all! But I think that they should not charge a shilling for it, and thus raise a revenue out of their own ill fame. It was not my fault that South Australia demanded the certificate. Considering all the circumstances, I think that they should give the passport, and say nothing about it.

South Australia

South Australia has a peculiar history of its own, differing very much from those of the other Australian colonies, though similar in some degree to that of New Zealand, which was founded after South Australia, and with aspirations of the same nature. . . . All the now existing Australian colonies, except South Australia, have either owed their origin to convicts, or have been at one period of their existence fostered by convict labour. But South Australia has never been blessed—or cursed—with the custody of a single British exile.

* * *

Perhaps no city, not even Philadelphia, has been laid out with a stronger purpose of regularity and order than has been shown in the founding and construction of Adelaide. Adelaide proper, as distinguished from North Adelaide, which has been allowed to deviate somewhat from the good manner of the parent city, stands in exact conformity with the points of the compass. The streets all run north and south, or east and west. There are five squares—or open spaces so designated—one in the centre, and the other four at certain fixed intervals. At the extremities of the town, on the northern, southern, eastern, and western sides there are four terraces. That, however, on the eastern side has been allowed to take a devious course, as the city to the south is longer than it is at the north. But there is a precise regularity even in this irregularity. This terrace on the map of the town takes the form of a flight of steps, for nothing so irregular as a sloping or diagonal line has been permitted in the arrangement of the streets. To me the Quaker-like simplicity of such urban construction never renders easy any practical conception of the topography. I find it quite as easy to lose my way in Philadelphia or Adelaide as I do in the old parts of Paris, or in the meandering lanes of such a city as Norwich. I forget which is north and which west, and what set of streets run at right angles to what other set. I never was able to find my way about Adelaide. But for a man with a compass in his pocket, clear calculating brain, and a good memory, the thing must be very easy. . . . King William Street, the High Street of the town, runs at right angles from the North Terrace to Victoria Square, which is the centre of the city. Here, in King William Street, is congregated the magnificence of Adelaide—comprising the Town Hall, the Public Offices, the Post Office, and various banks, and many of the most money-making shops.

The one building in Adelaide on which the town most prides itself—and of which at the same time the colony is half-ashamed because of the expense—is the Post Office. I was gratified by finding that the colonies generally were disposed to be splendid in their post-offices rather than in any other buildings, for surely there is no other public building so useful. At Brisbane, when I was there, they were building a fine post-office. At Sydney they had nearly completed a magnificent post-office. At Melbourne I found a very large post-office indeed—though, as I thought, one not very convenient to the public. And here at Adelaide the Post Office is the grandest edifice in the town. It is really a beautiful building, with a large centre hall, such as we had in London as long as we could afford ourselves the luxury. We have built up our hall, compelled by exigencies of space and money—compelled, as I think, by a shabby regard to space and money.

It will be long before the authorities of Adelaide will be driven to perpetrate a similar architectural meanness, for surely such a post office will be more than ample for the population for many a year to come. I went over the building, and knowing something of post-offices, I regret to say that the arrangements might have been improved by consultation with English officials. As regarded the building as a building, it is a credit to Adelaide, and would be an ornament to any city in Europe.

The government offices are not magnificent but are pleasant, commodious, and sufficient. The Town Hall is a fine room, and forms a portion of a very handsome building. In such luxuries as town-halls, large public concert-rooms, public ball-rooms, and the like, the Australian cities greatly beat our own. I do not say that there is any such an edifice on the Australian continent as St. George's Hall at Liverpool—but then neither is there any town with half the number of inhabitants that Liverpool contains. Adelaide itself has less than 30,000, and I doubt whether there be any town in England with double that number which has such a chamber for public purposes as that of which I am speaking. I am sure there is none with four times the number that has a theatre so pretty, so well constructed, and so fit for its purpose as the Adelaide Theatre. Even little Perth with its 6,000 souls has a grand town-hall. In almost every municipality—even in those of the suburbs of such a town as Adelaide—halls are erected for public purposes, for speeches, balls, concerts, and the like. In this respect our children in Australia take after their cousins in the United States. In regard to banks also Adelaide flourishes greatly. I must not name any one in particular, lest it be thought that I am making return for accommodation given; but, such was their grandeur, that I felt of them generally that the banking profits in South Australia must be very great, or such edifices could not have been erected. . . .

Adelaide is well provided with churches—so much so that this speciality has been noticed ever since its first foundation. It was peculiarly the idea of those who formed the first mission to South Australia, that there should be no dominant church—that religious freedom should prevail in the new colony as it never had prevailed up to that time in any British settlement; and that the word dissent should have no meaning, as there should be nothing established from which to disagree. In spite of all this the Church of England has assumed a certain ascendancy, partly from the fact that a liberal and worthy Englishwoman, now Lady Burdett Coutts, endowed a bishopric at Adelaide; but chiefly from the indubitable fact that they of the Church of England who have flocked into the colony have been higher in wealth and intelligence than those of any other creed. It would be singular indeed had it not been so, seeing that the country from which they came had for centuries possessed an established and endowed Church. But the very fact that the Church of England boasted for itself even in this colony a kind of ascendancy, and the other fact that the colony had been founded with the determination that there should be no such ascendancy, have together created great enmity among the rival sects. . . .

All round the city there are reserved lands, of which I may best explain the nature to English readers by calling them parks for the people. These reserves are of various widths in different parts, but are full half a mile wide on an average. They are now being planted, and are devoted to air and recreation. I need hardly explain that they cannot as yet rival the beauty and the shade of our London parks—but that they will do so is already apparent to the eye. And they will have this advantage—which, indeed, since the growth of the town towards the west belongs also to our London parks—that they will be in the middle, not on the outside, of an inhabited city. As Adelaide increases in population, these "reserves" will be in the midst of the inhabitants. But they will have also this additional advantage—which we in London do not as yet enjoy, in spite of efforts that have been made—that they will not be a blessing only to one side or to one end of the city. They will run east and west, north and south, and will be within the reach of all Adelaide and her suburbs. There are here also public gardens, as there are in every metropolis of the Australian colonies. The gardens of Adelaide cannot rival those of Sydney, which, as far as my experience goes, are unrivalled in beauty anywhere. Nothing that London possesses, nothing that Paris has, nothing that New York has, comes near to them in loveliness. But as regards Australian cities, those of Adelaide are next to the gardens of Sydney. In Melbourne the gardens are more scientific, but the world at large cares but little for science. In Sydney, the public gardens charm as poetry charms. At Adelaide, they please like a well-told tale.

The gardens at Melbourne are as a long sermon from a great divine—whose theology is unanswerable, but his language tedious.

The city has a background of hills called the Mount Lofty Range, so called by Captain Flinders when he made his first survey. The only pretension to landscape beauty which the city possesses is derived from these mountains. It was indeed said many years ago by one much interested in Adelaide, that she was built on a "pretty stream". The "stream" is called the Torrens, after one of the founders of the colony, but I utterly deny the truth of the epithet attached to it. Anything in the guise of a river more ugly than the Torrens it would be impossible either to see or to describe. During eleven months of the year it is a dry and ugly channel, retaining only the sewer-wards property of a river. In this condition I saw it. During the other month it is, I was told, a torrent. But the hills around are very pretty, and afford lovely views, and charming sites for villa residences, and soil and climate admirably suited for market gardens. As a consequence of this latter attribute Adelaide is well supplied with vegetables and fruit. By those who can afford to pay the price already demanded for special sites, beautiful nooks for suburban residences may still be obtained. . . .

I liked Adelaide very much—and I liked the Adelaideans; but I must confess to my opinion that it is about the hottest city in Australia south of the tropics. The heat, however, is not excessive for above three months. I arrived in the first week of April, and then the weather was delightful. . . . No city in Australia gives more fixedly the idea that Australian colonization has been a success, than does the city of Adelaide.

I have said that Adelaide has been called a city of churches. It has also been nicknamed the Farinaceous City. A little gentle ridicule is no doubt intended to be conveyed by the word. The colony by the sister colonies is regarded as one devoted in a special manner to the production of flour. Men who spend their energies in the pursuit of gold consider the growing of wheat to be a poor employment. And again the squatters, or wool-producers of Australia, who are great men, with large flocks, and with acres of land at their command so enormous that they have to be counted not by acres, but by square miles, look down from a very great height indeed upon the little agriculturists—

small men, who generally live from hand to mouth—and whose original occupation of their holdings has commonly been supposed to be at variance with the squatters' interests. The agriculturists of Australia generally are free-selectors, men who have bought bits here and bits there off the squatters' runs, and have bought the best bits—men, too, whose neighbourhood has not been a source of comfort to the squatters generally. In this way agriculture generally, and especially the growing of wheat-crops for sale, has not been regarded in the colonies as it is certainly regarded at home. The farmers of South Australia are usually called "cockatoos"—a name which prevails also, though less universally, in the other colonies. The word cockatoo in the farinaceous colony has become so common as almost to cease to carry with it the intended sarcasm. A man will tell you of himself that he is a cockatoo, and when doing so will probably feel some little justifiable pride in the freehold possession of his acres. But the name has been given as a reproach, and in truth it has been and is deserved. It signifies that the man does not really till his land, but only scratches it as the bird does.

* * *

I also visited a large cattle-station in the south of the colony, on the eastern side of the lakes. It belongs to a rich Scotch absentee landowner who sits in our parliament, and I will only say of it that I think I ate the best beef there that ever fell in my way. Like other things, beef must have a best and a worst, and I think that the Portalloch beef was the best. I heard that there was beef as good—perhaps even better—up at a large cattle-station far north; but the information reached me from the owner of the northern station who was with us at Portalloch. As I found his information on all other subjects to be reliable, I am bound to believe him in this. If it be so he must be the very prince of beef-growers. On the road from Adelaide to the lakes—on the lake side of the Mount Lofty hills—we stayed a night at the little town of Strathalbyn. Afterwards, on my route back to Victoria, which I made by steamer from Port Adelaide to Macdonnell Bay, and thence overland across the border, I stayed also at the little town of Gambier-Town, under Mount Gambier. I mention these places because they were the cleanest, prettiest, pleasantest little towns that I saw during my Australian travels.

I would say that they were like well-built thriving English villages of the best class, were it not that they both contain certain appliances and an architectural pretension which hardly belong to villages. When the place in question is dirty, unfinished, and forlorn—when the attempt at doing something considerable in the way of founding a town seems to have been a failure—the appearance of this pretension is very disagreeable. But at Strathalbyn and Gambier-Town there had been success, and they had that look about them which makes a stranger sometimes fancy in a new place that it might be well for him to come and abide there to the end. They are both in South Australia. Perhaps I was specially moved to admiration because the inns were good.

* * *

There are not a few in the colonies who declare that South Australia, as a name for the colony which uses it, is a misnomer. Nearly the whole of Victoria is south of nearly the whole of South Australia. Adelaide is considerably to the north of Melbourne, and but very little to the south of Sydney. Consequently those foolish English people at home are actually making the stupidest mistakes! Letters have been addressed to Melbourne, New South Wales, South Australia. The story is very current, and is often told to show the want of geographical education under which the old country suffers. I have not, however, been able to trace the address to later years, and at any time between 1837 and 1851 the details as given by the letter-writer were only too correct. Melbourne did belong to New South Wales, and certainly was in the most southern district of Australia.

But if the name South Australia was bad, or falsely described the colony, when first given, it is infinitely worse now. Then the proposed confines of the young settlement lay around Spencer Gulf, and Gulf St. Vincent, and Encounter Bay, which armlets of the sea break up into the land from the eastern extremity of the Great Australian Bight, as the curve in the sea line of the southern coast of the continent is called. The new colonists had settled themselves, or, when the name was chosen, were proposing to settle themselves, at the centre of the south coast, and the name was fair enough. But since those days South Australia has extended herself northwards till she has made good her claim up to a line far north of that which divides

Queensland from New South Wales, and now she is supposed to run right through the continent up to the Gulf of Carpentaria and the Indian Ocean, so that she thoroughly divides the vast desert tracts of Western Australia from the three eastern colonies, Queensland, New South Wales, and Victoria. As far as area is concerned, she is at present as much northern as southern. In some of our maps the northern half of these territories is separated by a line from the southern, as though it were a separate colony—but it has had no name of its own yet given to it; its lands are at the disposition of the government of South Australia; its very few inhabitants are subject to South Australian laws; and it is in fact a part of South Australia.

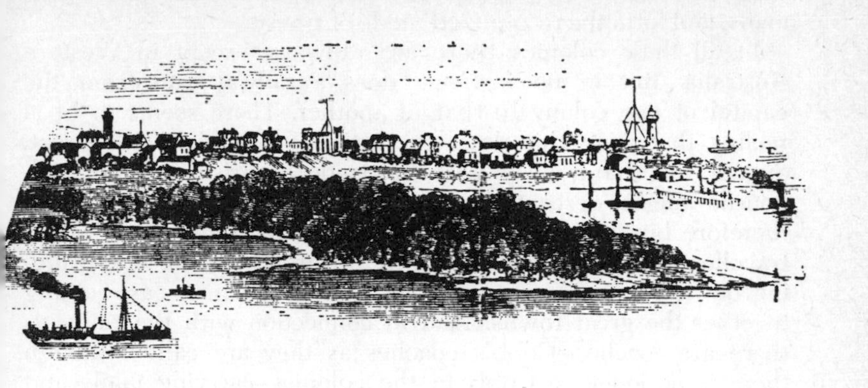

3 BY STEAMBOAT AND COACH

Travel by Sea

The mode of journeying from one colony to another in Australia is almost always by sea—and indeed in a great measure from one part of a colony to another part of the same. The inhabited portion of the Australian world consists of the eastern and southern coasts, with a belt of land varying in breadth—and a population ever becoming thinner as the breadth is increased. The capitals, Brisbane, Sydney, and Melbourne, are seaports, and Adelaide has a seaport, Port Adelaide, within seven miles. The same is to be said of many of the secondary towns. There is communication by coach from Brisbane to Sydney, from Sydney to Melbourne, and from Melbourne to Adelaide, supplemented in each case by the use of small detached railways; but no one travels in this fashion between any of those towns. There are steamers plying twice or thrice a week, and thus the journeys are made. The greater number of these boats belong to the firm of the Australian Steam Navigation Company. These steamers run from King George's Sound in Western Australia—which is regarded by the other Australian colonies as the Ultima Thule of the colonial world—round by Adelaide, to Melbourne, Sydney, and Brisbane and thence up the coast of Queensland to Maryborough, Rockhampton, and Cleveland Bay. They carry the mails, and form the recognized mode of transit.

In all these colonies there are railways, except in Western Australia. But in no instance does a railway run from the capital of one colony to that of another. There seems to be a feeling that were this done the intimacy would be too great. Sydney might run away with the trade of Brisbane, and Melbourne might destroy Sydney. The Australian railways are therefore bits of railways, giving a help here and there to the traveller who has to make his way inwards from the sea, bringing down wool and carrying back stores, but in no case joining together the great towns. And in connection with the railways there are coaches—Cobb's coaches as they are called, though there is no longer a Cobb in the colonies—carrying mails and passengers into remote districts, carrying mails and passengers to towns on the routes between the capitals. But travellers from one capital to another almost always use the steamers.

I had already made four voyages under the auspices of the A. S. N. Company, and I found the boats to be fairly comfortable when not crowded—but wretchedly uncomfortable when full. Everything is provided for the passenger and included in the fare paid—except of course, wine, or beer, or spirits. When the room at the table is ample, and the stewards and cook are not overworked, the food given is excellent, and a good sailor can enjoy his meals. As soon as the servants are overtasked everything becomes abominable. Nor is the trouble of the table by any means the worst trouble. Men who have travelled much know what it is to be "doubled up", and the doubling up on board the A. S. N. Company's boats is intolerable. It is probably only for two or three nights, and therefore the space allowed to each passenger is very small. That it should be so is, perhaps, reasonable. Larger vessels would create very much increased expense, and probably might not pay, and, north of Sydney, the towns lie on rivers which will not admit of deeper keels. I make no complaint, acknowledging that the company does its best to suit the traffic. But, looking at the matter from my own point of view, I protest that two or three nights passed with a couple of snoring strangers in one of the A. S. N. Company's cabins. without a peg on which to hang an article of clothing, with no spot to call your own except the narrow crib in which you are to lie, with the most meagre accommodation for washing that the ingenuity of a seafaring man can contrive, are—very painfully passed. A persevering man might probably succeed in making for himself something of a bed upon deck, and on an occasion I have done so. Everybody on board these boats is civil. I cheerfully acknowledge that the captains, and mates, and stewards never blow up or become tyrannical. But the man who would sleep upon deck comes to feel that the spirit of the ship is against him, and he slinks below, and is snored at and almost smothered in his wretched berth.

Such had been my lot when I went up from Sydney to Brisbane, sharing my cabin with two respectable commercial gentlemen against whom I have not a word to say. Snoring is not disgraceful, and their courtesy was complete. My temper had been acerbated early in the voyage by a slight accident in regard to the soup, of which a large allowance was poured over me by a too anxious steward; and then the utter peglessness of the cabin completed my unhappiness. North of Brisbane I had fared better—the company having fared much worse in regard to the number of passengers carried. On my return to Sydney I found that a boat not belonging to the A. S. N. Company was about to make the trip—as to which an allegation was made to me that she was slow, and that she habitually disgraced herself by carrying cargoes of coal from Newcastle, on her southern journey down to Melbourne. I instantly made inquiry and found that I—and a friend who was with me—could have separate cabins on board the *Blackbird.* On board the *Blackbird* we went to Sydney, and a very comfortable voyage we made. The captain was an excellent captain, no doubt thoroughly up to the work, for he ran us upon no rocks and stuck us upon no sand banks, and brought us into no trouble, and made the journey two hours shorter than his original promise. In regard, however, to his nautical acquirements I do not profess to be capable of forming a trustworthy opinion. But this captain had procured live turtle up the coast, and had a cook on board whom I can safely recommend to any embryo Lord Mayor. I forget that captain's name—but I never will forget his turtle soup.

It strikes an Englishman with surprise that he should meet all the paraphernalia of Custom Houses in going from one colony to another. One's shirts and socks are subject to be searched on entering Sydney Harbour from Brisbane, as undoubtedly as when taken into Prussia from Belgium. And I observed that the shirts and socks of some men were searched by Custom House officers on occasions. Personally I encountered no difficulty. I was asked some questions and allowed to pass without even a reference to my keys. As I have almost always been allowed to do so on the Continent, and even at New York, I presume that I have no trace of smuggling ingenuity in my countenance.

The Roads in the East

Hitherto my travelling had been chiefly by steamboat from one town along the coast to another. From Maryborough I determined to return to Brisbane by coach, in order that I might see Gympie, famous for its gold. . . .

I had been very much advised against the coach. I was told that the road, and the vehicle, and the horses, and the driving were so rough as to be unfit for a man of my age and antecedents. One anxious friend implored me not to undertake it, with an anxiety which could hardly have been stronger had I been his grandfather. I was, however, obstinate, and can now declare that I enjoyed the drive most thoroughly. It lasted three days, and took me through some magnificent scenery. Woodland country in Australia—and it must be remembered that the lands occupied are mostly woodland—is called either bush or scrub. Woods which are open, and passable, passable at any rate for men on horseback, are called bush. When the undergrowth becomes thick and matted so as to be impregnable without an axe, it is scrub. In Queensland the scrubs are filled with tropical plants, long vine tendrils, palms and the parasite fig-tree, and when a way has been cut through them the effect for a time is very lovely. The fault of all Australian scenery is its monotony. The eye after a while becomes fatigued with a landscape which at first charmed with its park-like aspect. One never gets out of the trees, and then it rarely happens that water lends its aid to improve the view. As a rule it must be acknowledged that a land of forests is not a land of beauty. Some experience in travelling is needed before this can be acknowledged as every lover of nature is an admirer of trees. But unceasing trees, trees which continue around you from six in the morning till six at night, become a bore, and the traveller begins to remember with regret the open charms of some cultivated plain. I had to acknowledge this monotony before I reached Brisbane—but I acknowledged also the great beauty of the scrubs, and found some breaks in the mountains which were very grand.

But the wonder of the journey was in the badness of the roads and the goodness of the coachmanship. I have been called upon by the work of my life to see much coaching, having been concerned for more than thirty years with the expedition of mails—and I remember well the good old patriotic John Bull conviction that go where one would round the world one could never find a man to drive like the English mail-coachman of the olden times. There was a fixed idea that coach-driving was a British accomplishment, and quite beyond the reach of any one out of Britain. Since that I have seen something of driving over the Alps and other European mountains; something also of driving in America; which lessened my belief in the "unapproachability" of the excellence of the Englishman. I have now travelled over the Gympie road, and I feel certain that not one of my old friends of the box—and I had many such friends—would, on being shown that road, have considered it possible that a vehicle with four horses should have been made to travel over it. There is often no road, and the coach is taken at random through the forest. Not unfrequently a fallen tree blocks up the track, and the coach is squeezed through some siding which makes it necessary for the leader to be going one way while the coach is going another. But the great miracle is in the sudden pitches, looking as though they were almost perpendicular, down which the coach is taken, and then the equally sharp ascents—not straight, but at a sharp angle—up and round which the coach is whirled.

The art of driving on such roads depends very much on the foot. The vehicle is supplied with strong machinery for dragging the hind wheels, so as almost altogether to stop their rotation, and this the coachman manages with his right foot. I heard of various accidents to the coach, but of none to passengers. I at any rate went through in safety, and I recommend others to make the journey. We slept during the night between Gympie and Brisbane at a place called Cobb's Camp, at which the pleasant manners of the pretty German hostess almost atoned for the miraculous profusion of fleas. It may be as well to observe here, that all stage-coaches in Australia and New Zealand are called Cobb's coaches—one Cobb, an American, having started a vast business in the coaching line. Two or three different companies now carry on the trade through the colonies. I here pronounce my opinion that the man who drove me from Cobb's Camp to Brisbane was the best driver of four horses I ever saw. Had he been a little less uncouth in his manners, I should have told him what I thought of him.

The coach journey from Maryborough to Brisbane takes three days; but as I stayed a day at Gympie and left Maryborough the evening before the coach, I was four days and a night on the road. I travelled the first twenty miles in an open boat up the Mary River, with a gentleman who owned the boat, and who had got together a crew of Polynesian rowers. None of the party, however, had made the journey before; and as it was done in the dark, and as the river is in part crowded with rocks, and as both I and my friend went to sleep while we were steering, and as we had to land at a spot which was in no way different from any other spot on the river bank, we were not without the excitement of some little difficulties. When we were ashore we had to walk a couple of miles through the forest in search of the village in which we were to sleep, a place called Tiaro, and when we found it, about two in the morning, the first innkeeper whom we knocked up, a German, took us for bushrangers and would not let us in. But there was a second innkeeper who was more courageous, who gave us brandy and water and beds, and who had been butler in the house of a friend of mine at home, or, rather, of my friend's father. He sent home many messages to Mr. John, and declared himself to be happy in his new career.

* * *

This travelling through the endless forest of gum-trees is very peculiar, and at first attractive. After awhile it becomes monotonous in the extreme. There is a great absence of animal life. One may go all day through a pastoral country without seeing a sheep or a kangaroo. Now and again one hears the melancholy note of the magpie, or the unmelodious but cheerful gobble of the laughing jackass, and sometimes the scream of a cockatoo; but even birds are not common. Travellers one meets occasionally

—a man on horseback, with his swag before him on his saddle, or a line of drays drawn by bullocks, or perhaps a squatter in his buggy—but they are few and far between. The road, such as it is, consists of various tracks, running hither and thither, and very puzzling at first to a "new chum"—till he learns that all these tracks in the bush are only deviations of one road. When the bullock-drays have so cut up a certain passage that the ruts are big enough and deep enough to swallow up a buggy or to overset the stage-coach, the buggies and the stage-coach make another passage, from which they move again when the inevitable bullock-drays have followed them. The Government shows its first care on these roads in making bridges over the streams, but even bridges are not absolutely essential. With some rough contrivance, when any contrivance is absolutely necessary, the vehicles descend and ascend the banks, though the wheels be down to the nave in mud. Over many of these bush roads, Cobb's coaches travel day and night, passing in and out through the trees, up and down across the creeks, sticking here and there in the mud, in a rough, uneasy, but apparently not very insecure fashion. Now and then one hears that a coach has been upset, and that the passengers have been out in the bush all night; but one very rarely hears than any one has been hurt, unless it be the coachman. The average pace of the travelling in New South Wales is about six miles an hour.

But more go in their own buggies than by coach, and perhaps more on horseback than in buggies. In Australia every one keeps horses—every squatter keeps horses by the dozen; and a buggy is as necessary a part of his establishment as a dinner-table. These vehicles are either American, or are built on the American plan, and are admirably adapted for bush work. They are very light, and go over huge logs and across unfathomable ruts almost without feeling them. To upset them seems to be an impossibility. They are constantly being broken—hopelessly broken to the mind of an ignorant stranger; but they go on apparently as well without a pole as with one, and are indifferent to bent axles and injured wheels. There are always yards of rope at hand, and supplementary timber can be cut from the next tree. Many scores of miles through the bush I have travelled in these buggies, and have sometimes felt the hours to pass by very slowly; but though there have been no roads—nothing that in England would be called a road—I have encountered no injury, nor have I been aware of any danger.

But the pleasantest mode of bush travelling is on horseback. It is open to this objection—that you can carry nothing with you but what can be strapped on to your saddle before you. Two changes of linen, a night-shirt, a pair of trousers, with hair-brushes, tooth-brush, and a pair of slippers, is about as much as can be taken. But, on the other hand, bush-life requires but little in the way of dress, and a man travelling on horseback is held to be exempt from rules which he should observe if he travelled in a buggy. The squatter travelling alone through the country generally takes two horses, leading one and riding the other, and in this way makes very long journeys.

The work which Australian horses will do when immediately taken off the grass is very surprising. I have ridden forty, fifty, and even as much as sixty-four miles a day, the whole weight on the animal's back being over seventeen stone, and have come to the end of the day's work without tiring the horse. According to the distance to be done, and the number of consecutive days during which you require your steed to travel, will be your pace. The fastest which I ever did from morning to evening was eight miles an hour throughout, resting two hours and journeying eight; but six miles an hour will perhaps be the average rate. The stories, however, that we hear are very wonderful—for in matters of horseflesh, gentlemen in Australia do not hide their lights under bushels. I have heard men boast of doing ten miles an hour for ten hours running; and one very enterprising horseman assured me that he had ridden seventy-five miles in four hours.

The bush horses are, generally, not shod, though I would always recommend shoeing for a long journey, and are very rarely stabled. They are expected—to us a bush phrase—to cut their own bread and butter, or, in other words, to feed themselves by foraging. The two paces which are commonly adopted by horsemen in the bush are walking and cantering. Men seldom trot, and consequently many horses altogether lose, or never acquire, the habit of trotting. I have been assured that Australian horses will get over the ground at a fast pace with greater ease to themselves by a continual canter than by changing that pace for a trot. That such a theory is altogether wrong I have not the slightest doubt. I have found in Australia, as all horsemen know in England, that horses carrying heavy weights will make much longer journeys if made to trot than they can do if required to canter hour after hour. The canter is the easier pace to the man, and therefore it has been adopted. Not uncommonly a horse will knock up with his rider on the road. On such occasions the rider turns into the nearest squatter's station, and borrows another. The fact that everybody's horses, and everybody's saddles and bridles, are always at somebody else's house and never at the owner's, is one of the most remarkable and perhaps not least pleasing phases of Australian life . . .

* * *

I cannot speak as highly of the coach roads as of the railways of Victoria. One effect of railways in a new country is to anticipate and supersede the creation of ordinary roads. A perfectly new country, hitherto known only to a few shepherds, is opened up by a railway—which is not carried hither and thither for the service of towns and villages, but creates them as it goes along. Then, the one great need of a central road having been achieved, neither the government nor the inhabitants are for a time willing to go to the expense of macadamization. The badness of the roads is, however, remarkable throughout Australia—and it is equally remarkable that though the roads are very bad, and in some places cannot be said to exist, nevertheless coaches run and goods are carried about the country.

A Victorian coach, with six or perhaps seven or eight horses, in the darkness of the night, making its way through a thickly timbered forest at the rate of nine miles an hour, with the horses frequently up to their bellies in mud, with the wheels running in and out of holes four or five feet deep, is a phenomenon which I should like to have shown to some of those very neat mail-coach drivers whom I used to know at home in the old days. I am sure that no description would make any one of them believe that such feats of driving were possible. I feel that nothing short of seeing it would have made me believe it. The coaches, which are very heavy, and carry nine passengers inside, are built on an American system, and hang on immense leathern springs. The passengers inside are shaken ruthlessly, and are horribly soiled by mud and dirt. Two sit upon the box outside, and undergo lesser evils. By the courtesy shown to strangers in the colonies I always got the box, and found myself fairly comfortable as soon as I overcame the idea that I must infallibly be dashed against the next gum-tree. I made many such journeys, and never suffered any serious misfortune. I feel myself bound, however, to say that Victoria has not advanced in road-making as she has in other matters.

* * *

The road from Launceston to Hobart Town is as good as any road in England, and is in appearance exactly like an English road. It is hard to say what are the features which make one road like another; but they who have travelled in France know that no French road, even when macadamized, is in the least like an English road. Every French road has a touch of despotism in it. Every English road looks as though it were ruled by a local board. The Australian roads are generally quite unlike our roads at home. They are made for the most part through dense forests. When they pass cleared lands, the divisions of the fields and paddocks are generally made either by fences with wooden frames and wire, or with two or three rough unpainted rails. The constructed part of the road, that on which the vehicles absolutely travel, is narrower than with us, but the allotted space for the road is very much broader—so much so that when the funds are low and the way gets out of repair, it is apt to meander hither and thither across its broad borders. A rut deep enough to bury a pony is avoided here, and there some slough of despond is circumvented by a cleverly contrived circuitous route. . . .

Such are Australian roads in general, but that from Launceston to Hobart Town is altogether unlike them. It was made throughout by convicts, and was manifestly made with the intention of being as like an English road as possible. The makers of it have perfectly succeeded. When it passes through forest land—or bush—the English traveller would imagine that there was a fox covert on each side of him. There are hedges too, and the fields are small. And there are hills on all sides, very like the Irish hills in County Cork. Indeed it is Ireland rather than England to which Tasmania may be compared. And, as I have said before, English—or Irish—coaches run upon the road; a night mail-coach, with driver and guard in red coats, and a day coach with all appurtenances after the old fashion. I found their pace when travelling to be about nine miles an hour.

We went by the mail coach as far as Campbelltown—a place with about 1,600 inhabitants, which returns a member to parliament, and has a municipal council, four or five resident clergymen, a hospital, an agricultural association, and a cricket club. Quite a place!—as the Americans say. When I asked whether it was prosperous, my local friend shook his head. It ought to be the centre of a flourishing pastoral district. It is the centre of a pastoral district which is not flourishing—because of the rabbits. This wicked little prolific brute, introduced from England only a few years ago, has so spread himself about, that hardly a blade of grass is left for the sheep! But why not exterminate him, or at least keep him down? I asked the question with thorough confidence that the energies of man need not succumb to the energies of rabbits. I was told that the matter had gone too far, and that the rabbit had established his dominion. I cannot, however, but imagine that the rabbit could be conquered if Tasmania would really put her shoulder to the wheel.

We passed a place called Melton, at which a pack of hounds was formerly kept—so called after the hunting metropolis in Leicestershire; and as I looked around I thought that I saw a country well adapted for running a drag. Foxes, if there were foxes, would all be away into the mountains. They used to hunt stags, but I should have thought that the stags would have taken to the hills. But the hunting had belonged to the good old prosperous convict days, and had passed away with other Tasmanian glories.

A Trip Through Gipps Land

I went by coach from Melbourne to Gipps Land with a friend, partly with a view of visiting that district generally, and partly that I might see the eastern gold-fields of the colony. I had indeed become very tired of gold—which, to a traveller who enjoys none of the excitement arising from the hope of acquiring it, is but a wearisome object. I did not desire to go down more mines, and yet I felt that I should not be strong-minded enough to save myself from further descents. I think I should have taken the Gipps Land gold-fields on credit, had I not been told that the scenery around them was peculiarly beautiful. I was specially desired not to miss Woods Point—which indeed is not in Gipps Land, but which could be visited from Gipps Land by any one who would trust himself among the mountains on horseback. From Woods Point I could return to Melbourne by a direct road, so as to avoid the disagreeable task of retracing my steps over the same path. As far as scenery was concerned, I was certainly repaid for the labour of a somewhat laborious journey. . . .

We started by one of Cobb's coaches at one o'clock in the day, and reached the little town of Rosedale in Gipps Land at ten the next morning. Cobb's coaches have the name of being very rough—and more than once I have been warned against travelling by them. They were not fit, I was told, for an effeminate Englishman of my time of life. The idea that Englishmen—that is, new-chums, or Englishmen just come from home—are made of paste, whereas the Australian, native or thoroughly acclimatized, is steel all through, I found to be universal. On hearing such an opinion as to his own person, a man is bound to sacrifice himself, and to act contrary to the advice given, even though he perish in doing so. This journey I made and did not perish at all; and on arriving at Rosedale had made up my mind that twenty hours on a Cobb's coach through the bush in Australia does not inflict so severe a martyrdom as did in the old days a journey of equal duration on one of the time-famous much-regretted old English mails. More space is allowed you for stretching your legs on the seat, and more time for stretching your legs at the stages. The road, of course, is rough—generally altogether unmade—but the roughness lends an interest to the occasion, and when the coach is stuck in a swamp—as happens daily—it is pleasant to remember that the horses do finally succeed, every day, in pulling it out again. On this road there is a place called the Glue Pot, extending perhaps for a furlong, as to which the gratified traveller feels that now, at any rate, the real perils of travel have been attained. But the horses, rolling up to their bellies in the mud, do pull the coach through. This happens in the darkness of night, in the thick forest—and the English traveller in his enthusiasm tells the coachman that no English whip would have looked at such a place even by daylight. The man is gratified, lights his pipe, and rushes headlong into the next gully. . . .

My friend and I bought two horses and two saddles, and

started from Rosedale on our journey to the mines. We had met some influential gentlemen of the district—a judge, a resident magistrate, and an inspector of police—who were united in their assurance that if we went without a guide we should certainly be lost in the bush. Now my friend was a man of mark, whose loss would have been severely felt by the colony, and for his security we were furnished with a mounted trooper, or policeman, to show us our way, and generally take care of us on our expedition. We certainly needed him, and, as I believe, would have been sleeping now in some Gipps Land gully but for his assistance.

Our first day's march was to Walhalla, a mining town of great wealth to which there is literally no road. Our journey was one of about forty miles—for the latter half of it, continuously through forest, and as continuously up and down mountains. These were so steep that it was often impossible to sit on horseback. As the weather was very hot our toil was great, and I shall never forget the welcome with which I greeted the beer-shop on the Thompson River. The scenery through these mountains is magnificent—when it can be seen. But such is the continuity and contiguity of the trees, that it becomes impossible for miles together to see either the hill-tops or the depths of the valleys. Going down to the Thompson River, and again down into Walhalla, we found it to be impossible to ride; and yet we knew that immense masses of machinery had been taken down by bullocks for the use of the miners. We were told that very many bullocks had been destroyed at the work. I could not have believed that there had been such a traffic across the mountains and through the forest, had I not afterwards seen thc things at Walhalla.

At last we got to the place, very tired and very footsore, and had bedrooms allocated to us in the hotel close to the quartz-crushing machine, which goes on day and night eating up the rock which is dragged forth from the bowels of the earth. The noisy monster continued his voracious meal without cessation for a moment, so that sleep was out of the question. To the residents of the inn the effect was simply somniferous. Their complaint was that from twelve o'clock on Saturday night when the monster begins to keep his Sabbath, to twelve o'clock on Sunday night when his religious observances are over, the air is so burdened by silence that they can neither talk by day nor sleep by night.

The mining town which has been dignified by the name of Walhalla lies at the bottom of a gully from which the wooded sides rise steeply. Through it meanders a stream which is now, of course, contaminated by the diggings, and pumpings, and gold-washing, and quartz-crushing, which have befallen the locality. Nevertheless it has a peculiar beauty of its own, and a picturesque interest arising in part from the wooded hills which so closely overhang it, but partly also from the quaintness of a town so placed. The buildings, consisting of banks, churches, schools, hotels, managers' houses, and miners' cottages, lie along the stream, or are perched upon low altitudes among the trees. There is something like a winding street through it, which is nearly a mile long—though indeed it is difficult sometimes to distinguish between the river and the street; but there is no road to it from any place in the world; and even the tracks by which it is to be left are not easy of discovery. We went down to it by the "Little Joe", the Little Joe being a hill-side, and I hope I may never have to go down the Little Joe again with a tired horse behind me. We left it by a path as steep, and so hidden that we should never have found it without a guide. As it was, the mayor conducted us out of Walhalla with some solemnity.

And yet in this singular place there are, or seem to be, congregated all the necessaries and most of the luxuries of life. There was a pianoforte in the hotel sitting-room, and framed pictures hanging on the wall—just as there might be in Birmingham. And there was a billiard-table—at which unwashed earth-soiled diggers were playing, and playing, too, very well. At what cost must the pianoforte and the billiard-table have been brought down the mountain track! Nevertheless the charge for billiards was no more than sixpence a game; and no charge whatever was made for the piano! . . .

We stayed but one night, and then proceeded on our journey, still taking our mounted guide, and for the first ten miles were under the special guardianship of the mayor, who was to be looked upon, I was told, as a deputation from the town in honour of my friend. A very pleasant fellow we found the Mayor of Walhalla, and we parted from him in great kindness, even though he did lose the way in the forest, and take us, all for nothing, up and down one mountain side. When he parted from us our trusty trooper was a safer guide. This man was, I believe, no more than an ordinary policeman. The rural policemen of the colonies, who have to pass over wide districts, are all mounted But they carry themselves higher, and stand much higher among their fellow-citizens, than do the men of the same class with us. We are apt to separate men into two classes—and define each man by saying that he is or that he is not a gentleman. This man was a private policeman. Had I not known the fact I should have taken him for a gentleman. Even as it is, I rather think that I regard him in that light. He was a fine, powerful fellow, well mannered, able to talk on all subjects, extremely courteous—and he amused us greatly by explaining to us why it was that a policeman must be always more than a match for at any rate two rogues. He was an Irishman—of course. In the colonies those who make money are generally Scotchmen, and those who do not are mostly Irishmen. He had probably come out because his family could do nothing for him at home. I hope that he may live to be General-in-Chief of the Victorian police. He took us through the mountains to an old and apparently worn-out diggings called Edwards' Reef—a miserable, melancholy place, surrounded by interminable forests, in which unhappy diggers had sunk holes here and there, so that one wondered that the children did not all perish by falling into them. But even at Edwards' Reef there was an hotel, though I was at a loss to imagine by whom it could be supported. It was a large wooden building, now nearly falling to the ground; though doubtless it had once been alive with the sound of miners' voices in the days when there was gold in those quarters.

From Edwards' Reef we went on to Woods Point, having changed our policeman. It seemed that the magistrates had ordered that we should be taken in safety as far as the latter place. We passed another day in traversing endless forests, and in ascending and descending ravines. We crossed the top of Mount Useful, of which, however, I make no boast as a mountain, acknowledging that it only claims to be 5,300 feet high. Had it been double the height the mist on the top of it could not have been thicker. Here and there, in the densest parts of the forests, we came on the old tracks of miners, finding the holes which they had dug in search of gold. How many a heart must have been broken—how many a back nearly broken, among these mountains! The ascents and descents here were very steep, and on one occasion we submitted to be pulled up, hanging on to our horses' tails—an operation which I had not seen since I hunted, many years ago, in Caermarthenshire. . . .

Woods Point, like Walhalla, is a gully or ravine—though less singular than Walhalla, because there is a coach-road running through it. The scenery around it is very lovely—so much so as to inspire a feeling of sorrow that so much beauty should be desecrated by miners. Altogether the beauty of the country through which we had passed, and through which we did pass on our way back to Melbourne, contradicted the too general assertion that Australia is destitute of lovely scenery.

Three days more, with a pleasant rest at a friend's house on the road, brought us back to Melbourne. On the way down we passed through a country now well known for its enormous trees, all gum-trees of various sorts, or Eucalypti as they are called by the learned. At the land office in Melbourne I heard tidings of one enormous tree which had lately been discovered in this region, prostrate over a river-bed, and of which the remaining portion—for the head had been broken off in the fall—measured 435 ft. in length. The gentlemen by whom this monster was found had been sent out by the commissioners of lands to inspect the timber in the ranges of the watershed of the Watts River, and a copy of his report was published in one of the Melbourne newspapers. It is, I believe, now admitted that the gum-trees of this district are the highest trees yet found in the world, surpassing altogether those world-famed productions of California, which have for a while been regarded as the kings of the forest. I believe I am right in asserting that no other measured trunk has been found equal in length to that above recorded.

At Melbourne I sold my horse and saddle for £3 10s. less than I had given for them, and I thought that I had made my journey with sufficient economy.

The Lonely Track

I travelled to Perth [from Albany] having made a bargain with the mail contractor to take us—not with the mail, which goes through without stopping in seventy hours, but by a separate

1 *Anthony Trollope*

2 *A Sketch on the Road*

3 *A Riverina Homestead*

4 *View of Hobart Town, Tasmania*

5 *Regatta Day on the Parramatta River*

6 *Overlanders Rounding up a Straggler*

7 *Great Extended Hustler's Mine, Sandhurst*

8 *King William Street, Adelaide*

9 *Flemington Race Course in the Morning: Training*

10 *Swearing in the Governor at the Treasury*

conveyance in four days, so that we might sleep during the nights. This we did, taking our own provisions with us, and camping out in the bush under blankets. The camping out was, I think, rather pride on our part, to show the Australians that we Englishmen—my friend, indeed, was a Scotchman—could sleep on the ground, *sub dio*, and do without washing, and eat nastiness out of a box, as well as they could. There were police barracks in which we might have got accommodation. At any rate, going and coming we had our way. We lit fires for ourselves, and boiled our tea in billies; and then regaled ourselves with bad brandy and water out of pannikins, cooked bacon and potatoes in a frying-pan, and pretended to think that it was very jolly. My Scotch friend was a young man, and was, perhaps, in earnest. For myself, I must acknowledge that when I got up about five o'clock on a dark wet morning, very damp, with the clothes and boots on which I was destined to wear for the day, with the necessity before me of packing up my wet blankets, and endeavoured, for some minutes in vain, to wake the snoring driver, who had been couched but a few feet from me, I did not feel any ardent desire to throw off for ever the soft luxuries of an effeminate civilization, in order that I might permanently enjoy the freedom of the bush. But I did it, and it is well to be able to do it.

No man perhaps ever travelled 260 miles with less to see. The road goes eternally through wood—which in Australia is always called bush; and, possibly, sandy desert might be more tedious. But the bush in these parts never develops itself into scenery, never for a moment becomes interesting. There are no mountains, no hills that affect the eye, no vistas through the trees tempting the foot to wander. Once on the journey up, and once on the return, we saw kangaroos, but we saw no other animal; now and again a magpie was heard in the woods, but very rarely. The commonest noise is that of the bull-frog, which is very loud, and altogether unlike the sound of frogs in Europe. It is said that the Dutch under Peter Nuyt, when landing somewhere on these coasts—probably near Albany—were so frightened by the frogs that they ran away. I can believe it, for I have heard frogs at Albany roaring in such a fashion as to make a stranger think that the hills were infested with legions of lions, tigers, bears, and rhinoceroses, and that every lion, tiger, bear, and rhinoceros in the country was just about to spring at him. I knew they were only frogs, and yet I did not like it.

The bush in Australia generally is singularly destitute of life. One hears much of the snakes, because the snakes are specially deadly; but one sees them seldom, and no precaution in regard to them is taken. Of all animals, the opossum is the commonest. He may be easily taken as his habits are known, but he never shows himself. In perfect silence the journey through the bush is made—fifteen miles to some water-hole, where breakfast is eaten; fifteen on to another water-hole, where brandy and water is consumed; fifteen again to more water, and dinner; and then again fifteen, till the place is reached at which the night-fire is made and the blankets are stretched upon the ground. In such a journey, everything depends on one's companion, and in this I was more than ordinarily fortunate. As we were taken by the mail contractor, we had relays of horses along the road.

After visiting Wallaroo, at the head of Yorke Peninsula in South Australia, Trollope had an even less inspiring experience of the lonely track.

The traveller to Wallaroo is forced to go from Adelaide either by coach or by steamer round the Gulfs. I was taken there by one of the great copper mining authorities of the colony, and we elected to go by coach, in order that I might see something of the country. The coach was a mail-coach, with four horses, running regularly on the road every day; but on our return journey we were absolutely lost in the bush—coach, coachman, horses, mails, passengers and all. The man was trying a new track, and took us so far away from the old track that no one knew where we were. At last we found ourselves on the seashore. Of course it will be understood that there was no vestige of a road or pathway. Travellers are often "bushed" in Australia. They wander off their paths and are lost amidst the forests. In this instance the whole mail-coach was "bushed". When we came upon the sea, and no one could say what sea it was, I felt that the adventure was almost more than interesting.

4 LIFE IN THE BUSH

The Darling Downs

I don't know that there can be a much happier life than that of a squatter, if the man be fairly prosperous, and have natural aptitudes for country occupations. He should be able to ride and to shoot—and to sit in a buggy all day without inconvenience. He should be social—for he must entertain often and be entertained by other squatters; but he must be indifferent to society, for he will live away from towns and be often alone with his family. He must be able to command men, and must do so in a frank and easy fashion—not arrogating to himself any great superiority, but with full power to let those around him know that he is master. He must prefer plenty to luxury, and be content to have things about him a little rough. He must be able to brave troubles—for a squatter has many troubles. Sheep will go amiss. Lambs will die. Shearers will sometimes drink. And the bullocks with the most needed supplies will not always arrive as soon as they are expected. And, above all things, the squatter should like mutton. In squatters' houses plenty always prevails, but that plenty often depends upon the sheepfold. If a man have these gifts, and be young and energetic when he begins the work, he will not have chosen badly in becoming a squatter.

The sense of ownership and mastery, the conviction that he

is the head and chief of what is going on around; the absence of any necessity of asking leave or of submitting to others—these things in themselves add a great charm to life. The squatter owes obedience to none, and allegiance only to the merchant—who asks no questions so long as the debt be reduced or not increased. He gets up when he pleases, and goes to bed when he likes. Though he should not own an acre of the land around him, he may do what he pleases with all that he sees. He may put up fences and knock them down. He probably lives in the middle of a forest—his life is always called life in the bush—and he may cut down any tree that he fancies. He has always horses to ride, and a buggy to sit in, and birds to shoot at, and kangaroos to ride after. He goes where he likes, and nobody questions him. There is probably no one so big as himself within twenty miles of him, and he is proud with the conviction that he knows how to wash sheep better than any squatter in the colony. But the joy that mostly endears his life to him is the joy that he need not dress for dinner.

* * *

From Warwick I got by railway to the first of the great Darling Downs stations, which I visited, and from thence went on across country from one to another till I had visited some six or seven of those which are the largest and most renowned. It is not my purpose to give any description of each, as I could hardly do so without personal references which are always distasteful when hospitality has been given and taken. To say that Mr. Smith's house is well-built or his wife agreeable is almost as great a sin as to declare that Mr. Jones's wine was bad or his daughter ugly. At all these houses I found a plentiful easy life, full of material comfort, informal, abundant, careless, and most unlike life in England. There were two great faults—namely these—that a man was expected to eat two dinners every day, and that no credence could be given when any hour was named for any future event. Breakfast at eight would simply mean to the stranger, after some short experience, that the meal would be ready some time after nine. A start promised for ten is thought to be made very punctually if effected at eleven. As regards the evening meal, the second dinner, there is no pretence of any solicitude as to time. There is nothing to be done after it, and therefore what can it matter? . . . The products of the colonies are always dear to the colonial mind, and sometimes praise is expected for colonial wine which a prejudiced old Englishman feels that he can hardly give with truth. I have also been frowned upon by bright eyes because I could not eat stewed wallaby. Now the wallaby is a little kangaroo, and to my taste is not nice to eat even when stewed to the utmost with wine and spices. . . .

It was a very pleasant life that I led at these stations. I like tobacco and brandy and water, with an easy-chair out on a verandah, and my slippers on my feet. And I like men who are energetic and stand up for themselves and their own properties. I like having horses to ride and kangaroos to hunt, and sheep become quite a fascination to me as a subject of conversation. And I liked that roaming from one house to another—with a perfect conviction that five minutes would make me intimate with the next batch of strangers. Men are never ashamed of their poverty; nor are they often proud of their wealth. In all country life in Australia there is an absence of any ostentation or striving after effect, which is delightful. Such as their life is, the squatters share it with you, giving you, as is fitting for a stranger, the best they have to give. Upon the Darling Downs the stations are large and the accommodation plentiful; but I have been on many sheep runs which were not so well found, at which bedrooms were scarce, and things altogether were less well arranged. But there is never any shame as to the inferiority, never any pretence at superiority. What there is, is at your service. If there be not a whole bedroom for you, there is half a bedroom. If there be not wine, there is brandy or rum; if no other meat, there is at least mutton. If the house be full, some young man can turn out and go to the barracks, or sleep on the verandah. If all the young men have been turned out the old men can follow them. It is a rule of life on a sheep run that the station is never so full that another guest need be turned away.

These houses—stations as they are called—are built after a very simple and appropriate fashion. There is not often any upper storey. Every room is on the ground floor. There is always a verandah, running the length of the house, and not unfrequently continued round the ends. The rooms all open out upon the verandah, and generally have no communication with each other. The kitchen is invariably a separate building, usually attached to the house by a covered way. When first building his residence the squatter probably has had need for but small accommodation, and has constructed his house with perhaps three rooms. Children have come, and guests, and increased demands, and increased house-room has been wanted. Another little house has therefore been joined on to the first, and then perhaps a third added. I have seen an establishment consisting of seven such little houses. Many hours are passed in the verandah, in which old people sit in easy chairs and young men lie about, seeming to find the boards soft enough for luxurious ease.

Attached to the station there is always a second home called the barracks, or the cottage, in which the young men have their rooms. There are frequently one or two such young men attached to a sheep station, either learning their business or earning salaries as superintendents. According to the terms of intimacy existing, or to the arrangements made, these men live with the squatter's family or have a separate table of their own. They live a life of plenty, freedom, and hard work, but one which is not surrounded by the comforts which young men require at home. Two or three share the same room, and the washing apparatus is chiefly supplied by the neighbouring creek. Tubs are scarce among them, but bathing is almost a rule of life. They are up and generally on horseback by daylight, and spend their time in riding about after sheep. The general idyllic idea of Arcadian shepherd-life, which teaches us to believe that Tityrus lies under a beech-tree most of his hours playing on his reed and "spooning" Phyllis, is very unlike the truth in Australian pastures. Corin is nearer the mark when he tells Touchstone of his greasy hands. It is a life, even for the upper shepherd of gentle birth and sufficient means, of unremitting labour amidst dust and grease, amidst fleeces and carcasses. The working squatter, or the squatter's working assistant, must be a man capable of ignoring the delicacies of a soft way of living. He must endure clouds of dust, and be not averse to touch tar and oil, wool and skins. He should be able to catch a sheep and handle him almost as a nurse does a baby. He should learn to kill a sheep, and wash a sheep, and shear a sheep. He should tell a sheep's age by his mouth—almost by his look. He should know his breeding, and the quality of his wool. He should be able to muster sheep—collect them in together from the vast pastures on which they feed, and above all he should be able to count them. He must be handy with horses—doing anything which has to be done for himself. He must catch his own horse—for the horses live on grass, turned out in paddocks—and saddle him. The animal probably is never shod, never groomed, and is ignorant of corn. And the young man must be able to sit his horse—which perhaps is more than most young men could do in England, for it may be that the sportive beast will buck with the young man, jumping up into the air with his head between his legs, giving his rider as he does so such a blow by the contraction of his loins as will make any but an Australian young man sore all over for a week, even if he be not made sore for a much longer time by being sent far over the brute's head. This young man on a station must have many accomplishments, much knowledge, great capability; and in return for these things he gets his rations, and perhaps £100 per annum; perhaps £50—and perhaps nothing. But he lives a free, pleasant life in the open air. He has the scolding of many men, which is always pleasant; and nobody scolds him, which is pleasanter. He has plenty, and no care about it. He is never driven to calculate whether he can afford himself a dinner—as is often done by many young men at home who have dress coats to wear and polished leather boots for happy occasions. He has always a horse to ride, or two or three if he needs them. His salary is small, but he has nothing to buy—except moleskin trousers and flannel shirts. He lives in the open air, has a good digestion, and sleeps the sleep of the just. After a time he probably works himself up into some partnership—and has always before him the hope that the day will come in which he too will be a master squatter.

* * *

I spent a very pleasant time on the Darling Downs—perhaps the more so because the rigid rule which prevailed in the wool-shed and at the wash-pool in regard to alcohol was not held to be imperative at the squatters' houses. I could hardly understand how a hospitable gentleman could press me to fill my glass again—as hospitable gentlemen did do very often—while he dilated on the wickedness of a shearer who should venture to think of a glass of rum. I took it all in good part, and preached no sermons on that subject. I had some very good kangaroo hunting, and was surprised to find how well horses could carry me which went out every day, eat nothing but grass, and had no shoes on their feet.

A Small Station

Although Trollope conceals the fact until later, the following description is of Mortray, the property of his own son, Frederick, near Grenfell, N.S.W.

When in New South Wales I spent a month at a small squatter's station in the distant bush, and as the difference between bush life in Australia and country life in England is more marked than I think any other difference between the two countries, I propose to describe the thing as I found it. I had already stayed at various sheep-stations in Queensland, but only for a few days at each; and these had been generally large places, where perhaps from one to two hundred thousand sheep were shorn—and into which consequently the comforts and luxuries of civilized life had been imported. These were hardly typical bush residences. At that to which I now went, a young squatter beginning life owned not much more than ten thousand sheep, and was living quite "in the rough". The number of sheep at these stations will generally indicate with fair accuracy the mode of life at the head station. A hundred thousand sheep and upwards require a professed man-cook and a butler to look after them; forty thousand sheep cannot be shorn without a piano; twenty thousand is the lowest number that renders napkins at dinner imperative. Ten thousand require absolute plenty, meat in plenty, tea in plenty, brandy and water and colonial wine in plenty, but do not expect champagne, sherry, or made dishes, and are supposed to be content with continued mutton or continued beef, as the squatter may at the time be in the way of killing sheep or oxen. During this month we killed mutton. After six months I returned to the same station, and beef was the provision of the day. Wool had gone up, and sheep had become valuable, and the squatter could not be persuaded to kill a sheep for love or money. He bought cattle as he wanted them, and found that his beef cost him 1½d. a pound.

The station I visited, and which I will call M——, was about 250 miles west of Sydney, and was decidedly in the bush. I have already endeavoured to explain that nearly every place beyond the influences of the big towns is called "bush"—even though there should not be a tree to be seen around—but in reaching this place I journeyed for three days after leaving the railway through continuous woodland, doing about forty miles a day in a buggy. The house stood on a small creek—hardly to be called a rivulet, because the water does not continually run, and in dry weather lies only in a succession of waterholes—and was surrounded by interminable forest. Close around it was the home-paddock, railed in, and containing about fifty acres. Such an enclosure about a gentleman's house in England is an appendage of great value, and constitutes with some who are ambitious almost a little park. In the bush it is little more thought of than as so much waste ground round the house. Two or three cows may run in it, or a horse or two for immediate use. It is generally found convenient to have a horse near the house for the sake of "running in" other horses. One horse in the stable to catch two horses in the home-paddock wherewith four horses when wanted may be run in from the horse-paddock, make together a combination which in the bush is considered to be economical and convenient.

At M—— the home-paddock was partially cleared of timber, and was pretty enough. Outside it, meeting the creek both before and behind, was the horse-paddock, containing about 250 acres. This was supposed to be the domain appropriated to the horses of the establishment needed for the working of it. At that time there were about twenty, and I believe that there was not one too many. My young friend also had his rams here during a portion of the year, but hardly expected more from so small an enclosure than food for the animals required for use. A public road, such as bush roads are, ran through the horse-paddock—very inconvenient in that it caused the gates to be left open, and brought travellers that way whose presence was hardly desirable, but not without compensation, as a postman with the mails passed each way twice a week. The postman was a great blessing. If he wanted food for himself or his horse, he got it; and in return he complied with all requests made to him, conveying letters, telegrams, and messages with wondrous accuracy. A mailman coming by—they are mailmen and not postmen in the bush—is a great addition to the comforts of bush life.

At the back of the horse-paddock was the wool-shed paddock, containing about 1,200 acres, with the wool-shed at one corner of it, distant about a mile from the house. For many reasons the wool-shed should not be close. The squatter does not want to have his shearers always in his kitchen, nor to hear their voices close to his verandah. But as it is well for his superintendent to be there constantly during the shearing, and for himself to be there often, any great distance is inconvenient. As my young friend sorted his own wool himself, he was generally in the wool-shed before the shearers, and did not leave it till long after they had "knocked off" work. The wool-shed was a wooden edifice, made of rough timber, roofed with bark, divided into pens, with room for eleven men to shear, and with outside pens for the shorn sheep as they leave the men's hands, a pen for each shearer. It was constructed to hold about 300 sheep, and that number would be put into it over night, so that, even should rain come, there might be so many ready for the shearers in the morning, for sheep cannot be shorn when wet. The form of the shed was that of the letter L, the base, however, being considerably larger than the upstroke. Along the base the shearers worked. At the corner were the sorting-table, and divided cribs for the different fleeces. In the upper part of the letter the wool was packed, and pressed, and stored, till the drays should come to take it away. My friend acknowledged that he did not think much of his own house, though he had built it himself—but he was proud of his wool-shed, which was also the creation of his own ingenuity.

About a quarter of a mile from the wool-shed was the shearer's hut, in which the men slept, and ate, and smoked their pipes. They had their own cook, who on this occasion was a Chinaman, and as is always the case with shearers, they gave their cook enough to do. He was generally to be seen outside the door of the hut chopping up onions. The cook had 25s. a week and his rations—the shearers were earning on an average about 7s. 6d. a day, which was considered bad work. There was rain, and the weather was against the men. The shearers bought their own food from the head station, paying at the rate of 7s. 6d. a week each for it.

There were three other paddocks on the run, one containing 12,000 acres, and the others 7,000 acres each. The greater part of the fencing necessary for these domains had been put up by my friend since his occupation at an average cost of £25 a mile. There were over forty miles of fencing on the run, made either with logs laid at length, on short round blocks—called in the bush chock and log—or of bushes laid lengthways and staked down with forked timber. This fencing suffices for sheep, but would be of no use at all on a run intended for cattle. When a run is not fenced, each flock of sheep requires a shepherd, and the sheep are brought up at night to an enclosure close to the shepherd's hut. When a run is "paddocked", shepherds are not required; but boundary riders are employed, each of whom is supplied with two horses, and these men are responsible not only for the sheep but for the fences. They should see every portion of their fences at any rate three times a week, and repair the breaches. A bush fence is easily broken down, but is as easily put up again.

The natural grasses of the bush in the locality of which I am speaking would carry in ordinary weather a sheep to three acres. When the weather was damp and warm it would do much more; when there was either frost or drought, it would not do so much. At M——— there was back ground outside the paddocks as extensive as the fenced area, and it was computed that the run might carry safely about 16,000 sheep. . . .

Almost all these pastoral homesteads are made up of various cottages, till sometimes the place assumes the appearance of a village. When the station is large there will often be a church and a school, and a separate house for strangers, and a shop for the stores, and an office. At M——— no such grandeur had as yet displayed itself. But there was a garden—in which the opossums would eat the vegetables—and an orchard had been commenced.

There was one house at a distance of only three miles, which was a great drawback to my friend's happiness—for it was inhabited by a free-selector and a publican. I rather liked the publican, as he got up a kangaroo hunt for me, but the vicinity of grog was looked upon as a serious evil by the squatter. And yet the men never drank when they were at work—would work for weeks without anything stronger than tea. But if, on an occasion, any one of the station hands did take to drink, he would stay and drink till he was turned out of the house on the plea that he had consumed all his money. This public-house was a blistering thorn in the side of my friend. A gold-field town, whence the letters came, was twelve miles distant, but this was visited as rarely as possible, and was regarded as almost obtrusive in having caused itself to be built in a pastoral district. The nearest neighbour for any social purpose was another squatter, twenty-five miles off.

Of social gatherings, such as we know them, there are none in the bush. Squatters do not go out to dine, or ask each other to dinner. As a rule, I think, they rarely invite each other for country visiting. But they make the freest use of each other's houses, so that society of a certain kind is created. They do not make visits exclusively of pleasure, but when business calls them from home they make no scruple of riding up to each other's doors, and demanding hospitality. . . .

I was at M——— during washing and shearing. I speak of course of the washing of sheep. It was the busiest time of the year, and the squatter himself was always out soon after five, and rarely back at the house in time for dinner at eight. He had two assistants, one of whom was his permanent first lieutenant on the run, and the other was borrowed for the occasion. The three, who were all young, certainly worked much harder than any other men about the place, and seemed to have more on hand than a British prime minister in June. I rode about at my ease—from the washpool to the wool-shed, and from the wool-shed to the kangaroos—giving now and then a fantastic opinion as to the doing of the work, criticizing the roughness of the mode in which the poor brutes were hauled into the water, or the cruelty with which they were wounded by the shearers. But my friends were terribly in earnest. Now and again a man would misbehave, and squatters' law had to be exercised with prompt decision. If a man would not work, or worked amiss, he was sent away with very curt warning —for the deed of agreement which is always drawn up gives the squatter the power of judging as to the man's deficiency, and of punishing him for being deficient. The sheep were always being washed, and always being shorn, but if the rain should come between the two operations all would be spoilt. Rain did come—but not thorough rain, and all was not spoilt. And then the "yarding" of sheep by hundreds at a time—getting them through one set of pens before washing, and through another set before shearing—having them ready for the morning's work, and finished off before the dark night came—weighing out tea and sugar and flour for the men, killing and preparing meat for them, sorting and packing the wool, pressing and labelling the bales—all seemed to demand more than Herculean energy. At large stations all this is done easily, because the greater number admit of divided labour. It seemed to me that the care of ten thousand sheep was the most difficult task that a man could have imposed upon him.

Those rides through the forest, either when I was alone, or when I could get my host to go with me—which was rarely, unless on a

Sunday afternoon—were very pleasant. The melancholy note of the magpie was almost the only sound that was heard. Occasionally kangaroos would be seen—two or three staring about them after a half-tame fashion, as though they had not as yet made up their mind whether it would be necessary for them to run. When approached they would move always in a line, and with apparent leisure till pursued. Then they would bound away, one here and one there, at a pace which made it impossible for a single horseman to get near them in a thickly timbered country. It was all wood. There arose at last a feeling that go where one might through the forest, one was never going anywhere. It was all picturesque, for there was rocky ground here and there, and hills in the distance, and the trees were not too close for the making of pretty vistas through them—but it was all the same. One might ride on, to the right or the left, or might turn back, and there was ever the same view, and there were no objects to reach, unless it was the paddock fence. And when the paddock fence was jumped, then it was the same thing again. Looking around, one could tell by no outward sign whether one was inside or outside the boundary—whether one was two miles or ten miles from the station.

Perhaps the most astonishing phenomenon on these runs is the apparent paucity of sheep. As a fact, there are thousands all around—but unless looked for they are never seen; and even when looked for by inexperienced eyes are often missed. If the reader will bear in mind that an enclosure of 12,000 acres contains more than eighteen square miles, he will understand how unlike to anything in England must be even the enclosed country in Australia. One seems to ride for ever and to come to nothing, and to relinquish at last the very idea of an object. Nevertheless, it was very pleasant. Of all places that I was ever in this place seemed to be the fittest for contemplation. There was no record of the hours but by the light. When it was night work would be over. The men would cease as the sun was setting, but the masters would continue till the darkness had come upon them.

There were four or five meals in the day. There was an early breakfast in the cottage for the young men—there was another breakfast at nine for those who were idle—for the ladies who were there and for myself. There was lunch at about two, to which one or two from the wool-shed might or might not rush in as things were going with them, and there was dinner at about eight o'clock.

My wife had brought a cook with her from England who was invaluable—or would have been had she not found a husband for herself when she had been about a month in the bush. But in spite of her love, and her engagement to a man who was considerably above her in position, she was true to us while she remained at M———, and did her best to make us all comfortable. She was a good-looking, strong woman, of excellent temper, who could do anything she put her hand to, from hairdressing and confectionery up to making butter and brewing beer. I saw her six months afterwards, "quite the lady", but ready for any kind of work that might come in her way. When I think of her, I feel that no woman of that kind ought, as regards herself, to stay in England if she can take herself or get herself taken to the colonies. I mention our cook because her assistance certainly tended very greatly to our increased comfort. The viands provided were mutton, bread, vegetables, and tea. Potatoes were purchased as an ordinary part of the station stores, and the opossums had left us lettuce, tomatoes, and a few cabbages. Dinner was always dignified with soup and salad, which must not, however, be regarded as being within the ordinary bush dietary. In other respects the meals were all alike. There was mutton in every shape, and there was always tea.

Tea at a squatter's table—at the table of a squatter who has not yet advanced himself to a man-cook or butler and a two-storied house—is absolutely indispensable. At this squatter's table there was colonial wine and there was brandy, produced chiefly to supply my wants; but there was always tea. The young men when they came in, hot and fagged with their day's work, would take a glass of brandy and water standing, as a working man with us takes his glass of beer at a bar. But when they sat down with their dinner before them, the tea-cup did for them what the wine-glass does for us. The practice is so invariable that any shepherd whose hut you may visit will show his courtesy by asking you to take a pannikin of tea. In supplying stores to men, tea and sugar, flour and meat, are the four things which are included as matters of course. The tea is always bought by the chest, and was sold by the merchant at the rate of 1s. 6d. a pound. There was but one class of tea at the station, which I found to be preferable to very much that I am called upon to drink in England.

The recreations of the evening consisted chiefly of tobacco on the verandah. I did endeavour to institute a whist table, but I found that my friends, who were wonderfully good in regard to the age and points of a sheep, and who could tell to the fraction of a penny what the wool of each was worth by the pound, never could be got to remember the highest card of the suit. I should not have minded that had they not so manifestly despised me for regarding such knowledge as important. They were right, no doubt, as the points of a sheep are of more importance than the pips of a card, and the human mind will hardly admit of the two together. Whist is a jealous mistress; and so is a sheep-station.

I have been at very many bush houses—at over thirty different stations in the different colonies—but at not one, as I think, in which I have not found a fair provision of books. It is universally recognized among squatters that a man who settles down in the bush without books is preparing for himself a miserable future life. That the books are always used when they are there I will not say. That they are used less frequently than they should be used I do not doubt. When men come in from physical work, hungry, tired—with the feeling that they have earned an hour or two of ease by many hours of labour—they are apt to claim the right to allow their minds to rest as well as their limbs. Who does not know how very much this is the case at home, even among young men and women in our towns, who cannot plead the same excuse of real bodily fatigue? That it should be so is a pity of pities—not on the score chiefly of information lost or of ignorance perpetuated, but because the power of doing that which should be the one recreation and great solace of our declining years perishes from desuetude, and cannot be renewed when age has come upon us. But I think that this folly is hardly more general in the Australian bush than in English cities. There are books to be read, and the young squatter, when the evening comes upon him, has no other recreation to entice him. He has no club, no billiard tables, no public-house which he can frequent. Balls and festivities are very rare. He probably marries early, and lives the life of a young patriarch, lord of everything around him, and master of every man he meets on his day's ride. Of course there are many who have risen to this from lower things, who have become squatters without any early education, who have been butchers, drovers, or perhaps shepherds themselves. That they should not be acquainted with books is a matter of course. They have lacked the practice in youth of which I have just spoken. But among those who have had the advantage of early nurture, and have been taught to handle books familiarly when young, I think that reading is at least as customary as it is with young men in London. The authors I found most popular were certainly Shakespeare, Dickens, and Macaulay. I would back the chance of finding Macaulay's Essays at a station against that of any book in the language except Shakespeare. To have a Shakespeare is a point of honour with every man who owns a book at all—whether he reads it or leaves it unread.

I have said that squatters marry early. The reasons for doing so are very strong; and those reasons for not doing so, which are terribly familiar to us at home, hardly exist in the bush. The man is alone, and can have at any rate no female companionship unless he marry. In ordinary life, as we know it, the unmarried man enjoys as many comforts—unfortunately, perhaps more luxuries—than do they who take to themselves wives. But in the bush the unmarried man is very desolate, and will probably soon become forlorn and wretched in his mode of life. He will hardly get a woman who will cook for him decently, or who will sew a button on his shirt when it is wanted. And he will soon care nothing how his dinner is cooked, and whether his shirt be with or without a button. On the other hand, the cost of his household when he is married will hardly be more than when he is single. If his wife know how to keep a bush house, her presence will almost be a saving to him. At home, in England, the young man when he marries has to migrate from his lodgings to a house; he must make up an establishment, buy furniture, hire servants, and enter altogether upon a new phase of life. He must have ready money in his pocket to begin with, and a future income probably very much in advance of that he has hitherto been expected to expend. But on a station there is nothing of the kind. There is the house, in which it may be necessary to put a few additional comforts. There is the establishment—already on so large a scale in consequence of the necessity of supplying men with rations that no recognised increase is created. When children come, and education is needed, expenses of course will grow; but at first the thing is so easy that the young squatter simply goes out in his buggy and brings home the daughter of some other squatter—after a little ceremony performed in the nearest church.

As a consequence of this, life in the bush is decent and moral. The bulk of the labour is performed by a nomad tribe, who wander in quest of their work, and are hired only for a time. This is of course the case in regard to washing sheep and shearing them. It is equally so when fences are to be made, or ground to be cleared, or trees to be "rung". The ringing of trees consists of cutting the bark through all round, so that the tree ceases to suck up the strength of the earth for its nutrition, and shall die. For all these operations temporary work is of course required, and the squatter seldom knows whether the men he employs be married or single. They come and go, and are known by queer nicknames or are known by no names at all. They probably have their wives elsewhere, and return to them for a season. They are rough to look at, dirty in appearance, shaggy, with long hair, men who, when they are in the bush, live in huts, and hardly know what a bed is. But they work hard, and are both honest and civil. Theft among them is almost unknown. Men are constantly hired without any character but that which they give themselves; and the squatters find from experience that the men are able to do that which they declare themselves capable of performing. There will be exceptions, but such is the rule. Their one great fault is drunkenness—and yet they are sober to a marvel. As I have said before, they will work for months without touching spirits, but their very abstinence creates a craving desire which, when it is satisfied, will satisfy itself with nothing short of brutal excess. Among the masters of these men—among squatters with their superintendents and overseers—drinking is not a common fault. I have seen a squatter drunk. I have seen a squatter very drunk. But he was a jovial exception.

Victorian Grazier

A writer attempting to describe England, and capable of doing so, would fill those chapters with the strongest interest in which he painted the various forms of English country life. He would know, and he would teach his readers, that the English character with its faults and virtues, its prejudices and steadfastness, can be better studied in the mansions of noblemen, in country-houses, in parsonages, in farms and small meaningless towns, than in the great cities, devoted as is London to politics and gaiety, or as are Glasgow, Manchester, Birmingham, and others like them, to manufactures and commerce. I doubt whether this be so in any other country. France has many aspects, but the Parisian aspect is more French than any other. Italy is to be seen only in her cities. In the United States the towns altogether overrule and subdue the country, so that the traveller who visits America under the most favourable circumstances rarely sees aught of her corn-fields and pastures, except in passing from one great centre of population to another. But the visitors to England who have not sojourned at a country-house, whether it be squire's, parson's, or farmer's, have not seen the most English phase of the country.

The same form and fashion of life is repeating itself in the Australian colonies. The race of farmers, such as are our own well-to-do farmers at home, does not, indeed, exist. The clergy are scattered at long distances, and hardly as yet form a distinctive social class—probably never will do so, as they do in England, and in England only. But the country gentlemen, almost all of whom were originally squatters, have fixed their homes about the colony, and have built their houses—not exactly after the English fashion in regard to architecture, because the climate is of a different nature—but with the English appurtenances of substantial comfort, with many rooms, with gardens, outhouses, and lawns, and with sweeping roads leading through timbered parks to the retired abode of the rural magistrate who owns the property. The visitor to Australia, who goes there under favourable auspices, will as surely find himself pressed to make his home at such country houses, as will the stranger in the United States be asked to enjoy the luxurious hospitality of her rich citizens, either in city mansions or in suburban villas. And such a one, if he have time on his hands, and can dally with weeks in idleness, may pass from station to station—from one gentleman's house to another—till he will hardly know who has sent him on, or on what ground he bases his claim to the hospitality of his new friends.

There is perhaps more of this in Victoria than in the other colonies, because the country gentlemen have more thoroughly established their fortunes there than elsewhere; but the same feeling prevails throughout Australia, and the same mode of life. They who rise to the top of the tree—or, in other words, the gentry, if I may use a phrase which is somewhat invidious, but which will be better understood than any other—seek to establish country houses for themselves; and homesteads of this class have sprung up with incredible rapidity. Nothing, I think, so clearly declares the wealth of the colony—which is not yet forty years old—as the solidity of her country life. When the stranger asks whence came these country gentlemen, whom he sees occasionally at the clubs and dinner tables in Melbourne, exactly as he finds those of England up in London during the winter frosts or in the month of May, he is invariably told that they or their fathers made their own fortunes. This man and that and the other came over perhaps from Tasmania, in the early days, joint owners of a small flock of sheep. They generally claim to have suffered every adversity with which Providence and unjust legislators could inflict a wretched victim; and, as the result, each owns so many thousand horned cattle, so many tens of thousands sheep, so many square miles of country, and so many thousands a year. Most of them have, I think, originally come out of Scotland. When you hear an absent acquaintance spoken of as "Mac", you will not at all know who is meant, but you may safely conclude that it is some prosperous individual. Some were butchers, drovers, or shepherds themselves but a few years since. But they now form an established aristocracy, with very conservative feelings, and are quickly becoming as firm a country party as that which is formed by our squirearchy at home.

I was able to speak of country life in New South Wales without reserve, because the small establishment which I described belongs to my own son. In Victoria I visited many houses of infinitely greater pretension, but I fear to speak of any one in particular lest I should commit that great sin—not always avoided as scrupulously as it should be by travelling authors—of putting some kind host into a book, with his wife, family, kitchen, and cellars. And yet, if it be possible, I would fain let English readers know what these houses are, and of what nature is the life contained in them. They are generally less remote from towns than are the habitations of squatters in the other colonies—the towns being more numerous and the roads more formed. The buildings themselves are generally of two stories—always having the tropical addition of a verandah, but not erected in that straggling, many-roofed, one-storied fashion which is common to tropical and semi-tropical countries. I like those straggling, many-roofed nests of cottages which are common in Queensland and New

South Wales. They betoken a gradually increasing prosperity. The squatter builds first a wooden hut which ultimately becomes his kitchen, then a wooden sittingroom and bedroom near to it; then a bigger sittingroom with two small bedrooms, still of wood —and so on. But when he has realized to himself the fact that he is a rich man he rushes into brick and mortar or stone, and erects a European country-house—with the addition of a wide verandah. This has been done now very generally by the landowners of Victoria. But still the place has rarely all the finished comfort, the easy grace, coming from long habit, which belong to our country seats at home. There is a roughness and a heaviness about it, a want of completion about the gardens, of neatness about the paths, and of close-shorn trimness about the plots and lawns, which strikes the beholder at once, and declares that though the likeness be there, it exists with a difference.

This difference is caused chiefly by the dearness of labour, a fact which influences not only the outside of the Victorian gentleman's house, but also every part of his establishment. Let his means be what they may, he never has the retinue of servants which is to be found in an ordinary English household. The high rate of wages and the difficulty of getting persons to accept these high rates for any considerable number of months together, cause even the wealthy to dispense with much of that attendance which is often considered indispensable at home even among families that are not wealthy. On the other hand, certain luxuries are common among Australian families, which few among us can enjoy without stint. He who has a carriage and horses at home is supposed to be a rich man. If a gentleman have daughters fond of riding he will perhaps have one horse for two girls. Young men can hardly hunt unless their fathers be wealthy. But horses on an Australian station are as common as blackberries on English hedges, and the possession of a carriage and pair of horses is as much a matter of course as the possession of a pair of boots. But horses are cheap and servants dear in Victoria.

I have spoken of sweeping roads through timbered parks. It must not, however, be conceived that I speak of parks such as those which are the glory of our English magnates. The Australian park is hitherto much as nature fashioned it. The trees are the gum-trees which the present resident or his father found there when he first drove his sheep on the pastures which had never yet known the foot of a white man. The grasses round his house he may gradually have changed, and have extirpated those indigenous to the soil by the use of English seeds. The road will probably be somewhat rough, and the fences which divide the paddocks still rougher. He is now a rich man, but he is rich because in all his expenditure he has thought more of a return for his capital than of the adornment of his place. He calls his park a paddock, and he has thought only of the welfare of his stock. But, nevertheless, there is that beauty about it which trees and grass, with the sky above them, always produce. And the territory is large and spacious, and all the magnificence of ownership is there. The man drives for miles through his own land. He has fortified himself on all sides against free-selectors. All those who frequent the place are his servants or his guests, and of every stranger whom he may see within miles of his house he is entitled to ask why he is there. He exercises a wide hospitality to the poor and the rich, and he is an aristocrat.

I imagine that the life of the Victorian landowner is very much as was that of the English country gentleman a century or a century and a half ago. In those days roads in England were very bad, so that it was a work of trouble to get from one house to another, a distance of twenty miles. Country houses of pretension were not numerous as they are now, and they who owned the halls and granges scattered through the counties rarely moved from their homes. There was great plenty, but of that finished luxury which is now as common in the country as in the capital, there was but little. Roast beef—or in winter powdered beef—and October ale were the fare. The men were fond of sport, but they did not go far a-field for it as they do now, hunting in the shires, shooting on the moors, and fishing on all lakes and rivers. They shot over their own lands, and hunted over their own land and that of a few neighbours who would join them. The ladies stayed at home and looked after the house, and much that is now trusted to domestics and stewards was done by the mistress and her daughters, or by the master and his sons. The owners of these country houses were Tories, aristocrats, proud gentlemen—but they were not fine gentlemen, nor, for the most part, were they gentlemen of fine tastes in art or literature. We know them very well from plays and novels—and know something of them too from history, as history has of late been written. The ladies' dresses, the books, the equipages, the wines, the kitchens, which are now found in English country houses, were in those days known only in the metropolis, or at the castle of some almost royal nobleman.

As were country houses and country life then in England, plentiful, proud, prejudiced, given to hospitality, impatient of contradiction, not highly lettered, healthy, industrious, careful of the main chance, thoughtful of the future, and, above all, conscious—perhaps a little too conscious—of their own importance, so now is the house and so is the life of the country gentleman in Australia. And as Justice Shallow in times still farther distant was ever anxious as to the price of a good yoke of bullocks or a score of ewes, so does the Australian country gentleman never omit his solicitude concerning those things which have made him what he is. The value of beef in the Melbourne market, and of wool at London, are continually in his thoughts, and as continually on his tongue, even though he may have reached the stage of prosperity which cannot be much affected by the transient rise or fall in prices. He has not at any rate reached that condition, be it good or bad, which enables the English country gentleman to drop all outward show of solicitude for the trade in which he is embarked, the trade namely of living upon his land, and to pursue the unruffled tenor of his way as though all good things came to him and were sure to come to him like manna from heaven. The Victorian wool-grower or grazier will be sure to tell you, if you visit him in his own home, what has been his produce of wool, and what prices he has realized for it, and will take you to his washpool, if he wash his sheep before shearing, and to his wool-shed; or he will show you his Durhams and his Herefords, and boast how he has led the markets. Out of the full heart the mouth speaks. He has made himself what he is by his sheep and his oxen, and the sheep and the oxen are still dear to him. His grandson or great-grandson will probably be as outwardly indifferent as an English country gentleman, who is no more given to talk of his rents than a banker is of his profits, and who is concerned wholly, perhaps with his hounds, perhaps with his library, perhaps with his politics, or perhaps with his cook.

I propose to devote a chapter to Australian sports, which belong quite as much to the towns as they do to the country, and therefore I will say but little of them here. They do not form so prominent a part of country life in the colonies as they do at home, partly because there are not so many idle men, and partly because there has not been as yet so great an expenditure of money with the view of creating sport. As years pass on both these causes will vanish. The idle men will be forthcoming, and game brought from England, Scotland, and Ireland, will be naturalized in the country. Hares in Victoria will be, I hope, not quite so plentiful as rabbits. There are deer already in the country, and they will soon abound with that prolific increase which seems to attend all animals brought from the old country to these colonies. Duck-shooting is much practised, and ducks abound. Pheasants are already more common in parts of New Zealand than in England, though not so plentiful, and will probably become equally common in Tasmania and Victoria. I despair, however, of fox-hunting. I think it improbable that that most anomalous, most irrational, most exciting, most delightful, and most beneficent sport should thrive elsewhere on the world's surface than in the British Isles. None but the British and Irish farmer will bear the invasion of a troop of horsemen. None but the British or Irish sportsman can have that tenderness in preserving and that stern perseverance in killing a little vermin, which fox-hunting requires. None but a British or an Irish gentleman can expend thousands in furnishing amusement for an entire county.

The fault of a country home in the Australian colonies is that it furnishes but little employment, and that its ordinary life seems to be antagonistic to industry, at any rate on the part of the visitor. The master of the house is or is not the working manager of his property. If he be so, his time is fully occupied. He is on horseback before breakfast, and seems never to slacken his labours till the evening dews have long fallen. The exclusive care of a large flock of sheep, which includes breeding, feeding, doctoring, shearing, selling, and buying, together with the hiring, feeding, inspection, and payment of a great number of by no means subservient workmen, taxes a man's energies to the utmost. Cattle probably impose less labour, but a man will have his hands fairly full who owns three or four thousand head of cattle, who breeds them by his own judgment, and himself selects them for market. But very many squatters and graziers really manage their properties by deputy. Serviceable men have grown up in their employment, and as years creep on the real work of the run is allowed to fall from their own hands into those of superintendents and overseers. Then the country gentleman, though he still talks of a "score of ewes" as did Justice Shallow, becomes an idle man. He comes down to breakfast at nine, and is impatient for his dinner before six, thinking that the clock must be losing time. The ladies no doubt look after their houses, order lunch and dinner, and superintend the servants. But they seem to be insufficiently provided with occupations over and above these. There is a piano in every house. There are always books—enough for reading though not enough for literary luxury. There may be croquet out of doors. There are horses to ride; and there is the unlimited bush, with its magpies, its laughing jackasses, and its bell-birds, if you be good at walking. But there is no provision made for the passing of time. There is no period of the day at which books fall naturally into the hands of men and women. Loitering is common, and the hours too often become foes instead of friends. This is specially the case during the long evenings. I fancy that the same fault might have been found with country-houses in England a hundred and fifty years ago.

Eating and drinking occupy so many of our thoughts, and contribute so much to the excitement and to the amusement of life, that I feel myself bound to say something of the Victorian country gentleman's taste. No table more plentiful or more hospitable was ever spread. Its chief distinctive feature is the similarity of the meals. The breakfast is nearly as substantial as the lunch and dinner, and between the lunch and dinner it was long before I could find out any difference. Two or three hot joints of meat and four or five dishes of vegetables, wine decanters, and not uncommonly a teapot, are common to both of them. As regarded the time allowed, or the appetite, or that addition to appetite which greediness furnishes throughout the world, I could not ascertain that there was any distinction between the two. With us at home the cook never exerts herself —or himself—for lunch, and is not indeed expected to do so. The Victorian cook is equally awake all the day long. At last I perceived that at luncheon there would never be more than two puddings. At dinner the number was not limited. As a rule, gentlemen in the colonies do not sit long over their wine; and, as a rule, also—and rules, of course, have their exceptions—the wine is not worth a long sitting.

But these little details of which I have spoken do but form the outside skin of society, whereas the bones, the muscles, the blood, and the flesh consist of the people themselves. Whether men and women dine at five or at seven, whether they drive out regularly or irregularly, whether they hunt foxes or kangaroos, drink bad wine or good, matters little, in regard to social delights, in comparison with the character, the manners, and the gifts of the men and women themselves.

5 GOLD

Trollope was highly skeptical about the rush for gold. As he wrote of the gold-seeker, ". . . 'something tells him' that he is to be the lucky man. There is a something telling the same lie to every man in that toil-worn crowd, as with sore feet and heavy burden on his shoulders he hurries on to the diggings. In truth he has become a gambler–and from this time forth a gambler he will live . . ." But, skeptical or not, Trollope was obviously in sympathy with the individual miner.

Queensland's Gympie

Gympie in its early days was a great rush–which means that when first the tidings were spread about through the colonies that gold was found at Gympie, the sudden flocking of miners to the place was very great. In those days, some ten years ago, when a new rush came out, the difficulty of supplying the men was excessive, and everything was consequently very dear. The rushes were made to spots in the middle of the forest, to which there were no roads, and to which carriage therefore was very difficult. In addition to this, men half-intoxicated with the profusion of gold, which is both the cause and consequence of a new rush, are determined to have, not comforts, for they are unattainable, but luxuries which can be carried. A pair of sheets will be out of the question, but champagne may be had. In this way a singular mode of life seems to have established itself—and the more singular in this, that the champagne element does not seem to have interfered with work. . . .

It may be well to remark here that Australian miners are almost invariably courteous and civil. A drunken man is never agreeable; but even a drunken miner is rarely quarrelsome. They do not steal, and are rough rather than rowdy. It seemed to me that very little care was taken, or was necessary, in the preservation of gold, the men trusting each other with great freedom. There are quarrels about claims for land, and a claim is sometimes unjustly "jumped". The jumping of a claim consists in taking possession of the land and works of absent miners, who are presumed by their absence to have deserted their claims. But such bickerings rarely lead to personal violence. The miners do not fight and knock each other about. They make constant appeals to the government officer—the police magistrate, or, above him, to the gold commissioner of the district—and they not unfrequently go to law. They do not punch each other's heads. . . .

Probably the class of miners which as a class does worst is that composed of young gentlemen, who go to the diggings, led away, as they fancy, by a spirit of adventure, but more generally, perhaps, by a dislike of homely work at home. An office-stool for six or eight hours a day is disagreeable to them, or the profession of the law requires too constant a strain, or they are sick of attending lectures, or they have neglected the hospitals—and so they go away to the diggings. They soon become as dirty as genuine diggers, but they do not quickly learn anything but the dirt. They strive to work, but they cannot work alongside of experienced miners, and consequently they go to the wall. They are treated with no contempt, for all men at the diggings are free and equal. As there is no gentility, such men are not subject to any reproach or ill-usage on that score. The miner does not expect that any airs will be assumed, and takes it for granted that the young man will not sin in that direction. Our "gentleman", therefore, is kindly treated; but, nevertheless, he goes to the wall, and becomes little better than the servant, or mining hodsman, of some miner who knows his work. Perhaps he has a little money, and makes things equal with a partner in this way; but they will not long be equal—for his money will go quicker than his experience will come.

On one gold field I found a young man whom I had known at home, who had been at school with my sons, and had frequented my house. I saw him in front of his little tent, which he occupied in partnership with an experienced working miner, eating a beefsteak out of his frying-pan with his clasp-knife. The occupation was not an alluring one, but it was the one happy moment of his day. He was occupied with his companion on a claim, and his work consisted in trundling a rough windlass, by which dirt was drawn up out of a hole. They had found no gold as yet, and did not seem to expect to find it. He had no friend near him but his mining friend—or mate, as he called him. I could not but think what would happen to him if illness came, or if his mate should find him too far removed from mining capability. He had been softly nurtured, well educated, and was a handsome fellow to boot; and there he was eating a nauseous lump of beef out of a greasy frying-pan with his pocket-knife, just in front of the contiguous blankets stretched on the ground, which constituted the beds of himself and his companion. It may be that he will strike gold, and make a fortune. I hope so with all my heart. But my strong and repeated advice to all young English gentlemen is to resort to any homely mode of earning their bread in preference to that of seeking gold in Australia.

I do not believe that gold-seeking in Australia has been remunerative to any class of men as a class. The gold found is sold to the mint or to the banks at prices varying from £3 10s. to £4 2s. the ounce. £3 15s. the ounce may perhaps be taken as an average price. I have been assured by those whose profession it has been to look into the matter, that all the gold in Australia has been raised at an expense of not less than £5 the ounce. For myself, I can only say that I fully believe the statement. . . .

All rates of wages and cost of living were so thrown out of gear throughout the colonies by the early gold rushes, that no exact calculation can be made. Shearers demanded and got

£10 a hundred for shearing sheep, whereas the present price may be about 17s. 6d. a hundred. £1 a-day was by no means extravagant wages for a groom. Everything for a while was on the same footing, because every man was taught to believe that he had only to rush to the gold fields to pick up a fortune. But the men who picked up fortunes are very rare. One never meets them. But the men who just failed during this time to pick up fortunes meet one at every corner. "Ah," says one, "If I had gone away from such and such a rush when I had that £7,000." "I might have walked off with £12,000 after the first three months at Ballarat," says a second. "I had £15,000 at one time out of Ophir," says a third. "Gympie was Gympie when I was rolling up £2,000 a month," says a fourth. Of course a question is asked as to what has become of these grand sums. The answer is always the same, though probably not always strictly true. The fortunes already made have been lost in pursuit of greater fortunes. It is not admitted that the money has been spent in useless, new-fangled luxuries; but that much has been so spent is certain. The Phœnix who has made his fortune at the diggings, and kept it, is a bird hardly to be found on Australian ground.

Gympie as a town was a marvellous place, and to my eyes very interesting, though at the same time very ugly. Its population was said to consist of about 6,000 souls, but I found throughout the country that no statement of the population of a gold field could be taken as accurate. The men go and come so quickly that the changes cannot be computed. It consists of a long street stretching more than a mile—up and down hill—without a single house in it that looked as though it had been built to last ten years. And probably no house had been built with any such ambition, although Gympie is now more than ten years old. The main street contains stores, banks, public-houses, a place of worship or two, and a few eating-houses. They are framed of wood, one storey high, generally built in the first place as sheds with a gable-end to the street, on to which, for the sake of importance, a rickety wooden façade has been attached. The houses of the miners, which are seldom more than huts, are scattered over the surrounding little hills, here and there, as the convenience of the men in regard to the different mining places has prompted the builders. All around are to be seen the holes and shallow excavations made by the original diggers, and scattered among them the bigger heaps which have been made by the sinking of deep shafts. When a mine is being worked there is a rough wooden windlass over it, and at a short distance the circular track of the unfortunate horse who, by his rotatory motion, pulls the buckets up with the quartz, and lets them down with the miners. Throughout all there stand the stunted stumps of decapitated trees, giving the place a look of almost unearthly desolation. At a distance beyond the mine-shafts are to be seen the great forests which stretch away on every side over almost unlimited distance. If at any place one is tempted to quote the *aurum irrepertum et sic melius situm*, it is at such a place as Gympie.

There is a hospital, and there are schools, which are well attended, and, as I have before said, various places of worship. I put up at an inn kept by a captain, which I found to be fairly comfortable, and by no means expensive. There were a crowd of men there, all more or less concerned in the search of gold, with whom I found myself to be quite intimate before the second night was over; and from whom—as from everybody at Gympie—I received much civility, and many invitations to drink brandy and water.

The Rush to Gulgong

I was in New South Wales in October, November, and December, 1871, and again in June and July, 1872. During my former visit very little was said in Sydney about gold or other metals. The tone of the public mind on the subject of mining was very different from that prevailing in Melbourne and Victoria generally. Indeed there seemed to be a feeling, in which I sympathized, that though goldfields when found should of course be worked, the finding and working them could hardly be regarded as an unmixed good to a community. Such operations led to gambling, disturbed the ways of legitimate commerce, excited men's minds unduly, and were dangerous. Victoria was very keen about gold, believed in gold, was willing to trust to gold for her greatness and population. Victoria prided herself on being a gold colony. Let it be so. New South Wales was conscious of a pride in better things. That perhaps may be taken as an expression of the general mind as I read it.

When I returned after an interval of six months all this was changed. No one in Sydney would talk about anything but mining shares. It was not only gold, nor, as I think, chiefly gold, that was in men's mouths. Copper had been found in the west, in the district between Bathurst and Orange, and tin in the north, in New England. It seemed that all they who had been so sober before were now as mad after mining shares as the gentlemen who congregate under the verandah in Melbourne. Everybody had shares in copper, and almost everybody shares in tin. Gentlemen went about with specimens in their pockets, and seemed to think that any conversation diverging from the one important subject was frivolous and unneeded. "You find us a little changed; don't you?" one old friend of the last year said to me. When I acknowledged that I had recognized an altered tone, he assured me that Sydney had now shaken herself and had ceased to be dull. Copper and tin were at the moment in the ascendant; but gold, too, was very "lively". The glories of Hill End, and of Hawkins's Hill in the Tambaroora district had culminated since I had before been in the colony, and Tambaroora itself had come to be talked about as perhaps the future greatest gold-field of Australia. I was asked whether "I had visited Tambaroora?" I replied that I had not, and now could not do so. Then I was told that I had then missed the one place in all that eastern world which more than any other would make Australia wealthy, happy, and great. . . .

To the stranger personally uninterested in the search, it seems that the known presence of gold beneath the earth begets a fury in the minds of men compelling them to search for it, let the risk, the danger, the misery, the probable losses, be what they may. That a thing in itself so rich, so capable of immediately producing all that men most desire, should lie buried in the dirt beneath their feet, loose among the worthless pebbles of the rivers, mixed at haphazard with the deep clumsy lumbering rocks, overcomes the imagination of the unconscious thinker, and takes possession of his heart and brain. For a while he makes no estimate as to the cost of his labours as contrasted with the value of his chance of success. It is gold that is there—gold that is customarily treasured, gold that is kept within bars and dealt out in tiny morsels as the recognized reward of the sweat of many hours, gold that is thought about, talked about, dreamed about, gold that is longed for, worked for, gambled for, and sinned for; and this gold may be got by the handful, if only the lucky sod of earth be turned. There is a feeling almost impersonal in the would-be miner's breast, as he feels it to be a shame that the dirty earth should hold, and hold without in any way using, the treasure of all treasures that is sweetest to the heart of man. *Cogere humanos in usus* should certainly be the motto of the gold-seeker.

When I was leaving Sydney in October, 1871, with the intention of travelling westward into the colony, the rush to Gulgong was the rush of the day, and to Gulgong I went in company with the gold commissioner of the district. I have already given some description of Gympie, in Queensland, but Gympie when I was there was an old-established place, and the rush thither was a thing quite of the past. The rush to Gulgong was recent. The great attraction proposed to one visiting a rush seemed to consist in the sight of a congregating together of a great many men, without any of the ordinary comforts of life, and with but few of those appliances which are generally regarded as necessaries. I was told there were 12,000 people at Gulgong, all of whom had collected themselves thither within a few months. The place had begun to be a place about a month since—but the real rush had only lately commenced. I confess that I felt an interest in seeing a town without streets, and people collected together with houses made of canvas and rough boards—an interest akin to that which induces others to see a criminal hung.

Our journey thither was one of three days from Bathurst, and was performed in the commissioner's buggy. As we went we saw parties of men, generally ten or twelve in number, either leisurely tramping along the road with their swags on their back, or taking their mid-day siesta under the gum-trees. The man who travels on foot in Australia, whether he be miner, shepherd, shearer, or simply beggar, always carries his "swag" with him, which consists of his personal properties rolled up in a blanket. The blanket is an essential necessity, because the man sleeps out in the bush beside a fire. And he carries also a pannikin and a "billy". The latter is an open pot in which he boils his water and makes his tea—for the bushman will always have a bag of tea within his swag. The billy is as essential as the blankets. A bushman of any refinement has the pannikin for drinking; but the rough old chum will dispense with it as a useless luxury, and will drink his tea out of his billy.

And these men were making a rush! They seemed to me to rush very leisurely. I hardly know what I had expected—whether to see each miner galloping on his steed, or running continually towards his goldfield at the rate of eight miles an hour. Though the influx of the men to such a place as Gulgong is a "rush", and when very numerous may be described as a stampede, the men themselves are orderly and slow. They have probably done it before, and know, if not the tale of the hare and the tortoise, at any rate the moral of the tale. But the men I saw were journeying some one way and some the other. Backs were turned upon Gulgong as well as faces towards it. Then I learned that such was the case with almost all rushes. Men would try their luck for a month, or perhaps for a fortnight, and if they failed, or did not meet success to satisfy them, would pack up their swags and would betake themselves elsewhere. In this way the population at a rush is very precarious, falling as quickly as it rises, receiving or losing a thousand in a few days, as the place gives or refuses to give its treasures. And, as a matter of course, the trade by which the place is supplied with meat and bread, with tea, sugar, and sweetmeats—the articles of food on which miners chiefly live—must be equally precarious.

On our route we passed the little town of Sofala, which was in point of time the second established goldfield in New South Wales, Ophir having been the first. Sofala is now a poor little town, containing 644 inhabitants, of whom a considerable portion are Chinese. It is built on a river, the channel of which contained the gold which created the town. The hills rise abruptly on each side of the stream, and give to the place a quaint picturesque appearance—as though it were altogether out of the world. Here we found about a dozen Chinamen "fossicking" after gold amidst the dirt of the river, which had already been washed by the first gold-seekers. These men "washed up" while we were looking on, and we saw them reduce the dirt collected during the day to a few dim specks of the precious metal. They then told us that they estimated their earnings for that day at 1s. each. They seemed to think that this was bad, but were not at all demonstrative in their disappointment.

Two days' travelling from Sofala took us to Gulgong; we stayed a night on the way at Mudgee, a clean little town, celebrated for the special breed of sheep produced in its neighbourhood. At Mudgee I was taken to visit the Mechanics' Institute, at which place I found a great number of well-thumbed novels. There were other books certainly; but the Mudgee shepherds certainly prefer novels. All these small towns have public libraries by one name or another. Mudgee boasts no more than 1,786 inhabitants, but it seemed to be very much better off in the way of churches, hotels, institutes, and schools than towns of more than double the size in England.

Gulgong was certainly a rough place when I visited it, but not quite so rough as I had expected. There was an hotel there, at which I got a bedroom to myself, though but a small one, and made only of slabs. But a gorgeously grand edifice was being built over our heads at the time, the old inn being still kept on while the new inn was being built on the same site. The inhabited part of the town consisted of two streets at right angles to each other, in each of which every habitation and shop had probably required but a few days for its erection. The fronts of the shops were covered with large advertisements, the names and praises of the traders, as is customary now with all new-fangled marts; but the place looked more like a fair than a town —perhaps like one of those fairs which used to be temporary towns and to be continued for weeks, such as some of us have seen at Amsterdam and at Leipsic. But with this difference, that in the cities named the old houses are seen at the back of the new booths, whereas at a gold rush there is nothing behind. Everything needful, however, seemed to be at hand. There were bakers, butchers, grocers, and dealers in soft goods. There were public-houses and banks in abundance. There was an auctioneer's establishment, at which I attended the sale of horses and carts. There was a photographer, and there was a theatre, at which I saw the *Colleen Bawn* acted with a great deal of spirit, and a considerable amount of histrionic talent. After the theatre a munificent banker of the town gave us an oyster supper, at a supper-room. It may be inferred, therefore, that the comforts of life had not been altogether neglected at Gulgong. In the middle of the day there had been a public dinner or lunch, at which there was much speaking. I cannot say that the Gulgong oratory was as good as the Gulgong acting, or the Gulgong oysters.

I think that the town of Gulgong, including its general inhabitants and mode of life, was more interesting to me even than the mines. I was charmed to hear that a few nights before there had been a most successful public ball. But I was distressed to find that there had been some heart-burning. Where was the line to be drawn in reference to the ladies? The postmistress would not attend the ball unless barmaids were excluded. The barmaids—I think very properly—were admitted, and the postmistress, who enjoyed the reputation of being the beauty of Gulgong, remained at home.

Of course, having come to Gulgong, I had to see the mines, and I went down the shaft of one, 150 feet deep, with my foot in the noose of a rope. Having offered to descend, I did not like to go back from my word when the moment came; but as the light of the day faded from my descending eyes, and as I remembered that I was being lowered by the operations of a horse who might take it into his brutish head to lower me at any rate he pleased—or not to lower me at all, but to keep me suspended in that dark abyss—I own that my heart gave way, and that I wished I had been less courageous. But I went down, and I came up again; and I found six or seven men working at the bottom of the hole. I afterwards saw the alluvial dirt brought up from some other hole, puddled and washed and the gold extracted. When extracted it was carried away in a tin pannikin—which I thought detracted much from the splendour of the result.

Of the men around me some were miners working for wages, and some were shareholders, each probably with a large stake in the concern. I could not in the least tell which was which. They were all dressed alike, and there was nothing of the master and the man in the tone of their conversation. Among those present at the washing up, there were two Italians, an American, a German, and a Scotchman, who I learned were partners in the property. The important task of conducting the last wash, of throwing away for ever the stones and dirt from which the gold had sunk, was on this occasion confided to the hands of the American. The gold was carried away in a pannikin by the German. Why should he not have put in his fingers and appropriated an ounce of the fragments to his own use? I know it is mean to suspect; but among us in England checks are necessary. No doubt the German to whom the pannikin was confided was respected far and wide for his honesty.

Of the courtesy of all these men it is impossible to speak too highly, or of the civility of the miners generally; and in saying this I do not allude to the demeanour of the men to myself or to other chance visitors, but to their ordinary mode of conducting themselves. The Australian miner when he is in work never drinks, and seems to feel a pride in his courtesy. It must be understood that his is not a submissive deportment, prone to the touching of hats and a silent reverence of his betters, but a manly bearing, which enables him to express himself freely, but which never verges on distasteful familiarity.

I found that miners working for wages at Gulgong were earning from £2 10s. to £3 a week; but I found also that many were there who could not get such work to do. No doubt a glut of labour would soon tend to lower the wages, but the population did not seem to be fixed enough to have produced that result. Men came, and tried their fortune on little speculations of their own, and failed. Then, if they could not at once get wages to their mind, they took up their swags and departed to some other rush. I found also that many men were employed on the most singular and easiest task that I ever met in my travels. When a mining speculator had taken out his claim to a piece of land, the law required him to occupy it. If he did not at once work it, he must hold it by his own bodily presence or by that of some deputy for at least two hours a day. I think I was told that this minimum of occupation for two hours must be before noon, either from nine to eleven or from ten to twelve. This duty was called "shepherding"—and the wages of a man to shepherd a claim were 25s. a week. But these mining shepherds are not miners. I asked a miner whether it would not suit him to earn 25s. a week by shepherding, and then to take a day's work, or a part of a day's work, at his own enterprise. But he gave me to understand that shepherding a claim was dishonourable for a miner.

It seemed to me, when I was at Gulgong, that the rush was not regarded as a success. The population was decreasing; and though much gold had been extracted, much useless labour had been expended on "duffers". A shaft sunk without any produce from it is a duffer. Looking around, an inexperienced stranger would think that gold about Gulgong was ubiquitous. There were holes everywhere, and the ugly masses of upturned clay which always mark the gold-seeker's presence. But of these excavations the majority were duffers. It is the duffering part of the business which makes it all so sad. So much work is done from which there is positively no return!

I came away from Gulgong with a feeling that I had hardly seen the rush in its most characteristic phase. The rush had been rushed before I reached it. The place had become to a degree settled—and people were going out at any rate as fast as they were coming in. But there was another rush to a place about 150 miles from Gulgong—a place called Currajong, which was described to me as being quite new, and I went there also. It was new, and a more wretched spot I never saw in my life. I was told by one inhabitant that there were over 2,000 people; by another that there were not above 500. Of the number I could not at all judge myself, either by the concourse of people or of habitations. There were a few public-houses roughly constructed of timber, and a shop or two for the sale of general articles. The miners and their followers were living in tents scattered here and there among the holes they were digging. When gold was "struck" at any of these holes—when enough had been found to be regarded as a probable forerunner of commercial success —a red flag was hoisted. Here and there I saw the red flag—but the holes and adjacent heaps at which there were no red flags were as legion to the distinguished few.

At Gulgong I had found satisfied miners, men who said that they were doing well; at Currajong everybody seemed to be disappointed, unhappy, and hopeless. The rush, it was found, was going to turn out a "duffer" altogether. The street of the place, if it can be said to have had a street, consisted of a bush road, wider and more trodden than usual, with the trees standing close around, though the undergrowth and shrubs had been burned or otherwise used and the trees themselves mutilated. Everywhere through the bush there were little tents, and holes and heaps. I visited one spot at which three men were working, one below filling a bucket, and two above drawing the bucket up. This they had been doing for a fortnight, and had found nothing. They did it for three weeks longer, and still finding no gold, had then gone away. One of them was the son of an English gentleman, who had thought that Australian gold-mining might probably be a road to easy wealth. He got his experience at Currajong, but he got nothing else. I can fancy no more heart-breaking occupation than the work of trundling dirt up out of a hole eight hours a day without results. There were drunken people about Currajong—which I had not seen elsewhere—and a rowdy aspect which made me think ill of the prospects of the place. I was told subsequently that for a while it was not a success, and that many left it in disgust; but that afterwards gold-bearing quartz was found in large quantities, and that they who stuck to the place through its early misfortunes did well there. Currajong, when I saw it, seemed to be the most hopelessly disappointing place I had visited in the colonies.

New South Wales contains coal as well as gold, and has coal-mines which are worked successfully. In this respect she is blessed above any other of these colonies. . . . In England we are accustomed to think that the possession of coal is the greatest blessing which Providence has bestowed upon us, and to believe that we owe to it our wealth, our population, and our greatness. I doubt whether there is a man of business in Great Britain who would wish to exchange our coal-mines for goldfields. When the idea is presented to our minds we at once feel that the really productive powers of coal must be much more fertile in producing actual wealth than any amount of a metal, the value of which is in truth little more than nominal. No increase in the production of coal would at all diminish the real value of the article; but were the production of gold to be increased suddenly, violently, and to a great extent, the value of the metal would fall away in a quickly increasing ratio in accordance with the increase of production. Its value depends on its comparative rarity; and, therefore, when we are told of some probable future development of Australian goldfields at a hitherto unprecedented rate; when we are assured that Australian gold is as yet in its infancy—as I have been assured very often—we feel that even should it be so, the expected wealth will not follow the new discoveries. Should it come very quickly, the dislocation of prices, which is now being effected slowly by the gradual increase in the amount, and therefore gradual decline in the value of gold, would become rapid—and therefore ruinous to many. In such a case the wealth of the world would be increased only as far as gold is required—not as wealth, but as a symbol of wealth. Whereas every additional ton of coal that we get will contain as much power as every ton of coal that was got before it. Therefore, although the coal of Newcastle and Wollongong, in the present price paid for it, falls very far behind the gold of New South Wales, I regard coal as being the more important produce of the two. Had there been no coal found in New South Wales almost every source of wealth in Australia would have been stunted. Steamers could not have plied, nor railways have been worked, unless at prices which would have made them inaccessible to the community. All machinery for mines and other works must have been procured from Europe. The copper must have been sent home unsmelted, and therefore at treble the freight now paid for it. It is useless to expatiate on this—as who is there that does not know that a country without coal is poor and miserable, and that a country with coal ought to be rich and blessed? . . .

It was believed of Australia, when Great Britain first planted her colonies there, that she would prove to be a country almost blank and barren in regard to minerals. It seems, however, now, that few countries on the earth are richer in ores than she is. If iron can be found on her hills, and worked, she will probably become as populous and as rich as the United States.

Fabulous Bendigo

My readers have, no doubt, heard of the Bendigo goldfields. I think it is by no means improbable that some of them—in England—may never have heard the name of Sandhurst as connected with gold. I had not done so when I first landed in Australia, though I had been often told of Bendigo, having some hazy idea that the place had called itself after a prize-fighter and therefore must be a very rowdy place indeed. I imagine that some such feeling must have been predominant with the people of the place when Bendigo, as a name, was dropped, and Sandhurst—which is not only euphonious, but which carries with it a certain mixed idea of youthful energy and military discipline—was chosen in its stead. Sandhurst means to go ahead, and become a great city. In regard to the production of gold it has gone very much ahead. As a city, when I was there, it was neither handsome nor commodious. It had the appearance, which is common to all new mining towns, of having been scratched up violently out of the body of the earth by the rake of some great infernal deity, who had left everything behind him dirty, uncouth, barren, and disorderly! Any one who has seen the mining towns as they rose in Cornwall and Glamorganshire must have observed the same ugliness. At Sandhurst you see heaps of upturned dry soil here and there, dislocated whims, rows of humble houses built just as they were wanted, shops with gewgaw fronts put up at a moment's notice, drinking-bars in abundance, here and there an attempt at architecture, made almost invariably by some banking company eager to push itself into large operations —but with it all a look of eager, keen energy which would redeem to the mind the hideous objects which meet the eye, were it not that the mind becomes conscious of the too speculative nature of the work done—of the gambling propensities of the people around—and is driven to feel that the buying and selling of mining shares cannot be done by yea, yea, and nay, nay.

In Melbourne there is the "verandah"; in Sandhurst there is a "verandah"; in Ballarat there is a "verandah". The verandah is a kind of open exchange—some place on the street pavement apparently selected by chance, on which the dealers in mining shares do congregate. What they do, or how they carry on their business when there, I am unable to explain. But to the stranger, or the passer by, they do not look lovely. He almost trembles lest his eyes should be picked out of his head as he goes. He has no business there, and soon learns to walk on the other side of the road. And he hears strange tales which make him feel that the innocence of the dove would not befriend him at all were he to attempt to trade in those parts. I think there is a racing phrase as to "getting a tip". The happy man who gets a tip learns something special as to the competence or incompetence of a horse. There are a great many tips in gold mines which fall into the fortunate hands of those who attend most closely, and perhaps with most unscrupulous fidelity, to the business of the verandahs. The knowing ones know that a certain claim is going to give gold. The man who has the tip sells out at a low price—sells out a certain number of shares, probably to a friend who holds the tip with him. The price is quoted on the share list, and the unfortunate non-tipped sell out also, and the fortunate tipped one buys up all. A claim is not going to give gold—and the reverse happens. Or a claim is salted—gold is surreptitiously introduced, is then taken out, and made the base of a fictitious prosperity. The tipped one sells and the untipped buy. It is easy to see that the game is very pretty; but then it is dangerous. It has certainly become very popular. One is told at Melbourne that all are playing at it—clergymen, judges, ladies, old ladies and young, married ladies and single—old men and boys, fathers unknown to their sons, and sons unknown to their fathers, mothers unknown to their daughters, daughters unknown to their mothers—masters and servants, tradesmen and their apprentices. "You shall go from one end of Collins Street to another," a man said to me, "and you will hardly meet one who has not owned a share or a part of a share." Gold-mining in Victoria is as was to us the railway mania some twenty-four years ago. Melbourne no doubt is the centre of the trade in shares, but low beneath the surface in the mines of Sandhurst lie the hearts of the gold gamblers.

At Ballarat the chief produce of gold is still obtained from alluvial dirt—from dirt which is indeed extracted by deep working out of the bowels of the earth, and not, as at first, from the channels of rivers and the crevices of mountain gullies—but still from alluvial dirt, which, when extracted, is washed. The gold remains after the washing, and then the operation is at an end. At Sandhurst the gold is got by quartz-crushing. The gold-bearing rock is brought up in great masses—thousands and thousands of tons of stone, which is called quartz. This is crushed by huge machinery, and the gold is separated from the dirt by the use of quicksilver and water. The washing of alluvial soil is the readier way of getting gold, but the quartz-crushing is the more important. Of the alluvial dirt there must, or at any rate there may, soon be an end. The geologists say that the crushers of quartz may eat up whole mountains, and still go on finding stone that will give gold. . . .

All prosperous trades have a slang of their own—certain terms used to keep outsiders at a distance, and to create that feeling of esoteric privilege which we all like to have in regard to matters which we think we understand. A man who only uses horses can never talk in professional language to a man who breeds them and deals in them and lives with them. A layman in politics, let him be ever so anxious for his country, is all abroad when conversing with a member of parliament about bills and acts, about notices of motion and the "previous question". It is very much so with mining. Everything is told to the visiting stranger, but I don't think he is intended to understand anything. What with tributes and claims, with leads and lodes, with shafts and levels and crosscuts and veins, with reefs and gullies, with quartz, amalgam, tailings, and mullock—I am by no means sure of the spelling of that last word—he is made to feel that he is an outsider, and that he cannot learn mining in a day. At Sandhurst I felt this very strongly—and my reader will probably feel as I did. He will simply acknowledge to himself the fact that a cake of gold containing 2,564 oz.—and worth about £10,000—is a very large cake indeed.

The names selected by various companies at the Sandhurst gold-fields deserve attention. Sandhurst, which now aspires to be the leading Australian gold-field, and which certainly turns out more gold than any other, boasts at present no less than 1,200 different companies. I should say that there were 1,200 in the early part of 1872. The number will probably be very greatly increased before these words are published. The names chosen for these companies are certainly very quaint. There are not less than fourteen "New Chum" Companies, and there are three or four "Old Chum" Companies. There are the Peg Leg, the Perfect Cure, the Who can Tell, the Great Extended Who can Tell, the Sons of Freedom, the Sir Walter Scott, the Sailor Prince, the Royal Louisa, the Lord Byron, the Little Chum, the Jonadab, the Hand and Band, the Happy Day, the Happy-go-Lucky, the Great Extended South Golden Pyke, the Go by Gold, the Charles Gavan Duffy, the Gladstone—indeed there are five or six Gladstone Companies—and, to be fair, I must add that there is a Disraeli Company; I do not, however, find it quoted among those that are paying dividends. But among all names at Sandhurst, the greatest name, the most thriving, the best known, and the name in highest repute, is—"Hustler". Whence came the appellation I do not distinctly know, but I believe that there once was—perhaps still is—a happy Hustler. If so, even the Marquis of Granby among publicans has not been a more prolific godfather than has Mr. Hustler among Sandhurst miners. What with original Hustler Companies and Tribute Hustler Companies, with simple Hustlers, and Extended Hustlers, and Great Extended Hustlers, with North Hustlers, and

South Hustlers, and with Extended North and South Hustlers, the companies who claim the happy name are difficult to count. There are at any rate two dozen of them, and all, or nearly all, are doing well. . . .

As regards the working miners, including all those who manage the works, and overlook the machinery, I am bound to say that they are a fine body of able and industrious men. This is so on all the large gold-fields, and nowhere more noticeably than at Sandhurst. They are intelligent, manly, and independent—altogether free from that subservience which the domination of capital too often produces in most fields of labour. I have spoken, perhaps, as strongly as I know how to speak, of the gambling propensities of the population of a gold-mining town. I should be wrong if I did not speak as strongly of the efforts which are made by such communities—which in Australia are always made when the communities become large and apparently fixed—to ameliorate the condition of the people. The hospitals are excellent, the provision for the indigent is so good as almost to promote indigence, the schools are well conducted and well filled, the churches are sufficient, and the clergymen are supported. The money comes freely and is freely expended. And in no community are the manners of the people more courteous or their conduct more decent. Of course there is drinking.The idle men drink—would-be gentlemen, who are trying to speculate, without apparent means of livelihood, drink—miners who are not mining, having what they call a spell, or holiday, will drink. But the working miner is a sober man, with a sober family; and of such the bulk of the mining population is made up. In England working men drink—work by day, and drink by night; then half work by day and double drink by night, till the thing comes soon to an end. In Australia, as a rule, the working man does not drink while he works. The shearer does not drink; the shepherd and boundary-rider do not drink; the reaper and ploughman do not drink; nor does the miner drink. Let them be idle for a while; let them take their wages and go away for a "spell" —then they will drink as no Englishman ever drinks, drink down in a fortnight the earnings of a year. But there is less of this with miners than with shearers or ploughmen. The miner gambles—and is so saved from the worse vice of drinking.

And the gambling of the miner has about it a certain redeeming manliness which is altogether wanting to the denizen of the racecourse or of the roulette table. Though he gambles, he works and produces. The gambling is but an excrescence on his genuine industry. The Sandhurst regular miner works in shifts, of eight hours each shift, throughout the day and night. The gold is being sought and found, dug out and dragged up, and crushed out of its matrix, the quartz, for four-and-twenty hours a day, during six days of the week. And the skilled miner, by eight hours' work a day, may earn at least 9s. a day, in a country in which he and his wife and children may live comfortably—and as regards food with absolute plenty—for 4s. a day. The gold-miner at Sandhurst who keeps himself simply to his work, and takes no part in New Extended Great Chum Tributes, has, as work goes in the world, by no means an unhappy lot.

I went down the shaft of one mine—the Great Extended Hustler, I think it was called—600 feet below the surface, and was received with the greatest courtesy. I am bound to say that I saw nothing that was worth seeing, and that I understood nothing of all that was told to me. This is an almost disgraceful declaration to make, after one has pretended to understand all that was said. But it was so with me, and is so I take it with all travellers. The experienced and good-natured professional miners who conduct the strangers are anxious that everything should be made plain. To them everything is plain. But the very A B C of their necessary knowledge is probably Hebrew to the listener, who is too grateful for the attention paid to him to tell the kind teacher how utterly unintelligible to him is the whole matter in question. It was so with me—but this I saw, and could have seen as well above the earth as by going below, that tons of grey stone were dragged up, that the grey stone was all stamped and crushed into powder by machinery, and that out of the powder gold was got in certain proportions, so many ounces, or more probably so many pennyweights, to the ton of stone, and that, as the result was good or bad, dividends were divided or were not divided among the speculators.

As a gold-field Sandhurst is now pre-eminent in Victoria. As a town it is not to be compared with Ballarat. As a town Ballarat is peculiarly attractive. Sandhurst, as I saw it, was equally repulsive. Everything was crowded, unfinished, and uncomfortable. At the inn, where we only breakfasted and dined, everything was done which civility could do to make our party comfortable

—and we dined and breakfasted well. But even the inn had that crowded air and brandy-scented atmosphere which are inseparable from hotel-keeping for many people with unfinished appliances. I was shown a bedroom in which beds stood thick as hops in a hop-garden—not a bed here and another there against a wall, so as to make that very objectionable inn chamber, a double-bedded room, but beds everywhere, as close as they could cluster, so that eight or ten might chum together. Men in search of gold are apt to dispense with many of the comforts of life, and will disregard the number of their chamber companions. I myself, luckily, was not called upon to stay a night at Sandhurst. An evening train took our party back to Melbourne.

6 THE UNDERPRIVILEGED

It is in his comments on Australian aborigines and on South Sea Islanders, brought to Queensland to work on the sugar plantations, that Trollope most clearly is seen to be writing in the context of another century. His arguments recall that context in a revealing way.

The First Australians

When in Gipps Land I visited an establishment called Rama Yuck, of a missionary character, maintained for the civilization, Christianization, and general improvement of the black races. Of these establishments there are many in various parts of Australia. . . . I did not think that Rama Yuck was flourishing, though I was convinced by what I saw that nothing was wanting to it which philanthropy and devotion could supply.

It has been only natural, only human, that efforts should be made by the invading race to ameliorate the condition of these people, and—to use the word most common in our mouths—to civilize them. We have taken away their land, have destroyed their food, have made them subject to our laws, which are antagonistic to their habits and traditions, have endeavoured to make them subject to our tastes, which they hate, have massacred them when they defended themselves and their possessions after their own fashion, and have taught them by hard warfare to acknowledge us to be their masters. We have done the work perhaps with as little cruelty as was compatible with such a job. No one I think will say that the English should have abstained from taking possession of Australia because such possession could not be secured without injury to the blacks. Had the English abstained, the Dutch or the French would have come, and certainly would not have come with lighter hands. There has been rough work—and how could rough work have been avoided when the cause for quarrel was so deep? The race was a savage race, hating tasks, ignoring property, and one which would not fall into our ways. Gradually we have seen them disappearing before us—sinking into the earth, as it were, as they made way for us. They have not retreated. Though personal property has been ignored, tribal property, the right of each tribe to its own territory, has been fully acknowledged among them—so that to retreat was impossible. The only land to which they could have retreated was already occupied. As we have scattered ourselves onwards these tribes have melted away. Their women have ceased to bear children, and their men have waxed prematurely old. Fragments of them only remain, and the fragments of them are growing still smaller and smaller. Within the haunts of white men, and under the tutelage of white men, they have learned to wear clothes, and to drink, and to be covetous of tobacco and money—and sometimes to do a little work. But with their rags, and their pipes, and their broken English, they are less noble, less sensitive of duty, less capable of protracting life than they were in their savage but unsubdued condition.

*　*　*

Children of mixed breed—of white fathers and black mothers—are found, but do not become a race as they have done in the western world. I have seen and heard of instances in which girls so born have been brought up as domestic servants. But it seems they always return to the bush and become some black man's gin—or strive to do so. I heard of one girl who had been trained to take care of children till she was fourteen. She had never known savage life, and had become docile and affectionate. But at fourteen she vanished into the bush. In another house I saw a girl about fourteen waiting at table, and was told that she had made repeated attempts at escape. I ventured to ask the lady by what right she was retained, and how caught when she had fled. The lady laughed at my scruples as to retention, and told me with a boast that she could always put a blackfellow on the girl's track if she made an attempt. Here at any rate was something like slavery, for the girl was not apprenticed, nor her position recognized by any legal transfer of service. She had been picked up, and bred, and fed, and used kindly—and was now the possession of the lady. When a little older no doubt she will escape and become a gin.

I once asked a member of Parliament, in one of the colonies, and a magistrate, what he would do—or rather what he would recommend me to do—if stress of circumstances compelled me to shoot a black man in the bush. Should I go to some nearest police station as any one would do who in self-defence had shot a white man?—or should I go on rejoicing as though I had shot a tiger or killed a deadly snake? His advice was clear and explicit. "No one but a fool would say anything about it." The aboriginal therefore whom you are called on to kill—lest he should kill you or your wife, or because he spears your cattle—is to be to you the same as a tiger or a snake. But this would be in the back districts, far away from towns, in which the black man has not yet learned to be a fine gentleman with dignified deportment, barely taking the trouble to open his mouth as he asks for sixpence and tobacco.

There can be no doubt that the law does hardly reach him in those distant districts for purposes either of punishment or protection. He cannot be numbered up and classified. If he disappears his absence is known only to his tribe, who do not recognize our law, and will not ask for its interference. He cannot be traced. The very hue of his face prevents evidence as to his identity. He cannot be found, and he is never missed. The distant squatter, whom he attacks or whose beasts he kills, knows that he must be redhanded himself, or that the black man will go unpunished—and he knows too that unless some black man be punished, life for him on his distant run will be impossible. It is not for petty pilferings that he is concerned—but for life and the means of living. The black men in his neighbourhood have determined to be his enemies, and as enemies he feels himself bound to treat them. No doubt he is unscrupulous, but scruples won't serve his turn. He has come to a country in which savage life prevails—and he finds it necessary to be, not savage, but ruthless.

In saying so much I have endeavoured to state the case fairly between the squatter and the aboriginal; for the real question at issue now lies between them. And I find that it resolves itself to this:—had the first English settlers any right to take the country from the black men who were its owners? and have the progressing colonists, who still go westward and northward in search of fresh lands, the right to drive the black men back, seeing as they do that they cannot live together? If they have no such right—that is, if they be morally wrong to do it—then has the whole colonizing system of Great Britain been wrong, not only in Australia, but in every portion of the globe? And had Britain abstained from colonizing under the conviction of conscientious scruples, would it have been better for the human race? Four nations struggled for the possession of Australia, the Portuguese, the Dutch, the French, and ourselves. It fell into our hands, chiefly through the enterprise and skill of Captain Cook. Should we have abstained when we found that it was peopled, and, so to say, already possessed? And had we done so, should we have served the cause of humanity? I doubt whether any philanthropist will say that we should have abstained—or will think that had we done so the Australian aborigines would at the present moment have fared better with Dutch or French masters than they are now faring with us. It is their fate to be abolished, and they are already vanishing. Nothing short of abstaining from encroaching upon their lands—abstaining, that is, from taking possession of Australia, could be of any service to them. They have been treated, I think, almost invariably with proffered kindness when first met, but they have not wanted and have not understood the kindness. For a time they would not submit at all, and now their submission is partial. In 1864 an expedition was made to take cattle from Rockhampton overland to Cape York, the northern extremity of Queensland, by two brothers, Frank and Alexander Jardine. The cattle were then driven up to save the lives of the occupants of a new settlement. The enterprise was carried through with admirable spirit and final success, after terrible difficulties. But their progress was one continued battle with black tribes, who knew nothing of them, and who of course regarded them as enemies. Which party was to blame for this bloodshed—the Messrs. Jardine who were risking their own lives to save the inhabitants of a distant settlement—or the poor blacks who were struggling against unknown and encroaching enemies? In this case there was certainly no cruelty, no thoughtless arrogance, no white man's indifference to the lives of black men. The Messrs. Jardine would have been glad enough to have made their progress without fighting battles, and fought when they did fight simply in self-protection. And yet the blacks were invaded—most unjustly and cruelly as they must have felt.

Of the Australian black man we may certainly say that he has to go. That he should perish without unnecessary suffering should be the aim of all who are concerned in the matter. But no good can be done by giving to the aboriginal a character which he does not deserve, or by speaking of the treatment which he receives in language which the facts do not warrant.

* * *

A story was told me by a lady which may serve to exemplify the trouble arising to squatters from the unfortunate aboriginals. She was on another station, belonging to her husband, in one of the back districts, and her husband was away. The only man about the place was a coolie cook, and this man was not very manly. She had babies—or a baby, and a nurse, and so forth. And things being in this condition, a black man made his way into the lady's kitchen and there took up his quarters. She asked him to go, but he declined to go, and there he remained—I forget whether it was one or two nights. He committed no great violence, but grinned, and demanded food, and gradually made himself very much at home. "What on earth did you do?" I asked. "My husband had a revolver," she said, "and I walked up to him with it and pointed it at him." "Well, and what then?" "I did it two or three times, and he didn't seem to mind it much." "And what next?" "I couldn't bring myself to shoot him, you know," she said. I quite sympathized with her there, remarking that it would be difficult to shoot a man who only grinned and asked for food. I went on to ask again what she did do—for an aboriginal who gets with ease all that he demands is likely in the end to ask for a good deal, and it may be a question whether, after all, the shooting him might not be the least of the possible evils. "I remembered," she said, "that my husband had a sword-stick. I went and got that, and drew it out before him. When he retreated I ran on at him and pricked him. He did not like it at all, so I pricked him again. When I pricked him the third time he ran away and never came back any more." It was a happy and in some sort a glorious termination—but then the lady might have had no sword-stick at her command, or might have lacked the courage to make upon a savage an attack so merciful and yet so persistent.

* * *

When at Gladstone I found that an "aboriginal" negro was to be tried for breaking into a shop, and I walked through the woods to the little court-house, which stands about a mile from the wharf, in order that I might see the ceremony. There I found a magistrate, four policemen, a young woman who attended as a witness, and the prisoner. The black man was described in the sheet as "Aboriginal Boney". He had taken away a slab from the corner of a wooden store in the hope of getting a bit of tobacco. He had been disturbed before making good his booty, and had left behind him a small pouch which he had taken from his waist to enable him the better to get through the hole. In this pouch there was elevenpence in silver—for even a black man will not condescend to carry copper in the colonies—and a lock of hair. Let us hope that it was a lock from the head of his favourite gin or wife. There was no evidence against him except his own, for the woman had only seen the form of a man escaping. Boney, when taxed by the sergeant, had confessed at once, seeming to have been more willing to bear the brunt of the offence than the loss of his purse. I wished I could have learned how much of his regret was sordid as attaching to the money, and how much tender as attaching to the lock of hair. He had gone, he said, for tobacco, but had got none, and had escaped when disturbed, leaving behind him his little property. The sergeant of police had it all his own way—examining the witnesses, putting himself into the box and giving his own evidence, taking the statement of the prisoner, and managing the matter in a manner that would be very serviceable if introduced at the Old Bailey. Aboriginal Boney was sentenced to six months' imprisonment, and seemed to be perfectly satisfied. He had, in fact, pleaded guilty—but had probably done so without comprehending much of the nature of the proceeding. I saw him afterwards in the prison at Rockhampton, and he seemed to be enjoying life in that retreat.

Trollope had most to say of the aborigines in his comments on Western Australia, both in writing of its history and in recalling his visit to the convict establishment on Rottnest Island.

All the first years of the colony's existence were saddened by contests with the blacks—by so-called murders on the part of the black men, and so-called executions on the part of their invaders. Looking at these internecine combats from a distance and by the light of reason, we can hardly regard as murder—as that horrid crime which we at home call murder—the armed attempts which these poor people made to retain their property; and though we can justify the retaliations of the white conquerors—those deeds done in retaliation which they called executions—we cannot bring ourselves to look upon the sentences of death which they carried out as calm administrations of the law. The poor black wretches understood no pleas that were made against them—were not alive even to the Christian's privilege of lying in their own defence, and of pleading not guilty. They speared a soldier here and a settler there, ran away with booty, fired houses, and made ravages on women and children, doubtless feeling that they were waging a most righteous war against a most unrighteous and cruel enemy. When caught, they knew that they must suffer. In the old records of the colony, one reads of these things as though all the injuries were inflicted by the blacks and suffered by the whites. Here, at home, all of us believe that we were doing a good deed in opening up these lands to the industry and civilization of white men. I at any rate so believe. But, if so, we can surely afford to tell the truth about the matter. These black savages were savage warriors, and not murderers; and we too, after a fashion, were warriors, very high-handed, and with great odds in our favour, and not calm administrators of impartial laws. . . .

It was impossible to explain to the natives that a benevolent race of men had come to live among them, who were anxious to teach them all good things. Their kangaroos and fish were driven away, their land was taken from them, the strangers assumed to be masters, and the black men did not see the benevolence. The new-comers were Christians, and were ready enough to teach their religion if only the black men would learn it. The black men could not understand their religion, and did not want it; and, to this day, remain unimpressed by any of its influences. But the white men brought rum, as well as religion, and the rum was impressive though the religion was not. It is common to assert, when we speak of the effect which our colonists have had on uncivilized races, that we have taught them our vices, but have neglected to teach them our virtues. The assertion is altogether incorrect. We have taught them those of our customs and modes of life which they were qualified to learn. To sing psalms, and to repeat prayers, we have been able to teach the young among them. Of any connection between the praises and prayers and the conduct of their lives, I have seen no trace. Many arts they have learned from us, the breaking and training of horses, the use of the gun, the skill and detective zeal of policemen—for in Western Australia and in Queensland the aborigines are used in this capacity—and some adroitness in certain crafts, such as those of carpenters and masons. But we have been altogether unable to teach them not to be savage. They will not live in houses except by compulsion. They will not work regularly for wages. They are not awake to the advantages of accumulated property. In their best form they are submissive and irresponsible as children—in their worst form they are savage and irresponsible as beasts of prey. . . . Their doom is to be exterminated; and the sooner their doom be accomplished—so that there be no cruelty—the better will it be for civilization.

The black men in Western Australia were certainly not treated with exceptional harshness—were perhaps treated with exceptional kindness—but they were very troublesome to the newcomers. There was much of spearing on the one side, and much of shooting and hanging on the other. There seem to have been two pertinacious chiefs, or resolute leading natives, named Yagar and Midgegoroo, who gave a great amount of trouble. They carried on the war for four or five years, by no means without success. The records speak of them as horrible savages. They were probably brave patriots, defending their country and their rights. Midgegoroo was at last taken and shot. What was the end of Yagar, or whether he came to an end, no one seems to know.

* * *

When I visited Rottnest there were sixty-five of these aboriginals in the island—not a large number, perhaps hardly sufficient to justify any special mention; but the special mention is made because it seemed to me that the black men whom I saw in the prison were very much nearer to a state of civilization, and were upon the whole in a better condition, and indeed happier, than any whom I encountered in other conditions. Of course they desired their liberty, though by no means with that pining desire which creates brooding melancholy; but they were clothed and fed and housed, and constrained to work—though by no means to work heavily—and had assumed the look and bearing of human beings. . . .

There is a governor, with five warders, and a doctor. There is no chaplain, nor is any attempt made to Christianize these savages. I believe that any such attempt, and that the presence of any chaplain, would be misplaced and useless. I know that for saying this I shall have against me the opinion of many good men—of the very men whose good opinion I should be most proud to win—but I do not believe in the result of the Christian teaching which these men are able to receive. Nor does it strike me with any special horror that sixty-five savages should be left without this teaching, when I know it to have been the will of God that hundreds of thousands such as they should die without it in their own countries. . . .

The crime and the violence of these men have altogether a different effect on the mind of the bystander than have the same deeds when done by white men. As we condemn them for much in that they are savages, so must we acquit them of much for the same reason. Our crimes are often their virtues; but we make them subject to our laws—of which they know little or nothing—and hang them or lock them up for deeds for which they are not criminal in their own consciences, and for the non-performance of which they would be condemned by their own laws. I was astonished to find how large a proportion of these black prisoners had been convicted of murder—and that the two who were awaiting their trial were both accused of that crime. But these murders were chiefly tribal retributions. A man in some tribe is murdered, or perhaps simply dies. It is then considered necessary that the next tribe should also lose a man—so that things might be made equal; and some strong young fellow is told off to execute the decision of the elders. Should he refuse to do so, he is knocked about and wounded and ill-treated among his own people. But if he perform the deed entrusted to him, he is tracked down by black policemen, is tried for murder, and has a life-sentence passed against him. When examined as to these occurrences they almost invariably tell the truth—never endeavouring to screen themselves by any denial of the murder done, or by the absence of sufficient evidence; but appealing to the necessity that was laid upon them.

Such an account one of those in the prison, who was to be tried, gave to me in the governor's presence, which was much as follows, though at the time demanding interpretation, which I hope the reader will not need:—"Him come,"—him being some old chief in the tribe—"him say, 'go kill Cracko' "—Cracko being the destined victim—"me no like; him say 'must'; me no like very much; him hab spear"—then there was a sign made of the cruel chief wounding his disobedient subject—"then me go kill Cracko." —"With a tomahawk?" suggests the governor. The prisoner nods assent, and evidently thinks that the whole thing has been made clear and satisfactory. In very many cases the murderer is acquitted, as the judge very properly refuses to take the prisoner's story as a plea of guilty, and demands that the crime shall be proved by evidence. If the evidence be forthcoming the young murderer is sent to Rottnest with a life-sentence, and—as I think —enters on a much more blessed phase of existence than he has ever known before.

In the evening it was suggested that the prisoners should "have a corroboree" for the amusement of the guests, and orders were given accordingly. At that time I had never seen a corroboree, and was much interested, because it was said that a special tribe from which sixteen or eighteen of these men came were very great in corroborees. A corroboree is a tribal dance in which the men congregate out in the bush, in the front of a fire, and go through various antics with smeared faces and bodies, with spears and sticks, howling, and moving their bodies about in time, while the gins, and children, and old people sit round in a circle. I am told that some corroborees are very interesting. I probably never saw a good one, as I did not find them to be amusing. This corroboree in the Rottnest prison was the best I saw, but even in that there was not much to delight. When the order was given, I could not but think of other captives who were desired to sing and make merry in their captivity. Here, however, there was no unwillingness—and when I proposed that five shillings' worth of tobacco should be divided among the performers, I was assured that the evening would be remembered as a very great occasion in the prison.

Trollope last met aborigines in South Australia.

At the Wallaroo mines I found a set of black natives employed on the surface work, at regular wages of 4s. 4d. a day, or 26s. a week. There were about ten of them, and I was told that they had been there for three months, and had been as regular in their attendance as white men. This was the only instance I found in Australia in which I myself came upon any number of these aborigines in regular and voluntary employment. . . .

I came across one of these men, who was supposed to be a little ill, and therefore not on duty at the moment. He was dressed in a very genteel manner—with clothes softer and finer than a white miner would wear even when on a holiday. He was very gentle and civil, but not very communicative. He bought clothes with his money, he said, and food—and the rest he put away. He did not resent the impertinence of my inquiries, but was not quite willing to gratify my curiosity. My desire was to learn whether he had realized the advantage of laying up and permanently possessing property. I doubt whether he had, although he did mutter something as to putting away his wages. He seemed much more willing to talk about the cold in the head under which he had been suffering than of his general condition in life.

From the South Seas

Trollope's argument is an interesting forerunner to later conflicts about Australia's immigration policy.

Queensland at present is supplying itself with labour from the South Sea Islands, and the men employed are called Polynesians, or Canakers, or Islanders; but it may be a question whether Queensland will be allowed to do so long. The philanthropists are hard at work to hinder them—working as they always do with the best intentions, working as they so often do in much ignorance.

I may as well go into the question of South Sea Island labour at once—premising, if I may be allowed to do so, that some years since I ventured to express an opinion, exactly similar to that I now entertain, in reference to the employment of coolie labour for the growth of sugar in Demerara and Trinidad, which colonies I found on the road to renewed success through the instrumentality of a body of imported workmen, who were treated with uniform kindness and care. Then as now there was a fear in England that these foreigners in a new country would become slaves under new bonds, and that a state of things would be produced, less horrible indeed than the slavery of the negroes who were brought into the West Indies by the Spaniards, but equally unjust and equally opposed to the rights and interests of the men concerned. And it was alleged then that benevolence and good intention on the part of those who might first institute such an immigration of foreign labourers, would not suffice to protect a crowd of poor ignorant strangers from the natural greed of the employer—who would carry on his operations far from strict control, far from the eyes of England, altogether out of sight of Exeter Hall. They who so argued did not fail to remember the benevolence, humanity, and thorough Christian kindness of the man who was in the first instance responsible for the exportation of the negroes from Africa to the West. Las Casas had desired to save the poor Indian from some of the horrors of his hated toil, and had therefore brought the negro to the West Indies. But the semi-divine Las Casas—not all divine, but blind as are men in general to future events—created that slavery in the West which has been its great disgrace, and which the humanity of mankind has not yet wholly succeeded in abolishing. Is it not, therefore, incumbent on philanthropy in the present age to see that no new form of serfdom be introduced—at any rate on soil owned by the British Crown—and to guard with all the eyes of Argus any approaches to the abomination of slavery? That is the argument from the philanthropical side, stated, I trust, fairly—and that argument I do not pretend to combat. Let us have no slavery, in God's name. Be careful. Guard the approaches. Defend the defenceless. Protect the poor ignorant dusky foreigner from the possible rapacity of the sugar-planter. But in doing this, know at any rate what you are doing, and be not led away by a rampant enthusiasm to do evil to all parties. Remember the bear who knocked out his friend's brains with the brickbat when he strove to save him from the fly. As ill-conducted enthusiasm may not only debar Queensland from the labour which she requires, but debar also these poor savages from their best and nearest civilization. Let philanthropists, at any rate, look into the matter somewhat closely before they make heavy charges against the Queensland government and the Queensland sugar-growers, because they employ Islanders in the colony. If they be in earnest let them send over some one who may learn the truth for them, some agent or messenger capable of finding out the truth and of telling them without prejudice what are the real facts of this trade. . . .

I will now describe "the state of things" as clearly as I can, and will explain what I believe to be the cause of opposition to it in the colony. These Polynesians are brought into Queensland in vessels under government superintendence, and in conformity with an act of the Queensland parliament passed with the view of protecting them from the rapacity of merchants and the possible evil of kidnapping by British or colonial captains. . . . The act, dated March 8th, 1868, is long and will hardly bear quotation; but all the clauses are arranged so as to protect the Polynesian labourer—to protect him specially in his act of emigration from home—and to insure that justice shall be done to him on his arrival in Queensland. His clothes and diet aboard ship are prescribed, his clothes and diet during his sojourn with his master are fixed; his wages are fixed, and the means of return at the end of three years' work in the colony, without cost to himself, are insured to him. . . . And he is to be provided with residence and medical attendance. He can be transferred from one employer to another, but not without the sanction of the government. He cannot be moved out of the colony till the expiration of the three years without his own consent and that of the governor. He cannot be punished otherwise than by appeal to a magisterial bench—in which case he would be dealt with as would be any other person accused of breaking the law. At the end of the three years he receives wages at the rate of £6 per annum—or £18 in all. This must be paid to him in money, and this he invariably lays out in the purchase of articles which he takes back with him to the islands—tools, calico, cloth, small pieces of furniture, boxes, ornaments, and the like. In considering the amount of money-wages the master will bear in mind that the man has been fed, housed and clothed, and that the wages represent his savings.

I have seen these men working under various masters and at various employments. No doubt their importance to Queensland mainly attaches to the growth and manufacture of sugar; but they are also engaged on wharves, about the towns, in meat-preserving establishments, in some instances as shepherds, and occasionally as domestic servants. I have told how I was rowed up the river Mary by a crew of these islanders. They are always clean, and bright, and pleasant to be seen. They work well, but they know their own position and importance. I never saw one ill-used. I never heard of any such ill-usage. The question, to my mind, is whether they are not fostered too closely—wrapped up too warmly in the lambswool of government protection. Their dietary is one which an English rural labourer may well envy—as he might also, if he knew it, the general immunity from the crushing cares of toil which these young savages enjoy.

But I am unaware that any serious complaint has been made either by the English philanthropists or by their informants, the colonists, as to the treatment which these men receive in Queensland. The charge is that they are kidnapped—taken on board the vessels from the islands surreptitiously—and that they are ill-treated on the journey; that the horrors of the middle passage—as we used to call it when we spoke of the sufferings of the poor Africans—are in some sort repeated. As regards the immigration into Queensland I believe the charge to be substantially without foundation. The vessels are worked under government surveillance, and every vessel employed in the trade is now accompanied by a government agent. . . .

No doubt the entire colony of Queensland is not in favour of Polynesian labour. It may be, and probably has been the case, that Mr. Raff lost his seat for East Moreton by opposition raised on this ground. But that opposition did not spring from the causes which are at work with the English philanthropists. With them the sole object is to prevent a possible return to some form of slavery, and the ill-usage of a certain number of their fellow-men. No one charges them with other motives, or believes them to be actuated by other than the purest feelings. But the motives and feelings which have produced the opposition to which they have adhered are other than theirs. Protection of white labour is the cause of that opposition to which Mr. Raff was indebted for the loss of his seat in the Queensland Assembly. In Queensland, as elsewhere throughout the world, the political questions which most strongly stir the minds of men are those which refer to the joint employment of labour and capital. The white man in Queensland who can now earn 15s. or 20s. a week and his food, would like to earn 25s. or 30s.—in which desire all the world will sympathize with him. And he believes that his desire may be best accomplished by preventing the use of cheaper labour than his own. In this belief, and in the efforts to which it gives rise, the world will not sympathize with him. The belief is as erroneous as the efforts are vicious. It is in some sort a repetition of the infantine political economy which many years ago induced rural labourers in England to destroy thrashing machines and burn out the farmers who used them.

It is not necessary for me now to adduce arguments to show that the greater the products of the colony the more general will be the aggregate prosperity of the colonists. The white labourer in Queensland, who is not a good political economist, does believe that cheaper labour than his own is injurious to himself, and therefore desires to keep the Polynesians away. He does not understand that the very business in which he is allowed to earn 4s. or 4s. 6d. a day would not exist—could not be carried on—without another class of labour at the rate of 2s. or 1s. 6d. a day. He therefore becomes quite as zealous in the cause as the philanthropist at home; but he in his zeal hates the shining Polynesian, whom he sees, with a warmth greater even than that which the philanthropist throws into his love for his unseen man and brother. There are a pair of hands, and a supple body, and a willing spirit, and a ready brain to be had for 2s. a day—underselling the white man's labour after a fashion most nefarious to the white labourer's imagination! How can this crushing evil be avoided? Are there no means by which good labour at 2s. a day may be made impossible—a thing not to be obtained in the colony of Queensland? Then the white labourer, with indistinct intelligence on the subject, hears something of his philanthropical friends at Exeter Hall, and begins to find that there may be common cause between them. White labour in the colony may be protected from Exeter Hall, though Exeter Hall itself has no such intention. The white labourer soon finds a go-between—soon comes into communication with some gentleman, anxious for his vote, who can make statements to the philanthropists at home. Under such circumstances it will not be strange to the mind of the ordinary English politician that Mr. Raff should lose his seat in the Assembly—especially when the ordinary politician remembers that almost every white labourer possesses a vote.

It may be taken for granted that the sole object in England on the part of those who object to the emigration of Polynesians to Queensland is to save the Islanders from suffering and oppression. It is said of these islanders that as they cannot understand English—and as they speak various languages among themselves, in regard to which it is impossible for us to send interpreters who shall understand them all—therefore they cannot understand the contracts made with them. That they understand the verbal niceties of these contracts no one can imagine. Their contracts to them are very much the same as are our legal documents to most of us at home. We sign them, however, because from various concurrent causes, we believe them to be conducive to our advantage—not because we understand them. We trust the person who asks for our signature; and, though we know that there is sometimes deceit and consequent misfortune, we believe that the chances are in our favour. Experience has taught us to trust. These Islanders are in precisely the same condition. Those who go to Queensland for three years are sent back to these islands with their hands full, in good health, and with reports of a life far better than that which Providence has given them at home. It is on the reports of these men that new contracts are now made—and it is by the experience thus gained that they who have served for one term of three years are induced to return for another term. . . .

According to "my lords", these Islanders will never willingly engage themselves to work away from home. As they have no work at home, my lords believe therefore that they will never engage themselves to work at all; or in other words that they are ineradicably savage, as is the poor Australian aboriginal—our friend Boney, for instance, who so willingly went to prison when he lost his pouch and could not get a bit of tobacco. But the very reverse is the fact as regards them. Civilization is within their reach—in spite of their island homes, their dusky colour, their various languages, and old cannibal propensities—because they will work, and are anxious to gather to themselves and to keep the fruits of their labour. They are unlike the Australian aboriginal, or even the African negro, who is indifferent to the fruits of work as long as he can enjoy the present moment; but they are like the Chinese and the Indian coolies, who know the comforts conferred and the power given by accumulated possessions, and who are therefore capable of receiving the blessings of civilization.

Work with fair wages has done infinitely more to civilize, and even to Christianize, the so-called savage races than has the energy of missionaries. Lessons in religion, even though they are accepted with gratitude and mastered with zeal, do not suffice to teach the practice of morality to men incapable of a desire of accumulating property by their own labour. The savage, who is inexorably savage, will sing psalms with almost an ecstasy of delight; but he will steal, and drink, and revel in his favourite vices almost as he sings them. He will not join in the psalm in any degree with the idea that the Power which he professes to praise should be obeyed. He does not put two and two together. He makes no attempt to see the reason of the thing. He never calculates, and therefore he will not work. But here is a race of men who do calculate, and who will work, and who by work may be civilized. The Islanders who are brought to Queensland all return, and not a man of them returns without taking with him lessons of civilization. On the planters' grounds in Queensland they learn each other's languages, they have to live as white men live—they have to cook, to sow, to dig, to plant and hoe canes, to clothe themselves and to be proud of their clothes—and they learn that continued work does produce accumulated property. These lessons they take back to the islands, and then they send their friends and return themselves, and so they are gradually being brought within the pale of civilization. But this is to be stopped, if the philanthropists be allowed to have their way, because there have been spread abroad stories that men have been kidnapped in the islands. "If not kidnapped for Queensland itself," say the philanthropists, "they have been kidnapped and taken to Tahiti, kidnapped and taken to Fiji. Let Queensland, even if she be pure herself, have nothing to do with a trade which may connect her, even though it may only be by idea, with the foul crime of man-stealing." Then they expatiate on the greed of merchants who want to make money out of the very bone and sinews of other men. To my intelligence, such as it is, there is no argument in all this. If good be done both to Queensland and to the islands by a system of emigration from the islands, it should not be stopped because evil is done by another system elsewhere. And as for that denunciation of the greed of merchants, it is worse than vain. To make money out of the bones and sinews of other men is the natural and serviceable desire of the employer of labour. I only wish that the English farmer could be constrained to treat his labourer, out of whose bones and sinews he makes money, with half the care that is used towards the happy Polynesian who is allowed to escape from the savage slavery of his island to the plenty and protected taskwork of a Queensland sugar plantation.

The Convicts of Port Arthur

In New South Wales with its enormous area, and in the absence of any sea barriers by which convicts could be hemmed in, the traveller does not at present hear much about convicts. They have wandered away whither they would. Now and then good-natured reference is made, in regard to some lady or gentleman, to the fact that her or his father was "lagged", and occasionally up in the bush a shepherd may be found who will own to the soft impeachment of having been lagged himself—though always for some offence which is supposed to have in it more of nobility than depravity. But in Tasmania the records are recent, fresh, and ever present. There is still felt the necessity of adhering to a social rule that no convict, whatever may have been his success, shall be received into society. "But if he should be a member of the Assembly?" I asked. Well, yes, my informant acknowledged, that there would be a difficulty. There are occasions on which a member of the Assembly may almost demand to be entertained —as a member of the House of Commons has, I imagine, almost a right to dine with the Speaker. It is not only that men and women in Tasmania do not choose to herd with convicts, but that they are on their guard lest it might be supposed that their own existence in the island might be traced back to the career of some criminal relative.

* * *

The interest of such an establishment as this of course lies very much in the personal demeanour, in the words, and appearance of the prisoners. A man who has been all his life fighting against law, who has been always controlled but never tamed by law, is interesting, though inconvenient—as is a tiger. There were some dozen or fifteen men, perhaps more, whom we found inhabiting separate cells, and who were actually imprisoned. These were the heroes of the place. There was an Irishman with one eye, named Doherty, who told us that for forty-two years he had never been a free man for an hour. He had been transported for mutiny when hardly more than a boy—for he had enlisted as a boy—and had since that time received nearly 3,000 lashes. In appearance he was a large man and still powerful—well to look at in spite of his eye, lost as he told us through the misery of prison life. But he said that he was broken at last. If they would only treat him kindly, he would be as a lamb. But within the last few weeks he had escaped with three others, and had been brought back almost starved to death. The record of his prison life was frightful. He had been always escaping, always rebelling, always fighting against authority—and always being flogged. There had been a whole life of torment such as this—forty-two years of it; and there he stood, speaking softly, arguing his case well, and pleading while the tears ran down his face for some kindness, for some mercy in his old age. "I have tried to escape—always to escape," he said, "as a bird does out of a cage. Is that unnatural?—is that a great crime?" The man's first offence, that of mutiny, is not one at which the mind revolts. I did feel for him, and when he spoke of himself as a caged bird, I should have liked to take him out into the world, and have given him a month of comfort. He would probably, however, have knocked my brains out on the first opportunity. I was assured that he was thoroughly bad, irredeemable, not to be reached by any kindness, a beast of prey, whose hand was against every honest man, and against whom it was necessary that every honest man should raise his hand. Yet he talked so gently and so well, and argued his own case with such winning words! He was writing in a book when we entered his cell, and was engaged on some speculation as to the tonnage of vessels. "Just scribbling, sir," he said, "to while away the hours."

There was another man, also an Irishman, named Ahern, whose appearance was as revolting as that of Doherty was prepossessing. He was there for an attempt to murder his wife, and had been repeatedly re-tried and re-convicted. He was making shoes when we saw him, and had latterly become a reformed character. But for years his life had been absolutely the life of a caged beast—only with incidents more bestial than those of any beast. His gaolers seemed to have no trust in his reformation. He, too, was a large powerful man, and he, too, will probably remain till he dies either in solitary confinement or under closest surveillance. In absolute infamy he was considered to be without a peer in the establishment. But he talked to us quite freely about his little accident with his wife.

There was another remarkable man in one of the solitary cells whose latter crime had been that of bringing abominable and false accusations against fellow-prisoners. He talked for a while with us on the ordinary topics of the day not disagreeably, expressing opinions somewhat averse to lonely existence, and not altogether in favour of the partiality of those who attended upon him. But he gave us to understand that though he was quite willing to answer questions in a pleasant, friendly way, it was his intention before we left him to make a speech. It was not every day that he had such an audience as a prime minister and an attorney-general—not to speak of a solicitor-general from another colony who was with us also, or of the commandant or of myself. He made his speech—and I must here declare that all the prisoners were allowed to make speeches if they pleased. He made his speech—hitching up his parcel-yellow trousers with his left hand as he threw out his right with emphatic gesture. I have longed for such ease and such fluency when, on occasions, I have been called upon to deliver myself of words upon my legs. It was his object to show that the effort of his life had been to improve the morals of the establishment, and that the commandant had repressed him, actuated solely by a delight in wickedness. And as he made his charge he pointed to the commandant with denouncing fingers, and we all listened with the gravest attention. I was wondering whether he thought that he made any impression. I forget that man's name and his crime, but he ought to have been a republican at home, and should he ever get out from Port Arthur might still do well to stand for a borough on anti-monarchal interests.

But of all the men the most singular in his fate was another Irishman, one Barron, who lived in a little island all alone; and of all the modes of life into which such a man might fall, surely his was the most wonderful. To the extent of the island he was no prisoner at all, but might wander whither he liked, might go to bed when he pleased, and get up when he pleased, might bathe and catch fish or cultivate his little flower-garden—and was in very truth monarch of all he surveyed. Twice a week his rations were brought to him, and in his disposal of them no one interfered with him. But he surveyed nothing but graves. All who died at Port Arthur, whether convicts or free, are buried there, and he has the task of burying them. He digs his graves, not fitfully and by hurried task-work, but with thoughtful precision—having one always made for a Roman Catholic, and one for a Protestant inmate. In this regularity he was indeed acting against orders—as there was some prejudice against these ready-made graves, but he went on with his work, and was too valuable in his vocation to incur serious interference. We talked with him for half an hour, and found him to be a sober, thoughtful, suspicious man, quite alive to the material inconveniences of his position, but not in the least afflicted by ghostly fear or sensational tremors. He smiled when we asked whether the graves awed him—but he shook his head when it was suggested to him that he might grow a few cabbages for his own use. He could eat nothing that grew from such soil. The flowers were very well, but a garden among graves was no garden for vegetables. He had been there for ten years, digging all the graves in absolute solitude without being ill for a day. I asked him whether he was happy. No, he was not happy. He wanted to get away and work his passage to America, and begin life afresh, though he was sixty years old. He preferred digging graves and solitude in the island, to the ordinary life of Port Arthur; he desired to remain in the island as long as he was a convict; but he was of opinion that ten years of such work ought to have earned him his freedom. Why he was retained I forget. If I remember rightly, there had been no charge against him during the ten years. "You have no troubles here," I said. "I have great troubles," he replied, "when I walk about thinking of my sins." There was no hypocrisy about him, nor did he in any way cringe to us. On the contrary, he was quiet, unobtrusive, and moody. There he is still, living among the graves—still dreaming of some future career in life when at last they who have power over him shall let him go.

Of the able-bodied men the greatest number are at work about the farm, or on the land, or cutting timber, and seem to be subject to no closer surveillance than are ordinary labourers. There is nothing to prevent their escape—except the fact that they must starve in the bush if they do escape. There is plenty of room for them to starve in the bush even on Tasman's peninsula. Then when they have starved till they can starve no longer, they go back to the damnable torment of a solitary cell. None but spirits so indomitable as that of the man Doherty will dare to repeat the agonies of escape above once or twice.

There was a man named Fisher dying in the hospital, who had been one of those who had lately escaped with Doherty, and had, indeed arranged the enterprise, and had gotten together the materials to form a canoe to carry them off. Before they started he had been possessed of £10, which—so the officers said—he had slowly amassed by selling wine and spirits which he had collected in some skin round his body, such wine and spirits having been administered to him by the doctor's orders, and having been received into the outer skin instead of taken to the comfort of the inner man. This, it was supposed, he had sold to the constables and warders, and had so realized £10. Now he was dying—and looked, indeed, as he lay on his bed, livid, with his eyes protruding from his head, as though he could not live another day. But it was known that he still had three of the ten sovereigns about him. "Why not take them away?" I asked. "They are in his mouth, and he would swallow them if he were touched." Think of the man living—dying—with three sovereigns in his mouth, procured in such a way, for such a purpose, over so long a term of years—for the man must have been long an invalid to have been able to sell for £10 the wine which he ought to have drunk! What a picture of life—what a picture of death—the man clinging to his remnant of useless wealth in such a fashion as that!

Among other works the convicts were making a railway—carrying it farther and farther into the bush in order that timber and firewood might be brought down. Here, as on all such works, there was a leading spirit—the clever man, who understood things and made things fit; who could measure beams, and make the rough material obey his hand by the exercise of his intellect. He too was a convict, named Dunn. I doubt whether I heard his antecedents, but he was spoken of with all that praise which is usually awarded to the clever man of an establishment in the presence of strange visitors. Perhaps Dunn may yet live to make his fortune on some public works.

In the evening and far on into the night the premier was engaged in listening to the complaints of convicts. Any man who had anything to say was allowed to say it into the ears of the first minister of the Crown—but all of course said uselessly. The complaints of prisoners against their gaolers can hardly be efficacious. So our visit to Port Arthur came to an end, and we went back on the next day to Hobart Town.

The establishment itself has the appearance of a large, well-built, clean village, with various factories, breweries, and the like. There is the church, as I have said, and there are houses enough, both for gentle and simple, to take away the appearance of a prison. The lunatic asylum and that for paupers have no appearance of prisons. Indeed the penitentiary itself, where the working convicts sleep and live, and have their library and their plays and their baths, is not prison-like. There is a long street, with various little nooks and corners, as are to be found in all villages—and in one of them the cottage in which Smith O'Brien lived as a convict. The place is alive, and the eye soon becomes used to the strange convict garments, consisting of jackets and trousers, of which one side is yellow and the other brown. If it were to be continued, I should be tempted to speak loudly in praise of the management of the establishment. But it is doomed to go, and, as such is the case, one is disposed to doubt the use of increased expenditure, of new farm implements, of a lengthened railway, of fresh enterprises, and of that extended energy which would be so desirable if the system were to be continued. . . .

All those whom I questioned on the subject in Tasmania agreed that Port Arthur must be abandoned in a few years, and that then the remaining convicts must be removed to the neighbourhood of Hobart Town. If this be done there can hardly, I think, be any other fate for the buildings than that they shall stand till they fall. They will fall into the dust, and men will make unfrequent excursions to the strange ruins.

* * *

Whether more of good or more of evil has befallen Australia generally from its convicts, is a question which will not be decided to the satisfaction of the English world at large for many a year to come—though the day for a general decision will come. But this may be said of the system with certain truth—as it may of all human institutions—that now, when the sweets of it have been used and are no longer sweet, the advantages are forgotten and the evils borne in mind. The Bill Sikes physiognomy of a large proportion of the population is to be seen daily throughout Western Australia. And the roads and buildings are also to be seen. But men remember whence Bill Sikes came, and why; but they forget how they got the roads and buildings.

7 MOUNTAIN AND RIVER

I have said that the scenery of the bush is monotonous. It is the complaint that has been made generally of all Australian landscape—so generally as to have reached England, and to constitute one of the few facts that are supposed to be known about the country. The "everlasting gum-tree" has become proverbial. Consequently no one visits Australia to see its scenery, and comparatively few of those who go there in pursuit of business, or to see men and women, make a search after the beauties of nature a part of their programme. The same feeling prevails with permanent settlers and with natives. It is taken for granted that Australia is ugly, and that the touring in quest of the picturesque, which forms so great a part of the delight of an Englishman's holiday, would be altogether time wasted and money misapplied if attempted at the Antipodes. Nevertheless, there is grand scenery in, I believe, all the Australian colonies. It is certainly to be found in Queensland and Victoria. Tasmania is one of the prettiest countries I ever visited. And in New South Wales I came across wonders almost as magnificent and charms as lovely as any that I have seen in Europe. As yet the localities are unknown, as yet the means of communication are unfrequent and uncertain, as yet popular taste has not settled herself in the direction of scenery, directing people to go here or to go there—and by her potency providing the means of encouraging them, feeding them, and amusing them. But the time will come in which Australian men and women will find that they need not go to Europe to delight themselves with mountains and rivers.

Of the extreme beauty of Sydney Harbour I have already spoken, and will only say of it further that its extent is so great as to require days for its examination. It is not a sheet of water which can be seen from one spot, and then be ticked off from the list of sights as a thing completed, and numbered among the lions which have been killed. That lion will demand four or five days before it can be killed to satisfaction, and will then bear to be rekilled by those who really take delight in natural loveliness.

Govat's Leap

The railway from Sydney to Bathurst passes through the Blue Mountains, which form a portion of the same dividing range. They presented a cruel, awful barrier to the early settlers, and for a long time debarred them from the land beyond, which they hoped to find flowing with all the requisites for milk and honey. The eastern strip, where Sydney is built and Parramatta, was singularly barren, though a little farther to the north and west there were river valleys, the soil of which was as singularly rich. It was felt by all the settlers that the Blue Mountains hemmed them in, making, as it were, a prison for them on the shores of Port Jackson. With infinite suffering and indefatigable energy, a way was at last found through the dark defiles of the hills, and the colonists made their way down to those plains, which are now called the Plains of Bathurst. Now a railway passes up and down through the wildest parts of the mountains, crossing their very summit, and passengers go from Sydney to Bathurst, thinking nothing of the struggles of their forefathers—and thinking very little of the wonders around them.

Close to the highest part of the range, with a fall to it so slight as to be hardly more than perceptible, and at a distance of about two miles from the railway, there is a ravine called Govat's Leap. Mr. Govat was, I believe, simply a government surveyor, who never made any leap into the place at all. Had he done so, it would certainly has been effectual for putting an end to his earthly sorrows. I had hoped, when I heard the name, to find that some interesting but murderous bushranger had on that spot baffled his pursuers and braved eternity—but I was informed that the government surveyor had visited the spot, had named it, and had gone home again. No one seeing it could fail to expect better things from such a spot and such a name.

It consists of a ravine probably more than a mile wide. I had no means of ascertaining the distances or heights of the place, but the whole was on so gigantic a scale as to deceive the eye greatly at the first sight. The only approach to it from the railway leads the visitor to the head of the ravine, at which he is stopped by a precipitous wall of rock, which runs round, in various huge curves, till on each side it loses itself in the distance. As you stand there, looking down, you see a world below you—a valley, but certainly not a happy valley, dark, awful, and inaccessible. Nowhere round these curves and lines of the rock can the eye find a spot at which it would be possible to descend. It is as though the ocean were below, and you were standing on the edge of a lofty cliff; but in lieu of the ocean there is this black valley, densely filled with forest timber, filled so densely that you see nothing but the continuous tops of the black foliage, which, though the wind is blowing hard above, never seem to move. In looking down from the cliffs upon the sea, one is conscious that the foot of the rocks may be reached. A boat, at any rate, will place you there, if the weather be fair. But here the mind becomes aware of no mode of entering the abyss. On reaching the edge it seems as though you had come upon a spot of earth which defied you to touch it, and which forbade the possibility of escape should you succeed in doing so. The idea is common to us when we look up at snowy peaks—and is not the less common because we know that men have learned the way to climb them. But to look down on a place which cannot be reached—into a valley full of trees, through which a stream runs, a green, dark, crowded valley—and to feel that you are debarred from reaching it by a sheer descent of four or five hundred feet of cliff all round, is uncommon. I would say double that descent only that I do not quite believe in their entirety some accounts of the place that I have heard. I never saw before so vast a gaping hole on the earth's surface.

At about half a mile to the right, as you reach the edge, a stream of water very much like the Staubach, near Lauterbrunner, in Switzerland, falls precipitously over the rock. I was there in winter, after rain, and there was water in plenty. I heard different altitudes named for the fall, ranging up to very high figures indeed. I believe it to be about 900 feet. From the spot whence it is seen it appears that the water is broken nowhere by striking against the rocks, and that therefore the descent is perpendicular; but this, no doubt, is a fallacy of the eye, caused by the distance. As we lay on the rock gazing at it, the wind would every now and then catch the long silver thread and sweep it away into the bend of the curve, so that it would disappear from sight. The forest trees above were wild with the wind, but the interminable thickets below were never stirred. I have said that we could not descend. There was not a spot at which we could think of making the attempt; but there was an easy track down to a jutting rock, about 200 feet below the top, and this we found to be the proper spot from whence to look down upon the awful grandeur of the scene below us. . . .

The nearest station, or stopping place, is Blackheath, at which the trains are pulled up if there be passengers. But there is no inn at this place. We, the young squatter of whom I spoke and myself—left the train at Mount Victoria, a station four miles distant from Blackheath, where we found very good accommodation at the house of one Mrs. Perry, whom we knocked up at two o'clock in the morning, and who took our somewhat noisy intrusion in perfect good humour. I would advise any stranger who finds himself at Sydney to make a visit to Govat's Leap, and to stop at the inn at Mount Victoria when doing so.

Grander Than the Rhine

Govat's Leap astonished me very much—but not, I think, so much as the scenery of the Hawkesbury River. A great portion of this is within forty miles of the town of Sydney, and might be as easily reached and much more quickly and cheaply seen than the Rhine—if only people knew of it, so that an hotel or two might be built on its banks, and a steamer built to ply upon it. A trip of two days from Sydney, at a cost of 30s. a head, might make the river known to every pleasure-seeker in Sydney—and if the expedition were customary, the Hawkesbury would soon be as much to Sydney as the mouth of the Clyde and the Kyles of Bute are to Glasgow. And yet who has heard of the Hawkesbury? As it is altogether unknown in Sydney, it is hardly surprising that the river should not have been much talked about in England. Had it been known in Sydney, it would have been talked about in England. I must own that when I was invited to join a party to visit the scenery of the river, I myself had never heard of the Hawkesbury, except as one of the first named rivers on the Australian continent —so called many years ago when Lord Liverpool was young.

The party which I was kindly invited to join was a very august party, consisting of nearly all the cabinet ministers, and a very considerable minority of the House of Assembly. The premier was at the head of it, and no man fitter for such an occasion ever held absolute dominion over hampers. It was by no means a partisan party; for I observed on my return to Sydney six months afterwards, when that premier had, alas, succumbed to the fate of premiers, and another head of the government reigned in his stead, that two of the most lively of our politicians on the Hawkesbury trip were sitting on the treasury bench. And we had been all so friendly then! I must confess that when I saw those two gentlemen on that bench, and saw that former premier opposite, turned out into the cold, partly, no doubt, by their efforts, I could not but say to myself that there could be ingratitude in New South Wales as deep as among the older nations of the earth.

We went by railway to the little town of Windsor, to which a branch line runs from the Sydney and Bathurst line—a quaint little place, inhabited by old settlers who came to this district as being singularly fertile. Very fertile it is; no land in the Australian colonies is perhaps more so; hardly any soil in any country is perhaps more so. But for this great gift it has to pay a proportionate penalty. Every now and then, perhaps once in six or seven years, it is so absolutely flooded by the Hawkesbury and its tributaries, that the farmers are forced to fly for their lives. And there have been floods so sudden and so high that all the farmers have not been able to fly with their lives. Windsor is built upon the Hawkesbury, here so called; but up above this it has another name and is called the Nepēān;—for it is the fashion in New South Wales to divide what with us at home would be the last syllable. From Windsor we went five miles down the river in open boats, and there found a steamer waiting for us. I must confess that during the first part of our journey I was disposed to think that I had been enticed away by false representations. Immediately below Windsor the river is not beautiful. It passes through a rich country, which gradually becomes narrower as the hills are approached; but for an hour or two the fertility of the land and the specialities, such as they might be, of its productiveness were the chief attractions. But gradually as we reached the bluffs and high banks of the lower reaches, the scene was changed, and as the afternoon wore itself away we steamed down among river scenery as lovely as any which I ever beheld.

There can, I think, be no doubt that among rivers the Rhine has the highest character for sustained beauty. There may be special points on other streams which have endeared themselves to the world—such especially as the Falls of Niagara, such as the Inn at Innspruck, or the Rhone at Geneva, or the Upper Lake at Killarney, which is, in truth, a river. But for continued scenery the Rhine stands first. There is a river, or rather a portion of a river, known to very few tourists, which I think beats the Rhine. This is the Upper Mississippi, for about 150 miles below St. Paul. It is not my business here to describe the Mississippi—but I mention it with the object of saying that in my opinion the Hawkesbury beats the Mississippi. I should not make the contrast unless there were many features in the two which are similar. At all of them the beauty consists in the breaking of the land on the very margin of the river, and is not carried far back into the interior. At all of them the banks rise suddenly, sometimes covered with timber and sometimes bald, sometimes sloping and sometimes precipitous, but at all of them the banks are broken here and there into lateral valleys, which give to the imagination the idea that the glory of the scene is far spread, and would repay pursuit. Unless it can convey this vague feeling of distant, unapproachable, and almost mysterious delight, scenery loses half its charm. On the Rhine, on the Mississippi, and on the Hawkesbury alike, there is created an idea that if the traveller would only leave the boat and wander inland, he would be repaid by the revelation of marvellous beauties of Nature—beauties which have perhaps never yet met the eyes of man. The Rhine has its castles and its islands—and it has, too, in its favour the bright colour of its waters. The Upper Mississippi has no castles, nor are its waters bright; but it has islands, and innumerable bluffs and headlands and varied valleys, and park-like timber, and its own fast-running rush of waters, which are to me more than compensation for the castles and the colour. The Hawkesbury has neither castles nor islands, nor has it bright clear water like the Rhine. But the headlands are higher and the bluffs are bolder, and the turns and manœuvres of the course which the waters have made for themselves are grander, and to me more enchanting, than those of either the European or American river.

It took us two days to descend the Hawkesbury to Broken Bay, and during the night our steamer lay at a bend in the river called Wiseman's Ferry, where there is a large dilapidated and unused church, showing how soon ruins may be instituted in a new country. Along the banks, at intervals from each other of a few miles, whenever a bit of alluvial soil gave an opportunity for cultivation, settlers had placed themselves, and lived by growing maize, potatoes, and fruit. These people, or their fathers, were among the earliest colonists of New South Wales, as the banks of the Hawkesbury had been soon reached. But civilization had passed by them and gone beyond them, and they were left now much in the condition in which their fathers were sixty or seventy years ago. A great portion of the banks are not approached by any road, and are accessible only by water. Small luggers from Sydney ply up and down the stream, taking the produce of the settlers to market, and bringing them back flour and tea in return. There can be but little intercourse even between families at ten miles' distance from each other, as a river is after all, but a poor road for the purposes of familiar intercourse. Life there must be very solitary and cheerless—but at the same time independent and plentiful. We saw children about, amidst the garden patches, but I fear that they were often out of reach of any school.

The lower part of the river, that between Wiseman's Ferry and Pitt Water—which is a large inlet of the sea, running southward from Broken Bay—is very much finer than the upper reaches. There are various spots, especially at Mangora Creek, Berowa Creek, and Mullet Creek, at which the expanse of water assumes the appearance of a lake, and from which the stream escapes under banks almost perpendicular, and, as we calculated, from four to six hundred feet high. At Broken Bay, after having steamed up to the head of Pitt Water, we got out into the sea, and within an hour and a half were in Sydney Harbour.

Up along the river banks there were numberless sites fit for private houses or for hotels—all of which might be reached within a few hours from Sydney. We saw but one house of any pretence, which, I was told, was occasionally inhabited by a gentleman's family. But residence here, except to a cockatoo farmer, or to a hermit, is at present impossible. Though the place be no more than forty miles from Sydney, it is altogether beyond reach—as many parts of the highlands of Scotland were some few years ago. In another space of a few years there will probably be daily means of getting to the Hawkesbury; and there will be villas dotted on its banks, and hotels of all descriptions for the accommodation of Australian tourists.

As of Australian scenery, so also is it generally said of Australian country houses, that they are without the charms and prettiness which are thought so much of at home by our squires and their wives and families. I do not think that I had many preconceived opinions as to country life in the colonies—but I certainly did think that the surroundings of it would be ugly. It is a matter of course that finished beauty at a homestead cannot be achieved to order by any given time. The surroundings of a house want years for the full creation of their charms. In England many an old ruined house is lovely, but who has ever succeeded in making a new country mansion pleasing to the eye? On this account landscape beauty of the domestic kind must be less frequent in a new than in an old country, and is, of course, less frequent in Australia than in Europe. But, nevertheless, it is to be found—and I saw the preparations for it frequent in many of the colonies.

Chudleigh Caves

I had gone to Deloraine in company with the governor and others on purpose to visit the Chudleigh caves.

The Chudleigh caves are one of the wonders of Tasmania—and, indeed, they are very wonderful. We went there in true gubernatorial style, with four horses—for it must be understood that throughout the colonies, when it is known that the governor is coming, things are done as they should be. Ours was a private little party, consisting of four, but we had four horses, and went to the caves magnificently. We had a very pleasant day, more than ordinarily so; but the Chudleigh caves should not be visited by any one lightly, and I think I may take upon myself to say that they should not be visited by ladies at all. On this occasion we were all males.

With our four horses we were driven some sixteen miles, till at last we were in the middle of thick bush without any vestige of a road. The road had become less like a road by degrees, and the fields less like fields. Where timber had been cleared away, wholly or in part, very heavy crops of oats were growing. The farmers are afraid to trust themselves to wheat because of the rust, and can hardly live by growing oats, so great is the cost both of labour and carriage, and so low the price of the grain. On our journey an old man attached himself to us, who seemed to have the caves under his peculiar care, and who assured us that he had shown all the governors over them. He came out upon us from a public-house, of which he was the proprietor, and promising us that we should have the benefit of his services, followed us on a wonderful rat-tailed mare, with which he jumped over every obstruction along the road, and made himself very busy, assuring the governor that no governor could see the caves aright without him, and taking command of the whole party with that air of authority which always carries success with it. I think his name was Pickett. We soon found that we were creatures in Mr. Pickett's hand.

We descended from the carriage, Mr. Pickett so ordering, but the order was not given till it was impossible for any carriage to proceed farther. We then walked about a mile through the scrub, descending at last into a hole which was the mouth of the cave. Stalactite caves are not uncommon in the world. Those at Cheddar in Somersetshire are very well known, and are very pretty—much prettier than the caves in Tasmania, as the stones drop into rarer shapes and are brighter and more picturesque. But the caves at Cheddar are nothing to the Chudleigh caves in bigness, blackness, water, dirt, and the enforced necessity of crawling, creeping, wading, and knocking one's head about at every turn. Mr. Pickett lighted the candles, told us that we should have to walk about five miles underground, gave us to understand that the water would never be more than up to our middles, that one could do it all in four hours, and that we were about to grope our way through the greatest wonder of the world. Then he led the way gallantly, splashing down into the mud, and inviting his Excellency to take heart and fear nothing. His Excellency took heart and went on. Whether he feared anything, I cannot say. I did—when I had broken my head for the third time, and especially when I had crawled through a crevice in which I nearly stuck, and as to which I felt almost certain that I should never be able to force my way back again. We were then more than a mile from the aperture, and innumerable black rivers, little Styxes, dark deceitful Acherons, cold as death, ran between us and the upper air. Pickett was instant with us to go on to the end. We had not seen half the wonders of the place—which by-the-bye were invisible by reason of the outer darkness. But we were cold to the marrow of our bones, wet through, covered with mud, and assured that, if we did go on, the journey must be made partly on our hands or knees, and partly after the fashion of serpents. At last we rebelled and insisted on being allowed to return. So we waded our way back again. I think that I will never visit another land cave. We had, however, brought fresh clothes. And when we had made a forest toilet, and demolished our chickens and sherry, we were able to smoke the pipe of peace in happiness and contentment under Mr. Pickett's auspices. Mr. Pickett told us, as we took our leave of him, that he should not enter the caves again till another governor should come to see them.

8 THE PASSION FOR SPORT

The English passion for the amusements which are technically called "Sports" is as strong in these colonies as it is at home. Why the taste should have transported itself to Australia and not to the United States I am not prepared to explain—but I think any one who has observed the two countries will acknowledge that it is so. Trotting matches and yacht-racing are no doubt in vogue in the States, and there are men, few in number, who take kindly to shooting—especially they who live near the Chesapeake and have canvas-back ducks within their reach. There is a set of betting-men at New York, who probably are beaten by none in the ferocity of their gambling. But "sport" is not a national necessity with the Americans, whereas with the Australians it is almost as much so as at home. Cricket, athletics, rowing matches, shooting, hunting, flat-racing, and steeplechasing are dear to them. There is hardly a town to be called a town which has not its racecourse, and there are many racecourses where there are no towns. As I was never either a cricketer nor an athlete, and know nothing of shooting or of racing, I am not qualified to describe the fashion in which our Australian cousins fulfil their ambition in these respects, but I can say that they are ambitious and are successful. In Queensland I saw kangaroos, wallabies, and iguanas shot down with precision. In Gipps Land I was witness to a great slaughter of wild ducks and black swans. At Hobart Town, in Tasmania, there came off while I was in the neighbourhood a regatta, for not being present at which I was much abused. And I know that I was wrong, for the scene must have been very lovely. No spot could be better arranged for boat-racing than the mouth of the Derwent, with the open public park rising high and close above the water. I was inspecting a lunatic asylum at the time, and think that the regatta would have been more amusing. Horse-racing I hate. As the horses run, I never can distinguish the colours; I generally lose sundry small bets; and I don't like champagne. But I did go to the Launceston races in Tasmania, in reference to which I can only remark that the number of betting-men who came over from Melbourne to make money out of the small performances on that occasion surprised me very much. When the meeting was over I went back to Melbourne with a ship-load of them, and was lost in speculation how so many carrion birds could live on so small an amount of prey. As to the professional activity of the confraternity, the diligence with which they worked at their trade, the unremitting attention which they paid to the smallest chances, I had no doubt. They all looked as though they would eat each other on board the boat, and I thought that some such unsatisfactory meals were made. Though the night was very cold I slept on the deck, as the banquet was going on below. The songs of triumph and the wailings of despair at such festivals do not make pleasant music for an outsider.

I went also to see some hurdle-racing and steeplechasing at the Melbourne racecourse—partly because I had been told that the course itself was especially worth seeing, and partly as having been invited to join a pleasant party. It had been impressed upon me as a duty that I should see at least one day's racing at Melbourne in order that I might report on the aspect of the racecourse, the skill of the riders, and especially on the manners of the people. The course itself is something under two miles round. The courses run can, here as elsewhere, be arranged to any distance. The races I saw were described as being about three and two miles, and were all leap-races. I can only say of the fences prepared that I never before saw any which appeared to me so dangerous. They consisted chiefly of timber built up so stiffly that no horse and rider could break them, and were about four feet eight inches high. There was also a wall or two in the distant part of the course—but I regard walls as very much less dangerous to men and horses than timber. The riding appeared to me bold to a fault, men being utterly reckless in riding beaten horses at barriers of built-up timber. The fashion and traditions of the place require that men shall so ride, and they certainly keep up the fashion and traditions. Consequently, on the occasion to which I allude there were almost innumerable falls. I think seven men and horses were down in one race, and four in another. I heard afterwards that the sports of the day were considered to have gone off with very harmless success. One jockey was a good deal crushed, and another had his collar-bone broken. Why half-a-dozen were not killed I cannot explain. Some of the horses jumped with admirable precision, taking just all the labour that was necessary and no more; but, as I afterwards learned, these horses will jump almost any amount of timber, but know nothing of fences, which are less dangerous, but more complicated and requiring greater skill. From the stewards' stand, and from the top of the great stand—and indeed from the seats below—every part of the course can be seen, so that with a good field-glass the working of any horse or any jockey may be watched throughout the whole race.

But perhaps the most remarkable feature of the performance was the demeanour of the people. From the beginning to the end of the day, I saw no one drunk; I heard no word that could shock any lady; I found no one rough, uncourteous, or displeasing. There was no thimble-rigging and no throwing of sticks. All the world was decent and decently dressed. Within a certain enclosure—if it was enclosed—ladies walked about with gentlemen; and outside of it, the world amused itself with orderly propriety. The meeting was not by any means the largest of the year, but I was assured by those who were qualified to give an opinion—among others by the Governor of the colony—that the conduct of the crowd was the same even when the crowd was the greatest. It should be understood at home that the people of these colonies are almost invariably decent in their behaviour when gathered together, decent in their dress, and decent in their language. There certainly was no reason why ladies should not be present at the races I saw—unless ladies dislike to see jockeys falling over high railings.

There was indeed a betting-ring, in which the usual applications were being made to some outside and invisible world to accept lavish offers of complicated bets. Men were walking about making unintelligible appeals apparently to each other—which nobody ever seemed to accept. I am bound to say that the Melbourne ring looked to be as villainous as any other ring that I ever saw. The men wore the same objectionable clothing, were conspicuous in the same manner for indescribably abominable hats, and talked in that tone which to ordinary ears seems to be in itself evidence of rascality sufficient to hang a man. There were present, perhaps, two or three dozen of them ready to pick out any man's eyes; but I could not discern the prey. There is prey no doubt, as the profession thrives and wears jewellery. But the betting-ring on the Melbourne racecourse will hurt no one who does not expressly seek its precincts.

On the following day there was a great hunt breakfast—or luncheon—and the opening meet of the season with the Melbourne staghounds. Of other sports I practically know nothing. In regard to hunting I have for many years been striving to do something. So much was known of me by certain kind friends, and I was therefore invited to the entertainment and provided with a horse—as to which I was assured that though he was small he was up to any weight, could go for ever and jump anything. The country would be very rough—so much was acknowledged—and the fences very big; but it was suggested to me that if I would only drink enough sherry I might see a good deal of the run. I thought of my weight—which is considerable; of my eyesight—which is imperfect; of my inexperience in regard to timber fences four feet six inches high—which up to that moment was complete; I thought also that my informant in respect of the little horse, though indubitably veracious in intention, might probably be mistaken in his information, never having ridden the horse himself. Wishing to return once more to England so that I might publish my book, I resolved that discretion would be on this occasion the better part of valour, and that I would save my neck at the expense of the ill-opinion of the Melbourne hunting-field.

Such a hunt-banquet I never saw before. The spot was some eight or ten miles from Melbourne, close up on the sea-shore, and with a railway-station within a quarter of a mile. It was a magnificent day for a picnic, with a bright sun and a cool air, so that the temptations to come, over and beyond that of hunting, were great. About two hundred men were assembled in a tent pitched behind the house of the master of the festival, of whom perhaps a quarter were dressed in scarlet. Nothing could have been done better, or in better taste. There was no speaking, no drinking so to be called, but a violent clatter of knives and forks for about half-an-hour. At about two we were out on a common smoking our cigars in front of the house, and remained there talking to the ladies in carriages till nearly three, when we started. I found the horse provided for me to be a stout, easily-ridden, well-bitted cob; but when I remembered what posts and rails were in this country, I certainly thought that he was very small. No doubt discretion would be the better part of valour! With such a crowd of horses as I saw around me, there would probably be many discreet besides myself, so that I might attain decent obscurity amidst a multitude. I had not bedizened myself in a scarlet coat.

We were upon a heath, and I calculated that there were present about 250 horsemen. There was a fair sprinkling of ladies, and I was requested to observe one or two of them, as they would assuredly ride well. There is often a little mystery about hunting—especially in the early part of the day—as all men know who ride to hounds at home. It is not good that everybody should be told what covert is to be drawn first; and even with stag-hounds the officials of the pack will not always answer with full veracity every question put to them by every stranger. On this occasion there seemed to be considerable mystery. No one seemed to know where we were going to begin, and there was a doubt as to the quarry to be chased. I had been told that we were to hunt a dingo, or wild dog; and there was evidently a general opinion that turning down a dingo—shaking him I suppose out of a bag—was good and genuine sport. We do not like bagged foxes at home—but I fancy that they are unpopular chiefly because they will never run. If a dingo will run, I do not see why he should not be turned down as well as a deer out of a cart. But on this occasion I heard whispers about—a drag. The asseverations about the dingo were, however, louder than the whispers about a drag, and I went on, believing that the hounds would be put upon the trail of the animal. We rode for some three or four miles over heath-land, nobody around me seeming to be in the least aware when the thing would commence. The huntsman was crabbed and uncommunicative. The master was soft as satin, but as impregnable as plate armour. I asked no questions myself, knowing that time will unravel most things; but I heard questions asked, the answers to which gave no information whatever. At last the hounds began to stir among the high heather, and were hunting something. I cared little what it was, if only there might be no posts and rails in that country. I like to go, but I don't like to break my neck; and between the two I was uncomfortable. The last fences I had seen were all wire, and I was sure that a drag would not be laid among them. But we had got clear of wire fences—wire all through from top to bottom—before we began. We seemed to be on an open heath, riding round a swamp, without an obstacle in sight. As long as that lasted I could go as well as the best.

But it did not last. In some three minutes, having ridden about half a mile, I found myself approaching such an obstacle as in England would stop a whole field. It was not only the height but the obduracy of the wooden barrier—which seemed as though it were built against ever-rushing herds of wild bulls. At home we are not used to such fences, and therefore they are terrible to us. At a four foot and a half wall, a man with a good heart and a good horse will ride; and the animal, if he knows what he is about, will strike it, sometimes with fore as well as hind feet, and come down without any great exertion. But the post and rail in Australia should be taken with a clear flying leap. There are two alternatives if this be not done. If the horse and man be heavy enough and the pace good enough, the top bar may be broken. It is generally about eight inches deep and four thick, is quite rough, and apparently new—but, as on this occasion I saw repeatedly, it may be broken; and when broken the horse and rider go through unscathed, carried by their own impetus, as a candle may be fired through a deal board. The other chance is to fall, which event seemed to occur more often even than the smashing of the rail. Now I was especially warned that if I rode slowly at these fences, and fell, my horse would certainly fall atop of me; whereas if I went fast I should assuredly be launched so far ahead that there would be room for my horse between me and the fence which had upset me. It was not a nice prospect for a man riding something over sixteen stone!

But now had come the moment in which I must make up my mind. Half-a-dozen men were over the rail. Half-a-dozen baulked it. Two fell, escaping their own horses by judicious impetus. One gentleman got his horse half over, the forequarters being on one side, and the hind on the other, so the animal was hung up. A lady rode at it with spirit, but checked her horse with the curb, and he, rearing back, fell on her. Another lady took it in gallant style. Of those before me no one seemed to flinch it. For a moment it seemed as though the honour of all the hunting fields in England were entrusted to my keeping, and I determined to dare greatly, let the penalty be what it might. With firm hands and legs, but with heart very low down, I crammed the little brute at the mountain of woodwork. As I did so I knew that he could not carry me over. Luckily he knew as much about it as I did, and made not the slightest attempt to rise with me. I don't know that I ever felt so fond of a horse before.

At that moment, an interesting individual, coming like a cannon ball, crashed the top bar beside me, and I, finding that the lady was comfortably arranging her back hair with plenty of assistance, rode gallantly over the second bar. For the next half-hour I took care always to go over second bars, waiting patiently till the top bar was broken. I had found my level, and had resolved to keep it. On one occasion I thought that a top bar never would be broken—and the cessation was unpleasant, as successful horsemen disappeared one after another. But I perceived there was a regular company of second-bar men, so that as long as I could get over a rail three feet high I need not fear that I should be left alone. And hitherto the pace had not been quick enough to throw the second-bar men out of the hunt. But soon there came a real misfortune. There was a fence with only one bar—with only one apparent obstacle. I am blind as well as heavy, and I did not see the treacherous wire beneath. A heavy philanthropist, just before me, smashed the one, and I rode on at what I thought to be a free course. My little horse, seeing no more than I did, rushed upon the wire, and the two of us were rolled over in ignominious dismay. The horse was quicker on his feet than I was, and liking the sport, joined it at once single-handed; while I was left alone and disconsolate. Men and horses—even the sound of men and horses—disappeared from me, and I found myself in solitude in a forest of gum-trees.

I was certain that we had been running a drag all the morning. As I wandered about I felt the ignominy of the whole thing. If a man does ride to a drag he should at any rate ride well, and not lose his horse and be alone after the first half hour. And in that wild country I might be wandering about for a week without seeing anything but a cockatoo or an Australian magpie. There does, however, always come some relief in these miseries. I first encountered another horseless man, then a second companion in misery, and at last a groom with my own little nag. As for the run, that, as regarded me, was of course over; but I had legs besides my own to take me back twelve miles to the place at which I was stopping.

As far as I could learn they ran a drag on that occasion for about seven miles, and then came upon a turned-down dingo. This animal they took alive after two miles. The sporting reader will perceive from this that an appearance was maintained of finding game, and hunting the game to the end. The Melbourne hounds do also hunt deer—sometimes turning down a deer from a cart as we do at home, and sometimes finding a wild deer. The sport, as I saw it in the neighbourhood of Melbourne, was as I have described.

But previously to this I had hunted kangaroos in Queensland and New South Wales, and I will say a word or two as to that sport. I confess that in the absence of fox-hunting I enjoyed it very much. Four of us went out in Queensland with four kangaroo-dogs amidst timber that was not thick, and found game in plenty. The kangaroo-dog—having that special name throughout the colonies quite as assuredly as any kind of hound has his own name in England—is a large rough greyhound that hunts both by sight and by nose. The difficulty consists in getting the dogs to settle upon any one head of game—and to settle upon the one kangaroo which the sportsman may select. And, indeed, there is the further difficulty of getting the men who are out to join in the same choice. The hounds scatter and the men scatter, and it will often happen that a man is attempting to ride down a kangaroo without a hound, and a hound making the same attempt without a rider. We found kangaroos in very large mobs—on one occasion I should think some hundreds of them together. On such occasions a great deal of cross riding takes place before any united action can be effected. If possible a very large, or "old man" kangaroo should be cut out and followed. They are very stout in running, but not as fast as the does and young ones. If a young kangaroo gets the chance of falling ground in his favour, he bounds at every leap to such a distance that it is impossible to keep near him. It is of course known by all readers that the kangaroo runs, or rather jumps, with his hind legs only. When not molested his arms come near to the ground, but when pursued he carries them high, and looks like some mixture of a man and deer springing through the forests. The pace in hunting them is always very quick, and it is necessary to turn with the greatest rapidity among the forest trees. Ten minutes or a quarter of an hour will generally see the end of a run. By that time either the hounds are at the throat of the animals, or else he has made good his escape. We killed, I think, seven in two days, and had other runs in which we lost our prey. The "old man" kangaroo when hard pressed will turn round and fight the hounds—or fight the man who comes up to knock him over. And he fights with great power, inflicting terrible wounds with his fore paws.

In New South Wales I saw a kangaroo which we were hunting catch up a terrier in his arms, and carry the little animal in his embrace throughout the run. He was not, however, able to hurt the dog, who, when the affair was over, seemed to come quite undismayed out of his difficulty. And I saw also a female kangaroo, when the hounds were after her, throw her kid out of the pouch in which she carried it. On that occasion the kid was killed and the mother escaped. They will carry their young one as long as it is possible for them, and then throw him out almost without losing a stride.

In this hunting there is not much jumping; but what there is requires a very quick horse. The turns are rapid, and the ground is strewed by prostrate forest trunks. There is danger too of riding against trees. This on one occasion I did, with great force; and could not use my leg for six weeks after the accident. In default, however, of anything better, kangaroo hunting is good sport.

9 POLITICS AND PARLIAMENTS

Tariffs and Rivalries

An Englishman cannot be a month in Australia without finding himself driven to speculate—almost driven to come to some conclusion—as to the future destinies of the colonies. At present they are loyal to England with an expressive and almost violent loyalty of which we hear and see little at home. There may be causes of quarrel on this or that subject of custom duties and postal subsidies. One colony may expostulate with a Secretary of State at home in language a little less respectful than another, in accordance with the temperament of the minister of the moment. But the feeling of the people is one of affectionate adherence to England, with some slight anger caused by a growing idea that England is becoming indifferent. The withdrawal of our troops, especially from New Zealand, has probably done more than anything else to produce an apprehension which is certainly unnecessary and, to my thinking, irrational. But the love of the colonies for England, and the Queen, and English government—what may best probably be described as the adherence of the colonies to the mother country—cannot be doubted. An Australian of the present day does not like to be told of the future independence of Australia. I think that I met no instance in which the proposition on my part was met with an unqualified assent. And yet it can hardly be doubted that the independence of Australia will come in due time. But other things must come first. Before that day shall arrive the bone and sinews of the colonies must be of colonial produce. The leading men must not only have lived but have been born in Australia, so as to have grown up into life without the still existing feeling that England is their veritable "home".

And I venture to express an opinion that another great change must have come first, as to the coming of which there is at present certainly no sign. The colonies will join themselves together in some Australian federation, as has been done with our North American provinces, and will learn the political strength and commercial advantage of combined action. But there are difficulties in the way of such a union, which existed indeed in reference to the Canadas, Nova Scotia, and New Brunswick, but which make themselves felt with much greater violence in Australia. Nova Scotia and New Brunswick were hardly strong enough to persist in their jealous fears of a stronger sister, and the two Canadas had already become one before the Dominion was framed. The Australian colonies are very jealous of each other, and in their present moods are by no means ready to unite. Victoria claims supremacy, New South Wales disputes it, and Queensland looks to a future in which she shall become as large as either. South Queensland, though thus ambitious, by no means desires separation; but in all probability separation not only of Queensland, but further separation of New South Wales and of South Australia will come before the federal union which will precede absolute independence. As Maine and New Hampshire were allowed to become States in the early days of American independence, as Kentucky was separated from Virginia, and Tennessee from North Carolina, so will Albertland—by that or another name—be divided from Queensland, the Riverine districts from New South Wales, and some great northern province from South Australia. Whether Victoria will ever submit to division I will not venture to prophesy —but even that may come. And thus a union of States will be formed infinitely stronger in its interests than can be any one of the colonies as they now exist.

Such may probably be the future condition of Australia, and doubtless any further immediate subdivision among the colonies would have a tendency towards producing it, but it cannot be said that the time has yet come for combined action, or that it is near at hand. There is no such feeling yet as Australian ambition. There is ambition enough—Victorian ambition, New South Wales ambition, Queensland ambition; and, above them all, there is British ambition, very pleasant to the ears and to the heart of an Englishman. The other will come, and separation will indirectly lead to it.

* * *

Sugar from Queensland has no preference in the other colonies over sugar from the Mauritius. Nor under the existing state of the British law as it affects the colonies could such preference be given. New South Wales, for instance, may decide for herself whether she will admit sugar free, or whether she will raise a custom duty upon its import; but she cannot take Queensland sugar free and refuse to take sugar free from other sugar-growing countries. As the colonies at present stand in reference to each other—with the existing feeling of jealousy, and occasionally almost of hostility—with a condition of things in which a minister in one colony speaks in his parliament of another as a "friendly colony", in the spirit in which our ministers at home call this or that nation a "friendly country", or an "allied country", laying stress on the alliance, when we know that we are on the brink of war with that country—with these mutual rivalries and almost antipathies, this British law, tending as it does to the separation of Australian interests, has no very strong immediate effect. The colonies are determined to be separate. Australia is a term that finds no response in the patriotic feeling of any Australian. They are Victorians, or Queenslanders, or men of New South Wales; and each is not at present unwilling to have the pleasure of taxing the other. But this will come to an end sooner or later. The name of Australia will be dearer if not greater to Australian ears than the name of Great Britain, and then the produce of the land will pass free throughout the land.

* * *

As the matter stands at present, Downing Street has simply notified her assent to a customs union between the colonies, should the colonies desire it. Two or three of them have agreed in principle to the arrangement, Tasmania having gallantly taken the lead. But the question has become so complicated among them by small diverse interests—the jam-makers of Victoria, for instance, objecting to the free introduction of Tasmanian jam—that no efforts made by some among them can, I fear, be successful. But if it were initiated from Downing Street—if Downing Street would arrange the measure, and fashion the clauses, and give her earnest influence towards carrying it out, it would be done. Victoria might not at first agree to it—or Queensland—or possibly New South Wales. But it would not require the agreement of all. Tasmania, South Australia, and New Zealand would agree. It is probable that the others would do so also, if the proposal were fairly made to them by the imperial government. But if three were combined—if only two were combined—not only with sanction from home, but also with British encouragement—the union would soon grow till it included the whole.

Trollope expected the further splitting up, or "separation", of the Australian colonies. North Queensland was one possibility (see pp. 23-29); the Riverina was another.

Why should not the Riverina be annexed to Victoria? The genuine Victorian thinks that annexation to Victoria would be a road to fame and fortune for any colony or any nation. The inhabitants of Port Phillip, having separated themselves from New South Wales, would annex their parent to-morrow without compunction. But they will first annex Tasmania and Riverina. The Riverinans, however, as also the Tasmanians, do not seem to be in love with Victorian practices. Their deputies would be lost in the Victorian Assembly—quite as much as those from the Riverina are now lost at Sydney; and after a while, lawyers from Melbourne would represent them, receiving £300 per annum for their labour in doing so. . . . The Riverinans do not much regard Sydney—but they prefer Sydney to Melbourne.

It is well that it should be so, as it cannot be for the interests of Australia at large that the colony which is at present the most populous and the most important should be made greater and more important by annexing her sisters. It is for the advantage of England and of Englishmen—for England will continue to feed Australia with Englishmen—and of Australia and Australians, not that Victoria should be ascendant, but that Australia should be well governed and prosperous. That good government and prosperity would be promoted by a federation of the colonies, no one, I think, denies—though there are various opinions as to the period at which such federation should, or can, be accomplished. As to the results which may be expected from federation, I will venture to speak elsewhere; but among the measures which will tend to produce it, none will probably be so efficacious as the division of those colonies which are now too large in area for government from a central parliament in itself too weak in its elements to spread its arms afar; and among those which might retard federation none certainly would be so fatally strong as the increased preponderance of any one colony over the others. The preponderance of Victoria is at present the drawback most to be dreaded—and to that a most injurious addition would be made, not only as regards population, but in pride also, were another colony or a section of one to add itself to the Victorian borders.

The only other remedy for the Riverina is Separation—or, in other words, a setting up for herself among the colonies. The argument which I have attempted to use against customs duties would undoubtedly be a strong argument against further separation, if the continuance of such a barrier between cognate colonies were a necessity. Who would willingly multiply such barriers, and accumulate the sure means of intercolonial irritation? But if we look forward to a grouping of those Australian colonies under some form of government which may be combined in regard to external matters, but be separate as to local matters—such as is the form of government adopted in the United States—then the arguments against a small colony, or a poor colony, or a colony sparsely inhabited, fall to the ground. In saying this I trust that I may not be considered as specially advocating what we at home call "American institutions". Of those institutions this is not the place to speak. But the institutions necessary for the combined colonies would be no inch nearer to American institutions, and would be no inch farther removed from British institutions, than those which are at present used. Indeed I know not that any institution would be changed—that any single "Palladium of British liberty" would be altered by the clipping of a hair. But I name the union of the American States as giving the best example which modern history affords us of a secure federation of self-governing communities. . . .

Whether the province should be separated entirely from New

South Wales, or become only semi-self-acting as proposed in the resolutions of 1864, may admit of discussion. Looking forward to a federation of the different colonies, with some system of central Australian government, I myself would wish to see the separation complete. I believe that the creation of smaller colonies on the Australian continent—if colonies is the proper name by which to call them—will conduce more quickly than any other step to this result. I believe that a community of many states would at once produce at any rate a customs union, and would put an end to the internecine absurdity of border duties.

Legislators in Action

In Queensland not long since the ministers of the day proposed a law by which paper money would have become inconvertible, and would have been substituted for gold as the legal tender of the country. The governor refused his acquiescence, and was supported by the Colonial Office at home. In this way the colonies are preserved from crude legislation, which would be the certain and natural result of inexperience in statecraft. In saying this I by no means intend to cast a slur on colonial ministers, or to imply that inefficient men have been chosen for high offices. I certainly make no such charge in regard to Queensland. But it cannot be expected that a colony with a population of 120,000 souls should be able to produce a ministry skilled at all points in questions of government and finance. Among such a population the minister chosen will usually be a gentleman intent on his own profession, whatever that may be; whose education and chances in life have made him a lawyer, a merchant, or a squatter. Such a man finds himself suddenly in parliament, and almost as suddenly a minister of state—a colonial secretary or prime minister, or perhaps a colonial treasurer or chancellor of the exchequer—backed by a majority in parliament, and enabled therefore, as far as the colonial parliament is concerned, to carry his own measures. His inexperience is brought face to face with the inexperience of a small chamber—just as the experience of a minister with us is encountered by the experience of a very large chamber. Though the interests of the colony are comparatively small—because the numbers are small—the benefits or injuries which may be the result of good or bad legislation will be as great to the few, as they are to the many in crowded communities.

It is by no means wonderful that it should appear expedient to six or seven gentlemen in Queensland that inconvertible paper should be the safest circulating medium for the colonists; but it would be highly prejudicial to the colony that such a question should be left to the unassisted wisdom of these six or seven gentlemen—and perhaps altogether ruinous. It may be that each of these six or seven should be superior in all good gifts, in eloquence, patriotism, and natural sense, to any Secretary of State at home. It is by no means to be supposed that a minister of state in England must be superior to a minister in Queensland, because the one is an Englishman and the other a colonist. But the concrete wisdom of thirty million people is greater than that of 120,000, and the experience of ages of legislation is needed to control the newness and rawness of a parliament that has existed but for a few years.

This probably is the strongest existing reason for maintaining the present dependent condition of the Australian colonies. There are other reasons, all strong, against immediate change—the possible need of protection in case of attack, which protection we should give with more heartiness and certainty to a colony than to an ally; the absence of any Australian feeling between the colonies of a nature strong enough to bind them into one whole; the doubt which would be felt both at home and in the colonies as to the form of government to be selected; the general dislike to a republic and the difficulties which stand in the way of the establishment of a monarchy—all these objections are valid against that idea of immediate independence which is not without its supporters in England. But strongest among them all is the necessary inexperience of colonial statesmen. The need for guidance and control is that of the youth who is no longer a boy but is not as yet quite a man. He may be better educated than his father, of a higher intellect, of finer aspirations, giving promise of almost Darwinian improvement in his descent—but he cannot be trusted to go quite alone till he has been taught by experience that paper, without gold to back it, will not long supply his necessities —till he shall have learned that and other worldly lessons which will not come simply from high intellect and fine aspirations.

Trollope compared the role of the colonial Legislative Councils to that of the House of Lords.

The Legislative Council in an Australian parliament is intended to be endowed with similar privileges and similar feebleness. Their sittings are short and uninteresting, but the chamber in which they are held is imposing and comfortable. The copy of the home institution is very faithful—with the exception of course of the hereditary element. As the members hold their seats for life, many of them are of course old, and as the age of the colony advances they will become older. Nothing can be more respectable and well-behaved than an Australian legislative council, and I believe that among legislative councils none is better behaved than that of Queensland. But the feebleness is there. It is at any rate supposed to be there. When you are told that a gentleman has been nominated to the upper house, it is intended that you should understand that he has been laid honourably on the shelf. It is, however, competent to him to come down from the shelf and again to enter upon the arena of true political action—a privilege which is altogether denied to members of the upper house with us.

The New South Wales Parliament led to these comments:

Border duties were so much in the ascendant, both when I first visited Sydney and when I returned thither, that I hardly heard other matters of much importance discussed in the New South Wales parliament. There was a divorce bill brought forward, and I then was surprised to learn that the people of New South Wales, alone among English-speaking races, are without any legalized means of separating a wife from her husband, or a husband from his wife. On this occasion the divorce bill was thrown out, and the peculiarity still remains. The practice of the British parliament as to counting out and observing the presence of strangers has been adopted, and is of course much more frequently used than it is at home. I was surprised to find how very large a proportion of the time of the House was occupied in personal discussions and appeals to the Speaker—as to some of which I could not but feel that the gentleman had by no means a bed of roses. A Speaker in an Australian House of Assembly should be a stout man, not thin-skinned, prone rather to content himself with a low level of conduct in his house than to attempt the maintenance of high dignified decorum—but capable of speaking a very strong word if a member should occasionally fall into a bathos lower than that low level. With some trains a driver feels that it is much to get along at all. The House at Sydney does certainly succeed in making its journeys. When there, I often felt that an exercise of some great act of authority would be useful—that an order to the Sergeant-at-Arms to carry away an offending member and lock him up in some parliamentary black-hole would be beneficial. I longed for the moment to be the Speaker, that I might be authoritative. But I perceived gradually that the work did get itself done, and that the gentleman in the chair knew what he was about. I was not so sure that he was right, when on an occasion —a new bill respecting the border duties being then in committee —he spoke from the benches as a member of the House, not simply on the clause under discussion, but with considerably party violence on the subject of the bill at large. I could not but think that his authority as Speaker would be injured by his descending into the political arena.

That a very commonplace man may make a fair debater was a lesson I had learned before I ever entered an Australian legislature. Such a one will not become a great orator. He will not overcome his hearers by reasons, or carry them away by passionate eloquence. But he may be very serviceable—as flour is serviceable in the fabrication of a pudding. Indeed a pudding with much flour and but few plums will answer its purpose better than one in which the plums have nothing to hold them together. In the House of Assembly at Sydney there was a sufficiency of farinaceous matter to prevent the plums from cloying the appetite and injuring the digestion.

* * *

The railways are still being extended, and it may probably be long before any material increase in the rate of direct profit will be realized; but that adequate profit of an indirect nature is realized, amply sufficient to justify the outlay, no one I think can doubt.

Nevertheless, these railways are open to an objection which strikes an Englishman very forcibly. With a few exceptions as to short lines for local traffic, all the Australian railways have been made by the Australian Government, and have necessarily been made under the authority of centralized officials. When it is determined to spend a million on railways, some individual has to determine whether the money shall be expended for the advantage of this or that district. No doubt the proposition must be sanctioned by parliament, but we all know what is the power of a man "in power"; and we know also how prone such men are to use their power, perhaps unconsciously, towards the promotion of their own parliamentary interest. They who do not know it would soon be taught the lesson by a visit to the Australian Colonies. When a change of Government is effected, and a new set of men obtains possession of the Treasury bench, the happy localities by whom the new ministers are sent to Parliament immediately become assured that roads and bridges will be showered upon them, and they become loudly expectant of railways. But these benefits are to be procured by money subscribed by the colony at large, which should therefore be expended on behalf of the colony at large. When the member for Wonga-jonga becomes the Honourable Secretary for Public Works, it is a matter of course that the inhabitants of the Wonga-jonga district should expect great things; and it is almost equally a matter of course that the Secretary for Public Works should do, if not great things, at least little things. He will do probably as little as may suffice to secure his popularity; but he will hardly be able to forget altogether his own interests in his public duty, and he certainly will not be encouraged to forget his own interest by the general feeling which prevails around him.

South Australia excited comments on the "ballot" (i.e., the secret ballot) and on the pettiness of many issues discussed.

I found the ballot to be generally popular—because it tended to make things quiet at elections. . . . I am bound to report this as the opinion which I found to prevail among almost all classes as to the use of the ballot in Australia. I give my evidence unwillingly, because I myself very much dislike the ballot for English use, and believe that a mistake is made by those who argue that because it suits the colonies, therefore it will suit ourselves. With us the object is secrecy, which I think should not be an object, and which I think also will not be obtained. In the colonies secrecy is not desired, but tranquillity is felt to be a blessing. It is clear that the ballot does assist in producing tranquillity.

But it may be questioned whether even tranquillity at elections is to be regarded as an unmixed blessing. Apathy is certainly not desirable, and it may be that tranquillity will show itself to be akin to apathy. Men are always eager as to that in which they are truly interested, and real human eagerness will produce excitement and noise. Broken heads are bad things, but even broken heads are better than political indifference. They who have framed the Australian constitutions and have selected the modes of election for the legislative chambers of the colonies, have had before their eyes an idea of human political excellence which has never hitherto prevailed, and never will prevail till that good time comes which we call the millennium. They have desired to produce great vitality in the electors without any excitement at the elections. Men are not to rush to the polls—certainly not to go thither under stress of fear, or bribery, or drink; but all men are to walk there in orderly strings, under the pressure of a high sense of national duty. They are to be debarred from the interest of personal contest by the ballot and other means—but are nevertheless to be constant in voting. The ballot, and the other means, are successful for the required ends—but the people are indifferent as to the results. It is the boast of Australian politicians that the elections are quiet. They are often too quiet. If it be the case, as a great man once said, that any first six men caught walking through Temple Bar, would make as good members of parliament as any other six men, the South Australian scheme of voting for members of the Legislative Council may be good—but under no other theory. . . .

The debates are fairly well conducted, at any rate without riot or that personal abuse and continual appeal to the Speaker which I have witnessed elsewhere. There is much useless and quite vapid talking—members making speeches without even an attempt at a new point or a new argument, to which no one listens, but which are endured with patience. It is understood that when a gentleman has taken the trouble to get a seat, and is willing to sacrifice his time, he should be allowed to air his voice, and to learn by practice to speak with fluency. Mr. Lowe and Mr. Childers have taught colonial legislators the possible results of such lessons; and why should any man throw away a chance? I heard a debate on the great question of cab-lamps—whether legislation should content itself with requiring simply cabs to be lighted at nights, or whether it should extend the precaution to other vehicles—on which subject two-thirds of a full House were eloquent. I heard impassioned eloquence on the question whether the excellent Bishop of Adelaide should be allowed to retain his right of walking out of the room before other people—a right which as it came from the Crown, the parliament could not take from him, but which he gracefully abandoned when it gave annoyance to scrupulous politicians. Their minds were much excited on this question. And I heard another debate as to the Governor's salary, carried on with much energy. The Lower House, with hot parliamentary zeal expressed in fervid words, decided on cutting off £1,000 a year from the salary of future governors. But the measure of retrenchment, though essentially a money measure, was lost, because no seconder would be found for it in the Upper Chamber.

There was another great debate when I was in the colony—of which, however, I only heard a small portion, and it gave rise to an incident which I will mention as giving an idea of the feeling displayed towards the House. It was decided, as a new measure that there should be after-dinner sittings, and on a certain evening there was an after-dinner sitting. There was a spirited debate, which was conducted with a fair amount of parliamentary animation. One of the leading Adelaide newspapers, giving its history of the affair on the following morning, described the speakers in round terms of having been—unfit for parliamentary work, because they had dined. On the following day one of the gentlemen attacked brought the matter forward on a question of privilege, and there ensued a debate in which it was at any rate shown that the accusation was altogether groundless. But nothing was done. No one seemed seriously to think that the writer of the article, or the editor, proprietor, or printer of the paper, should be punished for the insinuations made. On the next morning the newspaper in question ridiculed the complaining members for having adopted the only meaning of the words of the article which they would bear. I could not but think that had the *Times* or *Daily Telegraph* accused the House of Commons of being generally unfit for its duties because it had—dined, that the House of Commons would in some way have made its displeasure felt. But I was anxious to know why such an unwarranted attack should be made by one of the leading newspapers of the colony upon the parliament of the colony, and I received information on the subject. The newspaper in question had to report the debates, and disliked the trouble and expense of keeping reporters in the gallery late into the evening. . . .

In what I have said it will, I fear, be thought that I have intended to depreciate the parliament of the colony. I have not sought to do so, but I am merely giving my personal impressions of what I heard and saw. Parliaments, like puddings, should be judged by the proof of their results, as shown in the eating. One of the main works of all parliaments is so to adjust the financial affairs of the country entrusted to it, that the people shall not suffer from over-taxation, that the public credit shall be maintained, and that a sufficiency of revenue shall be collected to ensure the safety and general well-being of the community. If this be adequately done, a parliament need certainly not to be ashamed of its doings. And this is adequately done in South Australia.

A Sober Assessment

As I have gone along with my work through the different Australian colonies I have said a few words as to the legislatures and forms of government in each. . . . I do not think that we in England have paid very much attention to these parliaments, or even to the characters and political fitness or unfitness of the ministers. To those who sit in the Colonial Office in Downing Street the names of certain Australian statesmen are no doubt familiar—and now and again, they who are diligent in reading their newspapers learn that a change of ministers has been made at Melbourne, and that Mr. O'This has given way to Mr. MacThat. It is the same, to a much greater degree, in regard to India, as to which enormous dependency—the most populous and important that ever belonged to a nation, and conferring a higher political prestige on the ruling race than has ever been conferred by any other subject people—no Englishman at home can be got to interest himself in the slightest degree unless he be actually concerned in the government of it. No doubt the same apathy prevailed at Rome as to the Provinces, and among the Spaniards of Spain as to the western world over which the kings of Spain held dominion. They who live at the centre of a circle think only of the centre. To those who are half-way removed from the centre to the circumference so much of the area of the circle is of importance as lies between their line and the centre—to which they ever look wistfully. They who dwell on the outside, think much of the outside, but do so still with a consciousness that they are but outsiders.

In those colonies of which I have written men are often loud in abuse of the tyranny presumed to prevail at home. They denounce the pride of our aristocracy, the poorness of our people, the narrowness of our spaces, and the assumed decay of our energies. But they do so in a tone which to the attentive ear conveys more respect than censure. Their thoughts are full of England, and they are keenly alive to the attention or the want of attention which England shows in regard to their affairs. It is a standard joke among Australians, and one always repeated with some indignation, that Englishmen confound Botany Bay with Van Diemen's Land, and New South Wales with South Australia. Australians are essentially loyal—but are sore at the want of recognition of their importance which they think is displayed by the country on which they are affectionately dependent. It would be well if Englishmen at home could be induced to turn their thoughts somewhat more frequently to their cousins in the colonies, and to interest themselves in the political and social conditions of communities on which, in a few years, will hang much of the character and honour of the English-speaking race of men.

The Australian people as a whole are warmly loyal to Great Britain. In Victoria, but in Victoria only, there is perhaps a tendency among the Irish to republicanism—which means accelerated separation. Even in Victoria I have heard no politician announce this as his political creed; but I have thought that I have caught a difference of tone—a tone that has not struck my ear elsewhere—which has brought home to me a conviction that the tendency exists. But the traveller, taking as his guide the general expression of the national feeling, is impressed by the great loyalty of the colonies, and the determination to abide by British precedent in legislation and British authority in the execution of the laws.

* * *

It will probably be acknowledged that these colonial parliaments and colonial ministers are but stepping-stones to imperial action—or in other words to separation. . . . He must be a rash prophet or else a very wise man indeed who can name the years which must intervene before Australia shall become an empire. But it requires but little wisdom, and will be held to deserve no reproach on the score of rashness, to say that all that is now being done, both by statesmen at home and by statesmen in the colonies, is tending to the formation of a separate political nation.

Then the question arises whether that which is being done is being well done. It is not only needed that the colonies should rule themselves, subject to certain control from the Government at home, but also that they should learn to rule themselves when no such protection from any act of flagrant misrule shall be within their reach. The colonial parliaments and cabinets of the present day have to effect this double purpose. They pass land laws and make tariffs almost at their wills, and they are in the course of learning how to do so more efficiently when they shall have no extraneous assistance on which to depend.

These two are probably the subjects uppermost in their debates —unless we may regard the abuse and depression of one party by another as being in itself a separate subject of parliamentary interest. Perhaps in all parliaments this latter source of eloquence will be the most attractive of all. No doubt it is so with us. A vote of want of confidence not only fills our House of Commons so full that even gentlemen with seats can find no sitting-room, but crowds also the galleries with strangers and overwhelms the Speaker and members with applications for entrance. It sells all the newspapers, and gives a livelier joy to breakfast tables and a more stirring buzz to clubs than can be attained by any budget, or by any measure of reform. Internecine combat between two leaders, and hard hitting from party to party is the delight of parliamentary life. It would be both unjust and unwise to condemn the colonial parliaments for doing that which we not only do at home, but which we do with a result which we believe to be in the long-run beneficial and healthy. And it would be absurd to condemn the colonial parliaments for being occasionally ridiculous where we are wrong-headed, for being riotous where we are simply loud, for being foul-mouthed where we are only ill-natured, for being uneducated and illiterate where we are ill-informed and superficial, or even for being vulgar where we are severe.

It is not only that our House of Lords is to the manner born, and that we choose our House of Commons from the best of thirty millions of people, while they have no statesmen to the manner born, and can choose their parliaments in each colony from but a few hundreds of thousands. Perfect as might be their excuse for inferiority founded on that allegation, that is not their only nor their chief excuse. The colonies are peopled with men who have gone out to earn their bread and who are earning it—and from these have to be chosen their members of parliament. There is as yet among them no class of men capable of devoting their time and their energies to the public cause and to that only. There is no established wealth handed down from father to son, the possession or prospect of which enables the young legislator so "to learn the ingenuous arts that his manners shall be refined, nor ever allowed to become brutal". In the preparation of such a class of men much time is needed and many accessories. In the United States it has not as yet been created. Each State of the Union may possibly find two lawyers sufficiently polished, and at the same time sufficiently powerful, to make a senate capable of dignity; but their House of Representatives, and certainly their State Congresses will gain but little by comparison with our colonial legislatures. For the House of Representatives they elect from a population larger than our own, and for the Congress of each State they elect from populations much larger than those of our colonies. The States of Pennsylvania and New York together far exceed in numbers the people of Australia; but no Englishman need be ashamed—and certainly no Australian—to compare the tone and tactics of the Houses at Sydney, Melbourne, and Adelaide with those of Harrisbourg and Albany. But in neither land—in Australia or in the United States—has time yet been allowed for the creation of a class of men capable of bearing parliamentary honours with that habitual serenity which is essential to absolute fitness.

Perhaps nothing that a parliament can do towards disqualifying itself—making itself unfit for its own gravest and highest duties—is so injuriously powerful as the payment of its members. A measure to this effect offers an inducement to men to come forward as politicians altogether distinct from that ambition to move in public life and to influence public affairs which should be the personal motive to political aspirants. It is pleaded on its behalf that its adoption will enable men to enter parliament whose services, however valuable they might be to the State, would be lost to the State, unless they could be purchased by the State. It may be that some as yet inglorious Hampden, some unknown Somers, some youthful colonial Pitt or Canning, without fathers, uncles, or great party friends to bring him into notice, is tending sheep on some distant run, or cutting up bullocks for a meat-preserving company, because he has not the means of living while he is tearing unjust ministers to pieces at the capital of his colony. The payment of members has, as we all know, been for many years the law of the land in the United States; but it has not there produced youthful Pitts or Hampdens now glorious, who would have remained without glory had they also remained without their six dollars a day. The body of American legislators are lawyers, and many of them, no doubt, unsuccessful lawyers. The successful lawyers might have won their seats without payment, and it may well be questioned whether an unsuccessful lawyer is the man whom his country could profitably bribe into parliament with the hope of finding within his bosom true patriotism, backed by honest eloquence. In Victoria, and in Victoria alone among these colonies, the same political arrangement has been made. The members of each House are paid £300 a year for their services—so that any Victorian blacksmith, gardener, or shepherd may with seeming security leave his business if he can get himself elected into parliament. The very fact that a living is so to be made is favourable to the cause of the blacksmiths, gardeners, and shepherds. It is but reasonable to a working-man that he should give a vote towards getting a living for another working-man—but it cannot be for the welfare of the colony that one class of men should be debarred from parliament and another set brought into parliament, from such motives. Victoria, as being the richest colony of the group, and by far the most populous, should undoubtedly have the best set of men in her parliament. I will not make invidious distinctions, but I do not think that any stranger conversant with such matters—any travelling member of our own House of Commons—would be disposed to give her such pre-eminence.

* * *

The practice of counting out is quite as rife as with us. Application to the Speaker for interference is much more common—is so common as to have become the most prevailing fault in the conduct of these parliaments. In exciting debates gentlemen rise to order every minute. No doubt applications for order are very often necessary, for members do frequently allow themselves to use language which is disorderly. But as often as not the appeal to the Chair is made because the gentleman making it is too hot in his temper to keep his seat. He cannot endure that some orator whom he hates should have the undivided attention of the House, and by rising to order, and by that alone, can he excuse his ebullition. The Speaker asks for the point of order. There is none, and then the debate goes on, till the ebullition again takes the same form.

In watching the working of these chambers I became aware how much easier it is to rule a numerous assembly than a small one. The very number of the men congregated in a large house, the crowd of faces, and the spaces filled, lend a dignity and assurance to the elected master, and a magnificence, which of themselves confer power. Men rise to the situation in which they are placed, and find bulwarks for their greatness in the very accessories which their greatness is supposed to deserve. And the greatness of his empire makes it easy for the Speaker of a great House to govern his kingdom. The number of his subjects who are obedient, and who desire that their chief magistrate should be held in awe, enforces obedience even from the violent, and makes successful rebellion impossible. But in a smaller assembly an unruly and obtrusive unit is opposed to a weaker phalanx of order. A man will dare to misbehave himself before seventy members, and to howl like a maniac before thirty, who would be quelled into silence by three hundred. And one such unit, if successful, will soon have followers, and two or three will dominate the House and overawe the Speaker. I have thought when watching Australian debates that the Speakers might have been more powerful in enforcing order, and that they somewhat failed to use the means at their command. I express this opinion with the utmost diffidence, feeling that I could not judge the tempers of the men as they could judge them. But it seemed to me that these presidents of the debates were over anxious to make it understood that they never would attempt to coerce the House, although they might possibly be driven to coerce a member. If the House desired latitude of language, let there be latitude. If the House should wish it to be understood that "liar" was unparliamentary, and "miscreant" within the bounds, by all means let one gentleman call another a miscreant, though no gentleman be allowed to call another a liar. But on each separate occasion of the use of hard words the House cannot come to a decision, and the Speaker can. And there are precedents and rules, and the Speaker has the power of calling an offender to order even though no member should rise to ask him to do so. It seemed to me that almost all hard words were allowed to pass unchallenged, except those which convey a direct charge of falsehood—and that even in regard to those an offender was allowed to go on scot free, if, when called upon for retraction, he either laughingly withdrew the word with a whisper, or with some additional venom renewed the expression of his opinion, though he recalled the phrase.

I heard one gentleman call another a coward, and on appeal it was decided that "coward" was beyond the limits. But it was not at the moment withdrawn, and in the scuffle of retaliatory debate, the memories of those interested became hazy. Another offence was committed on the other side, and the offender would not "withdraw" his word because "coward" had not been withdrawn. Then there arose a debate whether or no "coward" had been withdrawn, the speaker of the word remaining silent while his party declared that that sin had been properly wiped out, and that the other sin therefore must be wiped out also. "Coward" had, they alleged, been duly retracted, and a second retraction was of course out of the question. At last the opposite side gave way, and a half-whispered jocose withdrawal of the other offensive term was effected. But the next day on reference to the colonial Hansard it was found that coward had never been withdrawn, and the "coward" party—the party supporting the gentleman who had used the word—was supposed to have obtained a signal triumph. . . .

Sitting as I did as a stranger first in one colonial House of Parliament and then in another, I could not but ask myself the question whether, were I resident there, I would endeavour to get a seat for myself. I have ever regarded a place in the House of Commons at home as the highest honour open to an Englishman. There are of course degrees of honour in that House, as there are many mansions in heaven; but an entrance into that House is the first stepping-stone to them all. It should be so also in the colonies if things could be made to fit into their right places. But certainly there would be drawbacks to the pleasure. It must be admitted that there are such also with us. Many subjects of debate are wearisome and uninteresting, and many debates are wearisome and uninteresting even on subjects which are full of interest. In the colonies I certainly thought that the drawbacks were very material. I have heard the speech of a Colonial Treasurer bringing forward a colonial budget, during no portion of which, though it extended itself over a whole evening, was I able to extract Mr. Lowe's *lucem ex lucello*. I have heard nearly a whole House—almost every member of it—discuss the propriety of enacting that vehicles should carry lamps. I have heard all the parliamentary indignation of a colonial House of Assembly poured forth on a question of social precedency. I have heard speech after speech of lingering length on the qualification of a gentleman to be appointed a magistrate after he had been committed for selling grog without a licence.

But I confess that I found a worse annoyance than this, a more serious drawback on the comfort of colonial parliamentary life, in the scope for continual speech which the checks or absence of checks in a small chamber allow to an individual member. At home we have had terrible bores, gentlemen whom it was hardly possible to keep from a daily performance for which they were qualified neither by nature nor education; but at home the Speaker is powerful, the House is powerful, and the reporters are powerful. The bore is silenced at any rate during the choicer hours of debate, and is, at last, after a certain fashion stamped out. The House will not listen when it has come to a general but unexpressed resolution that a certain member is never worthy of being heard. But in the colonial legislatures the brazen-faced bore seems to be too strong for any restraint that can be devised for him. And then in a small House his vote is of importance, and the party which is unfortunate in his adherence does not dare to join in snubbing him. Such a man there is in one of the colonies as to whom I wondered that the House should suffer him—that any side of the House should endure him even though he could have given a triple vote. That he spoke every day was nothing; many members did so. That he spoke on every subject was not much, for others, perhaps, did so too. That he always spoke a dozen times on every subject was by no means his heaviest offence; nor even that in all his speeches he never deviated into sense, or spoke a word worth hearing either on the score of argument, or from its eloquence or wit. There are offences worse than the offence of stupidity, even when stupidity be joined to arrogant presumption. In every word that this man spoke he either insulted an opponent, or attempted to pander to the prejudices of the multitude. There are tribunes of the people and would-be tribunes, fierce advocates of popular rights, as to whom it is often difficult not to think that their Demosthenic strain springs rather from their desire to please than to do good; and in listening to them the hearer turns his heart against them. Such men are flatterers and demagogues—but then they are probably capable of flattering and fitted by nature to seduce mobs. This man only aped the acts of such popular leaders, and aped them so badly, was so vulgar, so ignorant, so illiterate, so incapable in his attempts, so nauseous in his flights of oratory, so blasphemous in his appeals to religion, so impudent to the gentlemen around him, so weak in his language, so strong in his Billingsgate phrases, that I could think but little of a constituency which would return him, and marvelled at the patience of a House which would endure him. I felt that did I live in that colony and entertain a desire to sit in that House, I would certainly stand for the same constituency with that gentleman, so that we might not both sit there together. His continual presence must, I think, be to all those legislators a blistering thorn, robbing their position of all its pleasure and of most of its pride.

Of course there are parliamentary faults incidental to the infancy of these young parliaments. It was not to be expected that eloquence, wit, judgment, statesmanship, and above all that dignified serenity of manner which is essentially necessary to the construction of a great parliamentary assembly, should be brought to life at once in a young country, born as it were out of some Minerva's brain. Complaint is made that these colonial debates are sometimes noisy, often vapid, and always wordy. It was hardly possible that they should not be so. It requires the tuition and practice of at least a century to teach men that they should restrain themselves, confine themselves, and suppress themselves when assembled together to debate on public matters, and the lesson is much less easily taught in a small than in a large assembly. But the one thing necessary, the *sine quâ non* without which representative government could hardly be commenced, and certainly could not be continued, the very marrow of parliamentary life, without which any parliamentary effort can be no more than a galvanized convulsion without any motive power of its own—is vitality. It is essential to a parliament that the electors and the elected should be in earnest—that the constituencies should have an eager desire to send this or that politician to represent them, and that the politician should have an eager desire to represent this or that constituency. . . .

The strength of the Australian legislative chambers consists in the energy which they possess, in the anxiety which is felt concerning them by the colonists, and in their hot desire for action. They are all alive, and therefore will increase in strength with the growth of every year. We are apt at home to smile at their efforts because they change their ministries frequently. French kings and courtiers under the old régime, German statesmen and Russian diplomatists, have laughed at us, in England, on the same score. Even the Americans do so because they are bound to a ministry—to a president who is his own minister, and who need never change his subordinates—for four years. To our eyes the power of parliament to change a ministry at any time is the surest pledge of our freedom. Even the desire of one party to oust another, the very system of opposition which creates that continued warfare to which we are used at home, is as sure a proof as any that we have the vitality of our institutions. It is no less so in these colonies. Though their debates may be dreary, though their energy may be expended on small subjects, though an occasional member may be vulgar, noisy, and in every way objectionable, I do not doubt but that they will work satisfactorily, because they have got themselves set on foot in a proper spirit and with true life.

An Afterword

The phenomenon in regard to the Australian colonies which most powerfully strikes the observer is the intensity of the feeling of separate interest which divides one from another. There is at present very little tendency among them to that combination which seems to me to be essential to their future greatness. That they will at some time combine themselves I look upon as certain. When the leading politicians of the colonies are "colonial born" there will rise up among them a feeling of Australian patriotism —rivalling, and at last exceeding, that British patriotism which is at present felt as a passion among the people. Regard for the country of their birth will lead them to look for Australian greatness, and the way to that condition can be found only in Federation. And, as certainly, Federation will lead to ultimate Separation from the mother country. Here, in these few last words, I will not trouble the reader by repeating what I have already said on this tender subject. I will not again argue that they who love Great Britain well, may, without offence to her or her Colonial Empire, look forward with satisfaction to the future separation of Australasia. But I agree with those who think that the day for such a step has not yet come, and that much has yet to be done before it can arrive. Holding this view I can see with less regret that present fashion among the colonies of holding themselves aloof from each other of which I have spoken.

But there is a step which I regard as precursive of Federation which I think should be taken at once, and as to which I would hope that action might be commenced in aid of it by our Colonial Office in Downing Street. The immediate prosperity of the colonies is greatly injured, and their career impeded by the want of a customs union among them. They cannot consume the produce one of another, and therefore cannot lay themselves out for the productions for which they are best qualified, because prohibitory customs duties exist among them. Sugar from Queensland, wine from New South Wales, flour from South Australia, and fruit and hops from Tasmania cannot reach the Victorian consumers without a customs duty—and consequently the producers of those articles, each in his own colony, are restricted in their work of producing. Consequently also the people of Victoria are restricted in their consumption. My first immediate wish for the colonies is that they should join in establishing a customs union.

Here, in England, we naturally regard the colonies chiefly as the recipients of our redundant population. In that respect they are invaluable to us. We may probably be justified in saying that our great increase of people has been given to us in order that we might populate such lands. But we have much redundant population for which they are not fitted. The penniless young man who wants a genteel position, and who bases his claim to that condition of things on his education, will not generally find his claim allowed. If he go out with his position assured to him by interest it may be well with him; otherwise he will descend into the lowest grade of servitude, and will probably find himself a shepherd. The same fate in a different form will be the fate of ladies who emigrate hoping to earn by their talents and acquirements that bread which a too crowded market makes it difficult for them to find here. For their wares, excellent as they are, the market is also crowded there. Such are not the emigrants that Great Britain should be most urgent to send.

But for the men who can and will work with their hands, for women who can cook and be generally useful about a household, for girls who are ready to learn to cook and to be generally useful, these colonies are a paradise. They will find the whole condition of life changed for them. The slight estimation in which labour is held here will be changed for a general respect. The humbleness, the hat-touching, the servility which is still incidental to such work as theirs in this old country, and which is hardly compatible with exalted manhood, has found no footing there. I regard such manhood among the masses of the people as the highest sign of prosperity which a country can give.